D1393925

# PEACEMAKING IN CIVIL WAR

# PEACEMAKING IN CIVIL WAR

## International Mediation in Zimbabwe, 1974-1980

Stephen John Stedman

Lynne Rienner Publishers ▪ Boulder & London

The map of Zimbabwe is reprinted with permission from *Democracy in Developing Countries: Africa*, Larry Diamond, Juan J. Linz, and Seymour Martin Lipset, editors. Boulder: Lynne Rienner, 1988.

Published in the United States of America in 1991 by
Lynne Rienner Publishers, Inc.
1800 30th Street, Boulder, Colorado 80301

and in the United Kingdom by
Lynne Rienner Publishers, Inc.
3 Henrietta Street, Covent Garden, London WC2E 8LU

**Library of Congress Cataloging-in-Publication Data**
Stedman, Stephen John.
  Peacemaking in civil war : international mediation in Zimbabwe, 1974–1980 / Stephen John Stedman.
    p.  cm.
  ISBN 1-55587-200-X
  1. Zimbabwe—Politics and government—1965–1979. 2. Lancaster House Conference on Rhodesia (1979) 3. Mediation, International.
  I. Title
DT2981.S74 1990
968.91—dc20                                                      90-42271
                                                                      CIP

**British Cataloguing in Publication Data**
A Cataloguing in Publication record for this book
is available from the British Library.


Printed and bound in the United States of America

The paper used in this publication meets the requirements
of the American National Standard for Permanence of
Paper for Printed Library Materials Z39.48-1984.

# Contents

# Tables

# Preface

On March 4, 1980, Robert Mugabe was elected prime minister of Zimbabwe, formerly the "self-governing colony" of Southern Rhodesia and later the independently declared nation of Rhodesia. Less than three months before the announcement of his victory at the polls, Mugabe had been leading a guerrilla war that had engulfed Rhodesia for seven years and had cost between 30,000 and 40,000 lives. Throughout that period he demanded revolutionary change, fighting a war not just for political and racial equality, but for socioeconomic and political *transformation*. On the evening of his election, Mugabe appeared on television to address the peoples of Zimbabwe. For most whites in the country, this was the first time they had seen and listened to their new leader. Since as long as many of them could remember, Robert Mugabe had been portrayed as a communist terrorist, a single-minded, cold-blooded revolutionary who personally sanctioned the bayoneting of babies and the rape of widows. But the man on the television screen proved to be a different Mugabe than the caricature drawn by the Rhodesian propaganda machine. In masterly diplomatic fashion he called for a reconciliation and healing of wounds. He asked all citizens, black and white, to work together to help create a new nation.

Mugabe came to power by a most unusual path—a contentious three-month-long conference that produced a negotiated settlement, transition, and cease-fire, all leading to a competition measured by ballots instead of bullets. Events happened so suddenly that they took everyone by surprise. When the conference began in September 1979 at Lancaster House in London, one of the chief architects of the conference estimated there to be a one in one hundred chance of success. After the conference ended in December, but before the parties returned to Zimbabwe to compete for votes, the same diplomat believed there to be a one in twenty chance of a resolution of the war. One black opponent of Mugabe summed up the prevalent feeling when the election poll was announced: "The result—a successful settlement and election—stunned everybody."

As a student of revolution, peace, and war, I have been attracted to the Zimbabwean revolution. In particular, I became interested in Zimbabwe as a case study of a civil war that was terminated through negotiation rather than through the elimination or capitulation of one side. I wanted to sift through the Zimbabwean conflict to see if its resolution could help our understanding of how other civil wars could be ended through negotiation and could assist third parties that act as mediators in such conflicts.

When I started this study, I felt that the topic of negotiations and civil war was an important one. I am all the more convinced of that now. In 1987, twenty-four wars were fought, twenty-two of which were civil wars or wars of secession (Sivard 1988). All but four of these wars continue today. Such wars upset regional power balances, invite outside intervention, and cost millions of lives and billions of dollars. Yet, within the fields of war termination in international relations and revolution in comparative politics, termination of civil war remains, with few exceptions, an ignored subject. This stems from the perception that such conflict involves indivisible stakes and can have only one outcome: the elimination and total defeat of one side or the other (Gelb with Betts 1979, 165–166; Ikle 1971, 95; Pillar 1983, 24). There are cases, however, of successful negotiated termination of civil war; and even in some of the cases that ended in the defeat of one side, bargaining and negotiation led to the surrender that terminated the conflict. The purpose of this book is not to examine the broader question of how civil wars end, but rather to examine the possibilities of negotiated settlement of civil war and to investigate how third-party mediation can be a force for resolving such conflict.

I owe much to friends, family, colleagues, and teachers for emotional and intellectual debts accrued during the research and writing of this book. The book began as a doctoral thesis at Stanford University, where I was fortunate to have a thesis committee composed of Robert North, David Abernethy, and Alexander George. They and other members of the Stanford Department of Political Science—Marty Lipset, Alex Dallin, and John Ferejohn—are owed my thanks for the interest and concern they provided. I would especially like to single out my dissertation chair, Bob North, whose experience and wisdom helped me when I questioned the whole enterprise of graduate study.

Much of the support I received during the development of the thesis came from the Peace Studies faculty and students of Stanford. Two individuals in particular deserve special mention: Lincoln Moses and Byron Bland. Lincoln and Byron took it upon themselves to teach me about peace and the relationship between conviction and action. One of the joys of my years at Stanford was the time spent teaching peace with them.

Throughout my work I was blessed with friends whom I leaned on more than anyone had the right: Bill Caler, Larry Diamond, Emily Goldman, Joanne Liautaud, Bill Lowry, Mike McFaul, Donna Norton, Rick Olguin, Pierre Prentki, Eric Roth, Jenny Ruckelshaus, John Sanchez, Lewis Shepherd, Noreen Schertler, Kathy Teghtsoonian, and Holly Wunder.

Much of the work on this book took place at the Center for International Studies at the University of Southern California. While I was there I was lucky to meet many encouraging and helpful people: Tom Biersteker, Gerry Bender, Cecilia Cichinelli, Alex Hybel, Steve Lamy, Carol Thompson, and Al Yee. I particularly want to acknowledge Tom Biersteker's contribution. While acting in loco parentis for my committee, Tom displayed infinite wisdom in sending me to London and Zimbabwe to strengthen the historical chapters of the book.

The research for this book provided me with the trip of a lifetime. To all of those who availed themselves to be interviewed I give my heartfelt appreciation. I would also like to mention those who took the time and interest to put me in contact with participants who had been involved in the various Zimbabwean negotiations: Lord St. Brides, Sandy Katz, Peggy Watson, Willie Masarurwa, Marilyn Hunwick, and Masipula Sithole. Special thanks go to Masipula, who, as my big brother, took it upon himself to teach me the ins and outs of Zimbabwe. Some of my most memorable times there came from long, passionate discussions with him.

My research in Zimbabwe was made easy through the friendship of many folks there. In particular, I would like to thank Jenny Ruckelshaus, Chris Johnson, and Jane Reese for making 153 North Avenue, Harare, a home away from home.

Behind every book lies funding and many hours spent in library stacks. For the former I would like to thank the MacArthur Foundation and the Center for Arms Control and International Security at Stanford for summer support in 1986; the Center for International Studies at USC and the Center for International and Strategic Affairs at UCLA for their joint fellowship in security studies; the Pew Foundation and their Diplomatic Training Initiative Grants through the Center for International Studies at USC; the Lentz Peace Research Institute in St. Louis; and the Center for Political Economy at Washington University and its director, Douglas North. As for time spent in library stacks, I would like to thank the staffs of the National Archives in Harare, Zimbabwe, and the Hoover Institution Archives at Stanford, both of whom went out of their way to help me.

During the period of finishing this book, I was fortunate enough to be in the Political Science Department of Washington University amidst very supportive colleagues and friends.

Research assistance was provided by Michael Johnson, Heather

Rosen, and Diana Mosovich, who all did great jobs. At SAIS Arthur Rubin proofread the book, and Abby Harrison compiled the index. Special thanks go to my publisher, Lynne Rienner, and to my editor, Gia Hamilton, for their patience and enthusiasm.

Three individuals were incredibly generous with their time to read the manuscript and give me extensive comments—Roy Licklider, Donald Rothchild, and William Zartman. The ability of these scholars to be productive researchers and teachers and still take the time to offer detailed advice and suggestions troubles me—they are setting ridiculously high standards for junior colleagues to meet in the future.

It is customary to save for last the individuals whose contributions encompass more than single dimensions or span times and distances. I would like to thank my brothers and their families, my sister and her family, and my parents, who, even though not really understanding this quixotic quest of mine, were always there to back me up and believe in me. To steal a line from Rick Olguin, "Blind faith is a pretty rare thing." It's also something for which I will be eternally grateful.

Finally, I come to a very special individual: my brother Henry, who died in December 1985. More of a hell-raiser than a peacemaker, he had a penchant for speaking his mind and finding trouble wherever it was. But his love and generosity sustain me throughout my life, and the confidence he showed in me made this book possible. I love him and miss him. I dedicate this book to his memory.

*S.J.S.*

ZIMBABWE

# PEACEMAKING
# IN CIVIL WAR

# 1

# Negotiated Settlement of Civil War

*We had a chance to choose between rationality and madness. Just as Borges said about Switzerland, here you have a people who have taken the strange decision to become rational. We all want peace.* —Oscar Arias  Sanchez

*Once politics are introduced into a situation, it is very difficult to restore rationality.* —Jeffrey Pfeffer

Over the last five years, international leaders have become increasingly aware of the problem of negotiated settlement of civil war. During the summer of 1986, negotiations in the Philippines to reach a peaceful settlement of differences between communist guerrillas and the government of Corazon Aquino collapsed. In El Salvador in 1989 and 1990, the government met face to face with the FMLN in the hope of ending that country's brutal civil war. In Nicaragua in 1988 the Sandinista government negotiated a cease-fire with the U.S.-backed Contra guerrillas, the first step leading to the elections between the Sandinista government and its opponents in 1990. In Southern Africa, regional leaders have signaled their desire for the Angolan government to work with Jonas Savimbi's UNITA toward a settlement of the war that has plagued that country since long before its independence in 1975. Under the direction of Jimmy Carter, talks have recently taken place between representatives of the Eritrean separatist movement and the Ethiopian government. In 1987, Indian mediation in the Sri Lankan civil war was able to achieve an agreement between Tamil separatists and the Sri Lankan government, only to have the agreement collapse during implementation.

What, if anything, gives anyone any hope that negotiations in civil wars might succeed? The historical record of such negotiation is replete with failure; theories of war termination dismiss negotiated settlements of civil war as so improbable as not to warrant in-depth study; and the literature on civil war and revolution has barely addressed the topic.

This chapter sets out to better our understanding of negotiated settlement of civil war. I begin by challenging the conventional view that civil wars are nonnegotiable. Although civil wars provide special difficulties for resolution, I contend that there is no reason to assume a priori that such wars cannot be ended through negotiation. I then turn to understanding the conditions that could render civil war negotiable. I discuss key concepts from the literature on bargaining and conflict resolution, such as alternative leverage, problem solving, and rightness, and suggest how international mediation can help or hinder the resolution of civil war. I argue that current work on conflict resolution can be strengthened by focusing on politics within groups in conflict. Finally, I conclude the chapter by presenting the research design behind the book.

## War Termination Literature and Civil Wars

War termination theory argues that negotiated settlement of civil war is highly unlikely. According to Paul Pillar,

> the likelihood that the two sides in any dispute can negotiate a settlement depends greatly on whether compromise agreements are available. If the stakes are chiefly indivisible, so that neither side can get most of what it wants, negotiations are less apt to be successful. Stakes are usually less divisible in civil wars than in other types of war; the issue is whether one side or the other shall control the country. The very fact that a civil war has broken out indicates the weakness of any mechanisms for compromise, and the war itself tends to polarize whatever moderate elements may have existed. Furthermore, each side in a civil war is a traitor in the eyes of the other and can never expect the enemy to let it live in peace. The struggle for power becomes a struggle for survival as the options narrow to the single one of fight to the finish. (Pillar 1983, 24)

Similarly, Fred Ikle (1971, 95) describes civil war as "all-out" war in a limited setting. Even Adam Curle, an individual deeply devoted to peace and nonviolent settlement of injustice, writes, "Conciliation and bargaining are of very little use in revolutionary situations, or in situations that cannot be changed without a revolutionary adjustment of relationships" (Curle 1970, 24).

The problem with this formulation is that (1) the issues of dispute in civil war need not be indivisible; (2) historically, some civil wars have ended through negotiation and were not "fights to the finish"; and (3) some 16 negotiations of civil wars are under way in the summer of 1990 or have taken place in the last five years with varying degrees of success.

*Civil War: Divisible or Indivisible Stakes?*

First, do civil wars necessarily involve indivisible stakes? The crucial struggles over domestic political rule can be separated into issues of distribution, participation, legitimacy, penetration, and identity (Grew 1978). If the common war termination formulation is correct, then the only objective solution to such issues is all or nothing.

I will pass over the issue of distribution because it is self-evident that in terms of resources—either power or wealth—there are many possible solutions that fall between all or none. Likewise, in terms of political participation, compromise solutions exist whereby increasing the participation of challengers still leaves the government with the ability to be dominant in political processes. The evolution of mass suffrage in Western industrial societies provides many examples of compromise agreements.

Although the issue of participation in the abstract can be settled through compromise, in many instances actors in such crises perceive the stakes to be all or nothing: if actors perceive a struggle to be zero-sum, then they will act accordingly. This, however, is to put the explanation on the actors' perceptions of the conflict and not on the objective situation or issue. For example, contrast Poland in 1981, where the Communist party feared that allowing Solidarity limited participation in government decisionmaking would eventually render the party obsolete, with the Soviet Union in 1988, where Mikhail Gorbachev has argued that not allowing its citizens more participation in government decisionmaking will eventually render the party obsolete. My point here is that similar objective situations can engender different subjective views of possible choices.[1]

As to legitimacy, it may be the case that the conflict develops to the point where both sides make sole claims to this political good. Yet, when we think of compromises that have been reached in domestic conflicts, outcomes are possible where both parties recognize each other as legitimate participants in the political process. Two examples come to mind. In the English Revolution of 1688, the institution of the King of England probably had more legitimacy after the shift of power to the House of Parliament than it had immediately before the revolutionary assault. In a more recent example, in the accords between the Nicaraguan government and the Contra insurgents, signed in March 1988 at Sapoa, Nicaragua, the Contras recognized Daniel Ortega as the constitutional president, acknowledging him as the legitimate leader of the Nicaraguan people, while the Nicaraguan government recognized the Contras as a legitimate political force within Nicaragua that had the support of some of the people—a crucial preliminary step to the elections of 1990.

Penetration provides a more problematic category of issues.

Penetration refers to the ability of a state to extract resources from its peoples. In the strict sense, penetration on its own is an all-or-nothing issue: the state is either able to extract resources or it is not. A conflict over the rights or appropriateness of state penetration will either lead to the population submitting to the demands of the state or it will not. However, when penetration is considered in conjunction with the other issues of participation and distribution, trade-offs are possible on what the state is willing to concede in order to acquire submission. In the development of the nation-state in Europe, the extraction of resources from the population often involved trade-offs involving citizenship, participation, and social welfare (Tilly 1975).

When a civil conflict involves issues of distribution, participation, penetration, or legitimacy, a common identity can help foster cooperation among the parties. A foot soldier in the Nicaraguan army eloquently expressed an underlying sentiment that must be drawn upon if peace is to survive in that country: "We've lost friends, and they've lost friends. We're all Nicaraguans. We all have a right to live" (*New York Times*, March 27, 1988, 1). In the peace that followed the American Civil War there was an effort to emphasize that the North and South were bound together because, in the words of Ely Parker, Ulysses S. Grant's military secretary, "We are all Americans" (McPherson 1988, 849).

When the very conflict itself is over identity, however, as in the case of ethnic or religious wars, the room for compromise solutions becomes more constrained (Horowitz 1985).[2] If a people fights to be recognized as Tamils and their government insists that they are Sri Lankan, it is difficult to find a compromise that can satisfy the identity needs of both parties. What is particularly tantalizing about such conflict is that models of peaceful ethnic coexistence have been established whereby the identity needs of diverse factions are fulfilled (Lijphart 1977; Horowitz 1985; Adam and Moodley 1987). The most common reaction to this type of conflict, however, either attempts through coercion to impose an identity on participants or tries to emphasize shared values at the expense of what makes individuals and communities different. The vexing problem of conflict resolution in such instances is to understand "under what conditions and by what processes can there be a harmonious and cooperative society despite the absence both of shared values and coercion" (Burton 1979, 54).

## Past Outcomes of Civil Wars

It is one of my central contentions that civil wars can be negotiable; that there is no a priori reason to assume otherwise. To illustrate my point

I have compiled a list of civil wars from 1900 to 1989 to establish data on how such wars typically end. I have used Singer and Small's (1982) correlates of war data on civil wars and have chosen to limit myself to civil wars that have occurred only in the twentieth century. I have also added to the Singer and Small data civil wars that were excluded from their data because the conflict intersected with a foreign war,[3] and civil wars that ended in the 1980s.

Although endings to civil wars have been compiled twice before (Modelski 1964; Pillar 1983), I am not satisfied with those attempts, for various reasons. In the case of Modelski, the author presents a list of internal wars without stating his criteria for classification. Many of his cases are obscure, successful coup d'états, which the author admits biases his outcomes toward one actor defeating another. To eliminate this source of bias it would be necessary to include all cases of failed coups, or coups that terminated through negotiated settlement. In the case of Pillar, the author uses an amalgamation of cases from Singer and Small, and Wright (1965), choosing to omit from the former "instances of mass violence that some others would describe as riots rather than civil wars." This leads Pillar to ignore the Colombian civil war of 1899–1902 (100,000 deaths); the Mexican Revolution (250,000 deaths); the Russian Revolution of October 1917 and subsequent civil war (500,000 deaths); the Greek civil war (160,135 deaths); and the Sudanese civil war (250,000 deaths).

Following the criteria I mentioned above, Table 1.1 presents civil wars from 1900 to 1989. For my initial purpose I have classified how these civil wars have ended as follows: (1) elimination of the state or contender on the battlefield; (2) capitulation of one side, understood to mean the unconditional surrender of one side; (3) negotiated surrender by one side; (4) negotiated agreement of the participants; and (5) unstable negotiated agreement, whereby a settlement is reached but a violation soon leads to renewed fighting between the same combatants. Cases of elimination or capitulation where formal negotiations were previously unsuccessful in ending the conflict are indicated by (NEG-U). Mediation is indicated by (M) and mediation that failed to elicit formal negotiation by (M-U).

Table 1.1 shows that 41 of the 68 civil wars in the twentieth century ended in elimination or capitulation. Seven of the 68 cases were settled through negotiation, only to relapse into war. Three of those 7 unstable negotiated settlements ended in capitulation or elimination (China 1911, Jordan 1970, Laos 1973). Three of the 7 conflicts continue today (Angola, Cyprus,[4] Lebanon). One of the 7, Laos 1962, was settled before falling back into war that ended with another unstable settlement in 1973, and eventually terminated with the victory of one of the

Table 1.1  Civil Wars, 1900–1989

| Country | Years | Termination |
|---------|-------|-------------|
| Colombia | 1899–1902 | Negotiated Surrender (M) |
| Uruguay | 1903–1904 | Negotiation |
| Russia | 1905–1906 | Capitulation |
| Romania | 1907 | Elimination |
| Morocco | 1907–1908 | Elimination |
| Iran | 1909 | Negotiated Surrender |
| China | 1911 | Negotiation (Unstable) |
| Morocco | 1911 | Elimination |
| Paraguay | 1911–1912 | Elimination |
| Germany | 1919 | Elimination |
| Mexico | 1910–1920 | Negotiation |
| Hungary | 1919–1920 | Capitulation |
| Russia | 1917–1921 | Elimination (M-U) |
| Ireland | 1920–1922 | Elimination (NEG-U) |
| Honduras | 1924 | Negotiation (M) |
| Afghanistan | 1924–1925 | Elimination |
| Afghanistan | 1929–1938 | Elimination |
| Mexico | 1926–1929 | Negotiation |
| Brazil | 1932 | Elimination |
| Spain | 1934 | Elimination |
| Spain | 1936–1939 | Elimination (NEG-U) |
| Paraguay | 1947 | Capitulation (M-U) |
| Greece | 1945–1948 | Capitulation (NEG-U) |
| Yemen | 1948 | Elimination |
| Costa Rica | 1948 | Negotiated Surrender |
| Colombia | 1948 | Capitulation |
| China | 1927–1949 | Elimination (M) (NEG-U) |
| Indonesia | 1950 | Negotiated Surrender (M) |
| Bolivia | 1946–1952 | Capitulation |
| Korea | 1950–1953 | Negotiation |
| Indonesia | 1953 | Elimination |
| Philippines | 1948–1954 | Elimination |
| Guatemala | 1954 | Capitulation |
| Argentina | 1955 | Negotiated Surrender |
| Lebanon | 1958 | Negotiation |
| Cuba | 1959 | Capitulation |
| Iraq | 1959 | Elimination |
| Indonesia | 1956–1960 | Capitulation |
| Malaysia | 1948–1960 | Elimination (NEG-U) |
| 1st Laos | 1959–1962 | Negotiation (M) (Unstable) |
| Algeria | 1954–1962 | Negotiated Surrender |
| Congo | 1960–1964 | Elimination (M) (NEG-U) |
| Rwanda | 1963–1964 | Elimination |

*(continued)*

Table 1.1 (*continued*)

| Country | Years | Termination |
|---|---|---|
| Colombia | 1948–1964 | Negotiation |
| Cyprus | 1963–1964 | Negotiation (M) (Unstable) |
| Dominican Republic | 1965 | Negotiation (M) |
| Uganda | 1966 | Elimination |
| Yemen | 1962–1970 | Negotiation (M) |
| Nigeria | 1967–1970 | Capitulation (M-U) |
| Jordan | 1970 | Negotiation (M) (Unstable) |
| Guatemala | 1970–1971 | Capitulation |
| Sri Lanka | 1971 | Elimination |
| Pakistan | 1971 | Capitulation |
| Burundi | 1972 | Elimination |
| Sudan | 1963–1972 | Negotiation (M) |
| 2nd Laos | 1963–1972 | Negotiation (M) (Unstable) |
| Mozambique | 1964–1974 | Capitulation |
| Angola | 1963–1975 | Negotiation (M) (Unstable) |
| Cambodia | 1967–1975 | Elimination |
| Vietnam | 1957–1975 | Elimination (NEG-U) |
| Lebanon | 1975–1976 | Negotiation (Unstable) |
| Nicaragua | 1978–1979 | Capitulation |
| Iran | 1979 | Capitulation |
| Zimbabwe | 1972–1980 | Negotiation (M) |
| Uganda | 1981–1987 | Elimination |
| Chad | 1980–1987 | Negotiation |
| Namibia | 1964–1989 | Negotiation (M) |
| Nicaragua | 1981–1989 | Negotiation (M) |

| *Termination by Category*: | | |
|---|---|---|
| | Elimination | 26 |
| | Capitulation | 16 |
| | Negotiation | 14 |
| | Negotiated Surrender | 5 |
| | Unstable Negotiation | 7 |

*Key*: (M) Mediation
(M-U) Mediation that failed to elicit formal negotiation
(NEG-U) Elimination or capitulation where formal negotiations were previously unsuccessful

Table 1.2 Civil Wars Ended by Negotiation, 1900–1989

Colombia, 1902
Uruguay, 1904
Iran, 1909
Mexico, 1920
Honduras, 1924
Mexico, 1929.
Costa Rica, 1948
Indonesia, 1950
Korea, 1953
Argentina, 1955
Lebanon, 1958
Algeria, 1962
Colombia, 1964
Dominican Republic, 1965
Yemen, 1970
Sudan, 1972
Zimbabwe, 1980
Chad, 1987
Nicaragua, 1989
Namibia, 1989

challengers. Thus, if we eliminate the 3 continuing wars, and count Laos as one case, the ratio of elimination and capitulation to all civil wars increases to 44 of 64 cases in the twentieth century. Of those 44 cases, 3 experienced unstable settlement; 5 involved unsuccessful negotiations; 2 involved unsuccessful mediated negotiation; and 3 involved mediation attempts that failed to bring the parties together for negotiations.

Contrary to the expectations of the war termination literature, 20 of 65 conflicts were resolved through some form of negotiation. Table 1.2 is a list of those settlements that were reached through negotiation.

To take into account "special" features of cases on this list, I have further trimmed the cases by applying more stringent coding criteria. If we eliminate cases that are also colonial wars, cases that formalized one-sided agreements, and cases that ended in the negotiated partition of the country, we are still left with eleven cases of negotiated settlement: Uruguay, Honduras, Mexico 1929, Lebanon 1958, Sudan, Colombia 1964, Dominican Republic, Yemen, Zimbabwe, Chad, and Nicaragua. If we throw out of the larger sample the "special" cases, approximately 15 percent of the civil wars in this century were resolved through negotiation instead of elimination or capitulation. Of these eleven cases of negotiated settlement, six were terminated through international mediation.

Given that there are cases of negotiated settlement of civil wars, some would attempt to explain away such cases as exceptions or oddities. For example, in the Pillar study quoted earlier (Pillar 1983), the author recognized that negotiated settlements to civil wars have taken place. In a similar exercise to that here, Pillar classified six civil wars as having ended through negotiation. His cases differ from the cases above,[5] yet a major similarity between the two lists concerns the role of international involvement in the negotiated cases. Instead of seeing a puzzle to be explained, however, Pillar suggested that the mediated negotiation of civil wars is not a problem worth examining:

> Few civil wars end through negotiation unless they become highly internationalized. In all six of the wars. . . the country whose future was at stake had become a pawn in a larger conflict, with outside powers becoming directly involved as belligerents or negotiators. These include the two wars in Laos (in which the Vietnamese were participants), the Yemeni civil war (where Egypt became deeply involved), the fighting in Jordan in 1970 and Lebanon in 1975–1976 (both of which included Syria and the PLO), and the insurgency in Zimbabwe (in which Britain, as the responsible colonial power, arranged a settlement). (Pillar 1983, 24–25)

This observation, while correct in noting the presence of internationalization of these conflicts, leaves a number of questions unanswered. First, Pillar fails to specify what it is about international involvement that alleviates the problem of "indivisible stakes" he previously equated with civil war. What in particular about internationalization of civil war reduces the likelihood of a "fight to the finish"? Should we expect any internationalization of a civil war to mitigate the difficulties inherent in civil war negotiations?

If we turn to the example of Vietnam, Pillar himself argues indirectly that internationalization per se, or the presence of kingmakers (in this case the United States), need not contribute to the likelihood of political settlement. He discusses the inability of the United States to reach a stable agreement with the North Vietnamese over the Vietnamese revolution:

> The stakes in Vietnam centered on the fundamental question of who should rule South Vietnam, and that is the sort of issue on which compromises tend to be difficult and offer little satisfaction to either side. Solutions which leave open the possibility that the enemy eventually will take power are not highly valued because they pose a risk not only to one's political goals but even to one's life. Although during the period of American involvement it was an international war, and although this phase ended with a negotiated settlement as

most international wars do, the issues resembled those in most civil wars. (Pillar 1983, 162)

This prompts an obvious question: Why didn't U. S. involvement in the Vietnamese case mitigate against the issues resembling "those . . . in most civil wars"?

Some argue that it was U.S. involvement in Vietnam that precluded a negotiated settlement earlier in the conflict. George Kahin, for instance, documents how the Minh government, following the assassination of Diem in South Vietnam in 1963, wanted to enter into negotiations with the National Liberation Front opposition to form a coalition government that would be neutralist in character. This development so alarmed the U.S. government that some advisers instigated another coup to block any such talks from taking place (Kahin 1987, 182–202). In this instance, it was international involvement that hindered the domestic negotiation of a civil war. U.S. intervention in Vietnam defined the war as one of survival, as one where no compromise could exist.

Finally, one has to question Pillar's description of the domestic actors as "pawns" in a larger game. I find it difficult to think of such parties as big- or middle-power "yes-men." In the case that I am most familiar with, Ian Smith for fourteen years proved the impotency of the British to impose their will in Southern Rhodesia. After 1972, the British had found their plans for Rhodesia blocked three times by the obstinacy of Smith, and therefore resolved to avoid the conflict altogether. When they were brought back into the conflict, they did so with much reluctance. In the Jordanian example that Pillar cites, the settlement that was reached in 1970 was broken repeatedly by the PLO in the ensuing months, until King Hussein lost his patience and militarily defeated and disarmed them. This took place in a situation where many Arab leaders counseled caution and moderation to the PLO (Butterworth 1976). It is much too simple to assume that combatants in civil wars are putty in the hands of larger actors.

Regardless of the past efficacy of such negotiations, antagonists currently engulfed in civil war are searching for ways to resolve their conflicts. Table 1.3 presents civil wars in the world in 1989. For our purposes, the important point is that formal negotiations have taken place in thirteen of these seventeen civil wars. Of these thirteen negotiations, two have been partially successful by either reducing the conflict, establishing a cease-fire, or prompting some of the actors to choose a different method of political competition than war: Sri Lanka and Colombia. Although it is impossible to say whether these talks will lead to stable settlements, their progress provides more reason for examining such negotiations.

## Table 1.3 Civil Wars, 1989

| Country | Duration[a] | Deaths | Negotiations[b] |
|---------|-------------|--------|-----------------|
| Colombia | 3 | 20,000 | Y* |
| El Salvador | 11 | 65,000 | Y |
| Peru | 8 | 15,000 | N |
| Guatemala | 23 | 138,000 | Y |
| Lebanon[c] | 14 | 162,000 | Y |
| Ethiopia | 15 | 539,000 | Y |
| W. Sahara | 13 | 10,000 | N |
| Mozambique | 13 | 415,000 | N |
| South Africa | 4 | 4,000 | Y |
| Sudan | 5 | 506,000 | Y |
| Afghanistan[c] | 10 | 725,000 | Y |
| India | 5 | 12,000 | Y |
| Indonesia | 14 | 106,000 | N |
| Kampuchea[c] | 11 | 64,000 | Y |
| Philippines | 17 | 75,000 | Y |
| Sri Lanka | 5 | 9,000 | Y* |
| Angola | 14 | 341,000 | Y |

*Source*: Ruth Leger Sivard, *World Military and Social Expenditures* (World Priorities: Leesburg, VA, 1989)

[a]In years

[b]Y = negotiations are currently under way or have occurred; N = no negotiations; * = negotiations partially successful

[c]War also interstate

## Is Negotiation in Civil War Different from Negotiation in Other Conflicts?

Although some civil wars have been terminated through negotiation, many end in the elimination of one of the parties. This differentiates the termination of civil wars from the termination of most international wars, which tend to be fought over limited goals and rarely end by one side physically eliminating its adversary (Schelling 1966). As Schelling points out, if one side fights a war to force an enemy government into making a specific change, then it has a stake in preserving that government so that it will carry out the desired policy.

If indivisible issues do not account for the total war character of many civil wars, we are left with a puzzle. Why do so many civil wars end in capitulation or elimination? I suggest the following possible reasons why this should be so: (1) civil wars often concur with revolutionary struggle and involve individuals who place principles before interests, thereby rendering such conflicts nonnegotiable; (2) the mere presence of such individuals in the conflict and their rhetoric of elimination of the enemy establishes a key strategic bargaining dilemma that renders negotiations less likely; (3) since an essential part of power-sharing agreements is the willingness for the combatants to accept vulnerability and make their security dependent on mutual arrangements rather than self-help, individuals in civil war may fear settlement more than they fear continued fighting; (4) since insurgent and government leaders must be aware of their own political survival within their party, and because peacemaking is such a risky endeavor, leaders may not be able to commit to negotiations for fear of losing power within their own party; and finally (5) the mere fact that negotiated settlements are so difficult can lead to escalatory processes that may negate the possibility of any compromise. I will take up these issues in turn.

*Insurgency and Conflict over Principles*

One explanation for the total character of civil war would note the concurrence of such wars with revolutionary struggles and posit a theory of revolutionary leaders and unwillingness to compromise. I would anticipate the following characterization: Certainly what differentiates revolutionaries from others is that they will not compromise under any circumstance. They are ideologically and philosophically committed to their programs and will display an incredible indifference to costs in order to achieve their ideological goals. Even if they were to negotiate a settlement to the civil war, it would only be for tactical reasons. Lenin, for instance, went so far as to advocate parliamentary democracy while never losing sight of his long-term goal of seizing power.

Such an objection is, in part, well taken. I would broaden it first, however, to include not only insurgents but also government officials who are fighting to keep power. Second, I would argue that such ideologically committed individuals are to be found in revolutionary movements and governments that oppose them, but that it would be rare to find unanimity among leaders and followers concerning the desirability of fighting at all costs, or the willingness to compromise the basic goals of the revolution. Indeed, I wish to argue that often in revolutionary struggles there is little consensus as to the goals of the revolutionary movement.

In revolutionary struggles, some individuals may see the conflict as involving conflicting principles, whether they be alternative visions of a future society, or values, for instance, placing justice before security, or dignity before democracy (Laitin 1987). In such instances the conflict may be, for some, a clash of incommensurable principles. Objections to settlement are then philosophically derived and leave no room for compromise. The participants in the conflict see different worlds, speak different languages, and have no basis for settlement because the conflict takes on an ideological character that renders it nonnegotiable.

The distinction between conflict derived from interests and conflict based on principles is an old one but essential to understanding strategic calculations in revolutionary bargaining. For example, Martin Gilbert, in his study *The Roots of Appeasement*, discusses Edmund Burke's belief that war with the colonies in America was folly because it was a conflict over interests and therefore had a basis for compromise and reconciliation. Twenty years later, Burke urged war with France because the issues at hand concerned doctrines and ideas, an ideological conflict with no room for compromise.

The difficulty of such a distinction, as Gilbert points out, is that for leaders there is little basis for judgment and much room for error in determining conflicts whose roots stem from differences in interest and those that concern philosophical objections:

> It is for the individual to decide, by means of whatever evidence is at his disposal, whether a particular war springs from a clash of interests which by better management could be shifted from the battlefield to the conference table, or from a conflict of ideologies which can only be resolved—indeed, some would say must be resolved—by war.
>
> The personal dilemma creates a number of difficult problems. Can an individual, even a politician inside the government circle, know for certain that he has enough evidence at his disposal to make a valid judgement? Can a politician, however much evidence is at his disposal, be certain that he is not unduly influenced by personal or popular prejudice, the result, perhaps, of decades of imperceptible yet insidious propaganda? (Gilbert 1966, 2–3)

The chances of a compromise settlement with the Ayatollah Khomeini in 1979 were probably nonexistent. A compromise with Abimael Guzman, the leader of Sendero Luminoso in Peru, is also unlikely.[6] These individuals define the revolutionary conflict as a battle of principles, and the attainment of their goals precludes the possibilities of compromise and negotiation. Such leaders are completely indifferent to alternatives other than winning and are able to withstand horrendous losses in pursuit of their objectives.

On the other hand, revolutionary leaders such as Mao and Lenin occasionally recommended negotiations. Whether such recommendations were purely tactical is difficult to judge because their revolutions succeeded, and therefore there is an overwhelming tendency to consider such instances as part of an all-knowing, grand strategy that would not have accepted less than full power in the long run.[7]

## *Strategic Dilemmas in Civil War Negotiation*

The mere presence of actors who seek elimination of their adversary produces key strategic dilemmas in civil war negotiation. In any civil war there are individuals who seek a total transformation and the complete elimination of their opposition. But insurgent movements also contain leaders who will accept far less than that, if they believe their opponent will bargain in reasonably good faith. Governments, too, are rarely unified on their goals: while some participants may define the battle as a war to the death in which any concession will be interpreted as weakness, there will be other individuals who believe a compromise agreement to be both possible and desirable.

Insurgent movements thus are composed of diverse factional elements who, although at least informally united in their opposition to the current regime, may have very different and even competing goals and objectives, ranging from changing specific government policies to replacing specific regime personnel, increasing political participation, redistributing wealth, or transforming societal values. Rather than being internally homogeneous, revolutionary movements may be characterized as a heterogeneous coalition of distinct factions in terms of preferred end-states.

The panoply of goals within the revolutionary movement is mirrored within the government. There are factions whose goals include total preservation of the status quo and factions that desire limited change in personnel or policies. As with the revolutionaries, these factions are based on preferences as well as strategies.

In any civil war a government must try to recognize whether the insurgency is dominated by those who want complete change or those who want limited change. Can the insurgent movement be stemmed by concessions, or will those concessions spur the insurgents on to newer, stronger demands? If it is the latter, then the mere act of conceding will endanger the government's position in this battle to the death.[8] Insurgents, too, must judge the character of a government that shows a willingness to negotiate. Is it sincere? Is its cooperation a tactic to weaken the insurgency in order to triumph over it for good?

In any civil war there is the risk that either party may be willing to enter into negotiations or agreements solely for short-term tactical advantage. If we think back to the two experiences of cooperation between the CCP and the KMT in China, on both occasions the United Front between them ended because the KMT sensed an opportunity to obliterate the communists outright and slaughter their "allies."[9]  In

Nicaragua in 1934, Augosto Sandino was assassinated by Somoza after he had agreed to enter into negotiations to ending the revolution in that country (Macauley 1967). In the Zimbabwe case, this issue was a real concern (with good reason) among blacks during the cease-fire and among whites after independence. Therefore, the settlement had to establish protections and guarantees to produce the expectation that neither would eliminate the other.

## The Fear of Settlement

Leaders may recognize the value of settlement and cooperation but so fear being double-crossed that they are incapable of putting their followers at risk. For example, John Womack (1969) depicts Emilio Zapata, the Mexican revolutionary leader, as a leader who desperately wanted peace but was paralyzed to negotiate a settlement because the chance that his supporters would be tricked and eliminated weighed so heavily on his conscience. In that instance, a negotiated settlement emerged between the various revolutionary parties only after Zapata was killed and replaced by Magana.

This points to a different source of all-or-nothing outcomes of civil war: the lack of trust in an opponent in the face of incomplete information about his or her goals. Stated somewhat differently, an important reason for revolutions ending in the elimination of one party is that the actors come to fear the results of settlement more than they fear continuing fighting.

Moreover, the very issues involved in negotiating the termination of a civil war are fraught with risks and danger. Arrangements such as the integration of armed forces and police, the establishment of transitional governments, and the initiation and maintenance of a cease-fire provide opportunities for one adversary to take advantage of another. For such settlements to succeed the parties must accept vulnerability and place their security in the others' hands.

Finally, negotiations to settle civil war must inevitably lead to a consideration of the conditions for stable power-sharing arrangements. Polyarchy or power-sharing should be seen as an arrangement in which competing parties agree to place bounds on their competition. The essence of this arrangement is the expectation that whatever happens in the short term, the victor will not use its position to eliminate the loser. There is an expectation that competition will continue into the future and the loser will have the opportunity to contest for power at a later date.

A principal problem concerns how parties come to expect that their competition will stretch into the infinite future. How do players come to believe that their opponents will not use political power to eliminate them, take advantage of them economically, or exclude them politically? Constitutions, although they are statements of purpose concerning institutions, protections, and guarantees for keeping competition within bounds, do not in and of themselves provide such protections. And the expectations that one's competitor will abide by the rules of the game are deeply affected by the recent past of violence, bloodshed, and political chicanery that are part and parcel of civil war.

## Political Leaders and Internal Conflicts

Leaders of insurgencies and governments must negotiate with one face looking outwards to the opponent and one face looking inwards to political competition within their own parties. Political leaders of insurgencies and governments must calculate their actions in terms of their ability to keep their own positions. Often such individual political considerations work against possible conciliatory moves towards one's adversaries.

When analyzing civil war, it is tempting to see the main actors as governments and insurgency movements. Yet, in the overwhelming number of cases with which I am familiar, insurgencies are composed of either various parties fighting together against the government or single parties that contain within them different factions organized on many dimensions, including the crucial questions of what the overall goal of the insurgency is and what outcome it would be willing to live with. Examples of the former include Angola from 1962 to 1974, Zimbabwe from 1965 to 1980, Afghanistan from 1980 to the present, Russia in 1917, Iran in 1979, South Africa from 1962 to the present, El Salvador at present, Nicaragua from 1977 to 1979, and the Philippines in 1985. Examples of dominant insurgent parties marked by the presence of factional politics include the CCP in China, the Bolsheviks in Russia in 1917, ZANU in Zimbabwe, and the FLN in Algeria.

As to governments and factionalism in civil war, Fred Ikle observes that "nothing is more divisive for a government than having to make peace at the price of major concessions. The process of ending a war almost inevitably evokes an intense internal struggle if it means abandoning an ally or giving up popularly accepted objectives" (Ikle 1971, 59). Ikle goes on to argue that in almost any war the government faces a battle from within based on factions that he labels "hawks" vs. "doves." These factions differ on the important dimensions of what the war is all about and under what circumstances the war should end. Moreover, they tend to seek information that will bolster their interpretation about the course of the war in order to strengthen their position in the internal debate (Ikle 1971, 74).

Although Ikle's focus is on international war, his remarks also apply to governments and revolutionary movements in the throes of civil war. One instance that he cites, for example, concerns the Greek civil war:

> The Communist insurgency in Greece ended in 1949 with the national government in control of the entire country and the Communist party banned. In an earlier phase in the Greek civil war, the Communists could have chosen to give up their armed struggle while surviving as a party more or less free to use nonviolent means of opposition. But in the internal conflict among Communist "hawks" and "doves," Zachariades, the "hawkish" proponent of an all-out fight against the government army prevailed. . . . In the end, Zachariades managed to blame his opponents within the Communist party for the defeat (which he had engineered) and denounced them as "traitors"—the Communist equivalent of the stab-in-back legend. (Ikle 1971, 95)

In the article that preceded his *Essence of Decision*, Graham Allison discusses the implications of his model typology for the United States' war with Vietnam. He contrasts rational actor explanations of war termination that rely on calculations of losses and gains for governments taken as single actors with his Model III focus on intergovernmental politics:

> Model III suggests that surrender will not come at the point that strategic costs outweigh benefits, but that it will not wait until the leadership group concludes that the war is lost. Rather the problem is better understood in terms of four additional propositions. First, strong advocates of the war effort, whose careers are closely identified with the war, rarely come to the conclusion that costs outweigh benefits. Second, quite often from the outset of a war, a number of members of the government (particularly those whose responsibilities sensitize them to problems other than war, e.g., economic planners or intelligence experts) are convinced that the war effort is futile. Third, surrender is likely to come as the result of a political shift that enhances the effective power of the latter group (and adds swing members to it). Fourth, the course of the war, particularly actions of the victor, can influence the advantages and disadvantages of players in the loser's government. Thus, North Vietnam will surrender not when its leaders have a change of heart, but when Hanoi has a change of leaders (or a change of effective power within the central circle). How U.S. bombing (or pause), threats, promises, or action in the South affect the game in Hanoi is subtle but nonetheless crucial. (Allison 1969, 718)

To provide a more recent example, in the Nicaraguan peace talks between the Sandinistas and the Contras in February 1988, the Nicaraguan government made internal concessions demanded by the Arias peace plan. These concessions took place a couple of weeks before a vote in the U.S. Congress on whether to keep providing support to the Contras. In the week preceding the vote, the Nicaraguan government cracked down on internal opposition in direct conflict with some of the concessionary moves they had made earlier. Stephen Kinzer, a *New York Times* reporter not known for his sympathy for the Sandinistas, reported that factional infighting had broken out in the Nicaraguan government between Daniel Ortega and Tomás Borge on the issues of compromises with the Contras. Ortega supported concessions that Borge stridently opposed.

At the time, Ronald Reagan was lobbying heavily for the continuation of U.S. aid to the Contras. He argued that military pressure had brought the Sandinistas to compromise and that only by continuing pressure would the Sandinistas continue to make concessions. The crucial question then becomes: At that particular point were the Sandinistas of one mind on negotiating, or were the peace talks a highly divisive political issue that had split the leadership? If the negotiations had split the Nicaraguan government, and also assuming that the United States truly wanted a negotiated settlement,[10] then it should have acted in terms of strengthening Ortega's hand against Borge. The appropriate strategic move would have been for Reagan to be conciliatory so that Ortega could point to the benefits accrued from his negotiating stance. Instead, the Reagan regime continued to press for more Contra aid, thereby reinforcing the claims made by the Borge group that *no concession whatsoever by the Sandinistas would matter to the United States and that they should therefore play a tough strategy throughout.*

### Negotiation and Escalation

If antagonists in civil wars fear settlement and fail to move toward negotiated peace, escalation may render the conflict nonnegotiable.

The literature on escalation tells us that it has two aspects.[11] First, it is any action in war that involves the crossing of a limit. Second, not only does the action cross this limit, but it also alters the participants' expectations about the course and outcome of the war. The basic implication of this definition is that escalation is interactive: it involves both parties and therefore depends on one's perception and expectation of one's own actions and a perception and expectation of one's opponent's actions, expectations, and beliefs.

There are two prevailing images of escalation. Some see escalation as a deliberate process that can be controlled by the actors involved. Others see escalation as a process that has its own dynamic and that, once set in motion, naturally tends to lose control as an action-reaction cycle keeps the escalation moving to higher and higher levels. Following the lead of Richard Smoke (1977), I would like to suggest that it can be either or both. Under certain circumstances it can be controlled, but there always exists the potential for violence to increase out of control. There are at least two images of this: (a) the escalation-counterescalation process continues upward "out of control" in the sense that it reaches levels neither side wanted or expected at the outset; or (b) one side escalates in expectation of reaching a stable plateau but the other side "overreacts" with a massive escalation. This risk is particularly high in negotiations when an opponent, to bring pressure on the adversary, increases its use of violence within what it believes to be the implicit acceptable limit. The conflict may then escalate because of misperception on the part of the adversary—he reads the violence as crossing the threshold and reacts strongly. Or the cumulative level of violence may foreclose negotiations as an option: solutions that were possible at the beginning of a conflict may not be available later. There are three reasons for this.

First, as one's investment in something increases, the stakes become bigger, so there exists a temptation to stay involved and not cut one's losses. And while at some point the operative principle may become "don't throw good money after bad" (or, in war, don't waste live bodies after dead ones), this point may be far in the future and not reached until much has been lost. The U.S. experience in Vietnam and the French experience in Algeria are examples of this phenomenon.

Second, the objectives one pursues in war are related to ongoing events and tend to shift with them—so that as one's means escalate, so often do one's objectives: in Kenneth Boulding's words, "Sacrifice creates value." This dynamic is captured in the words of Saad Dahlab, an Algerian leader of the *Front de Libération Nationale*, who in 1958 stated, "France must understand now that a negotiation can no longer be entered into today on what Ferhat Abbas demanded with moderation in 1943. Our people have not eaten grass and roots in order to obtain a new statute given as a concession" (Horne 1987, 461).

Third, the work of Pruitt and Rubin (1986) argues that "as conflicts escalate, hard-to-reverse changes occur in the individuals and groups involved, thereby increasing the likelihood of further escalation. . . . Examples of such changes are the development of rigid, unfavorable perceptions of the adversary and the emergence of militant leadership on both sides" (Pruitt 1986, 239; Pruitt and Rubin 1986).

The changes that Pruitt and Rubin describe can lead to a fourth reason why prolonged conflict may escalate and preclude any more negotiations. As militant leadership emerges within groups, individuals within the insurgency or the government may attempt to escalate the conflict on their own, against the commands of those nominally in control. Adam and Moodley (1987, 255) describe such a scenario for South Africa: "Once bombs go off in factories and discotheques, planes are hijacked, and public figures are assassinated, a single minor symbolic event can trigger chain reactions on both sides that none of the more responsible leadership can control. Once this threshold has been passed, negotiations for power-sharing come too late. The option then will be surrender or 'victory': a fight to the death."

A common pattern in civil conflict is that at the beginning of civil wars, the insurgent movement makes demands that fall short of a complete political, social, and economic transformation. Governments, either because they perceive the opposition to have complete transformational goals instead of limited goals, or because of their optimism about defeating the movement outright, tend to avoid concessions and fight. At later stages of the fight, the government may believe that concessions are necessary, only to find that the demands of the insurgency have increased and what would have originally bought them a settlement is now rejected. There are two explanations for this. First, it is possible that those in the insurgent coalition whose demands were at first limited have defected to a hard-line faction. Alternatively, the increase in demands may be the product of a discount factor on the movement's side: the insurgency raises its demands to make up for the costs incurred in combat with the government. Even though the insurgents' goals fall short of complete transformation and elimination of the government, they have increased their limited goals.

With these possibilities in mind I will now turn to developing a framework for analyzing negotiated settlement of civil wars.

## *Negotiation: Bargaining,*
## *Problem Solving, and the Power of Alternatives*

In this book I follow Robert North (1990) in making processes of bargaining, leverage, and coalition formation central to my analysis. North, citing Schelling (1960), defines bargaining "as verbal and non-verbal interchanges in situations where the ability of one actor to gain his ends depends to an important degree on the choices or decisions that the other actor will make." Leverage refers to the "efforts by one bargainer to influence the choices or decisions of the other actor." Actors in situations of interdependence seek to use their leverage (resources, rewards, threats, coercions) to induce or compel desired behavior from other actors. Often, individual actors join coalitions to increase their resources "to effect socially what they cannot accomplish singly."

One of the important developments in the recent literature on bargaining focuses on alternatives as the crux for understanding whether agreements are reached between individuals in bargaining situations, what parties might benefit disproportionately from such agreements, and the likelihood of agreements being fulfilled. As Lax and Sebenius observe, "The basic test of any proposed joint agreement is whether it offers higher subjective worth than that side's best course of action absent agreement. Thus moves 'away from the table' to shape the parties' alternatives to agreement may be as or more important than tactics employed 'at the table'"(Lax and Sebenius 1986a, 163).

The relationship between alternatives and negotiation also works in the reverse direction. That is, the search for alternatives or the unilateral attempt to win a conflict outright is affected dramatically by the likelihood and progress of negotiated settlement. As Lax and Sebenius point out, "Especially in complex, protracted negotiations, new information and interpretations may become available about the external environment and about the bargaining situation itself (the real interests, aspirations, and tactics of other participants; subjective probabilities of reaching different outcomes; as well as the likely costs in money, energy, and time required for a settlement). Thus decisions on the extent and intensity of moves to affect alternatives should be conditioned by current assessments of the bargaining's future course" (Lax and Sebenius 1986a, 164).

Alternatives are directly related to issues of power between the actors: "Along with overtones of differing preference intensities . . . 'power' in dependent relationships thus can be understood as a variable combination of two key elements . . . the ability to change another's alternatives and the attractiveness of one's own competing alternatives" (Lax and Sebenius 1986a, 174–175).

The emphasis on alternatives is particularly useful for our purpose. In civil war there is a strong temptation to look solely for unilateral ways out of the conflict. That is, as long as alternatives exist apart from the bargaining table that may bring a better outcome for a party, that party will choose to explore such alternatives. Thus, in thinking about the bargaining aspects of civil war, it is wise to pay attention to "the strategic aspects of alternatives or to negotiators' complex moves to shape, protect, and improve them [alternatives]"(Lax and Sebenius 1986a, 164).

The interrelationship between alternatives and bargaining concerns the search to maximize the gains from a bargain vis-à-vis what one could gain "away from the table." The fruits of negotiation, however, not only depend on value that is claimed at the bargaining table, but also involve moves to create value at the table. Often, a possible agreement might be reached through negotiation that would prove superior to both parties' unilateral alternative, only to be unattainable because of the parties' intransigence in sharing information. For any negotiation to succeed, the parties must also search for common ground in order to identify sources of joint gain. What I would like to suggest is that negotiation is a process combining elements of bargaining and elements of problem-solving and that negotiations often fail because the adversarial nature of the bargaining component of negotiations overwhelms the problem-solving aspects.

In 1958, March and Simon characterized bargaining and problem solving as different modes of resolving conflict, with bargaining "appropriate when there are values to be distributed, and problem solving when there are values that are shared and must be achieved jointly" (Diesing 1966, citing the distinction made by March and Simon, 1958). A problem that immediately comes to the fore, however, is that negotiation typically involves both the distribution of values and the joint achievement of shared values. Both processes coexist in negotiations, often as a tug of war between maximizing individual gain and reaching a mutual settlement that makes possible said maximization.

As Paul Diesing points out,

> A bargaining process in which utilities are to be distributed brings with it the necessity of problem solving, because whenever there are utilities that cannot be shared, the process of distributing them creates a situation which is shared and creates values which are shared. For instance, in bargaining in terms of power, if you make a threat and it is answered, and you reach a solution in terms of power, you have created a situation in which there is a shared need to maintain a power distribution. In bargaining with norms—forcing your opponent to be fair—you create a situation in which you have to maintain these norms to protect them; in communication of information you must maintain communication lines. Bargaining always brings problem solving with it.
>
> The converse is also true. In any problem-solving situation, any discussion process, or any joint attempt to reach a common good, any ceremony or ritual creates a distribution of utilities, and this problem solving goes on through bargaining. Put in a more general way, human behavior is simultaneously an attempt to maximize expected utility as things are distributed, and the participation in a joint endeavor in which the emphasis is on spontaneous involvement. (Diesing 1966, 189)

Azar and Burton (1986) argue that conflict resolution is dependent on the analytical aspects of problem solving. The participants in struggle must redefine their conflict in such a way as to minimize the adversarial aspects of bargaining. In John Burton's words, "There is an implied assumption that *the analysis of a particular conflict*, within this analytical framework, *itself leads to the resolution of the conflict.* There is a hypothesis that once relationships have been analyzed satisfactorily, once each side is accurately informed of the perceptions of the other, of the alternative values and goals, of the alternative means and costs of attaining them, the possible outcomes acceptable to the parties are revealed" (Burton 1982, 122).

From civil war and the goal of eliminating one's opponent to the accurate awareness of one's opponents' needs, values, and goals—in essence their identity—takes us down a long road that is seldom traveled. Is it possible for actors involved in such intense conflict to be able to identify what is common to them and their enemy and what solutions may be possible that can address both of their needs? I am doubtful. But I believe that outside actors can help bring about such a process and will now turn to their role in peacemaking in civil wars.

## The Components of Mediation

For any potential mediator or negotiator, what I refer to here as leverage and what Lax and Sebenius label power "is associated with the ability to favorably change the bargaining set," that is, the ability to create alternatives away from the table for oneself and the ability to lessen the desirability of alternatives away from the table for one's adversary. Based on an array of sources, Lax and Sebenius suggest that such leverage comes from five sources: coercion (the "stick"), remuneration (the "carrot"), identification ("charisma"), normative conformity (appeal to values, principles, and norms), and knowledge (information).

The effective use of leverage depends on appropriate strategy and tactics. Strategy for a mediator consists of achieving a good fit between "substance, authority and resources, and administration." Strategy demands that individuals combine a clear idea of their goal, an understanding of what is needed to attract and sustain support, and a feasible plan of administration and implementation. Often such coalescence of factors comes from learning and creativity: "The process of integrating the different required factors is iterative, somewhat ad hoc, and even requires a kind of esthetic judgement" (Lax and Sebenius 1986b, 255–264).

In this conception of mediation, the ability of a would-be mediator is an independent variable that affects the success or failure of negotiation. To carry out the demands of strategy "requires preparation, analysis of interests, alternatives, and possible agreements, as well as, sometimes, careful sequencing of meetings, and so on." Lax and Sebenius also suggest that strategy has a coalition-building component that involves the skills of "creating consistent networks of linked agreements" (1986b, 264). Mediators must build coalitions around the alternatives they put forth and block any possible adverse coalitions that may attempt to derail the negotiations. The authors suggest that the tool of "backward mapping" is particularly useful; that is, a mediator should try to envision where opposition to a joint alternative may come from, and then work backwards from that individual or group to create an agreement that will attract or isolate that actor.

A key to creating such "networks of linked agreements" lies in the art of adding or subtracting parties to the negotiation. Often it is necessary to tie current negotiations to relationships beyond the parties and issues in the main confrontation. As Lax and Sebenius observe, "Adding or subtracting parties who have an interest in a settlement may alter the original zone of agreement . . . [and] . . . may spread or elevate risks from the bargain of the original participants." While such linking of negotiations may be crucial for success, it creates a heavy burden on the planning abilities of mediators: "The more parties (and issues), the higher the costs, the longer the time, and the greater the informational requirements tend to be for settlement" (Lax and Sebenius 1986b, 228–229).

The tactics of negotiation can also serve as leverage for skilled mediators. The manipulation of agendas, the control of information, and the structuring of the negotiation (decisions on appropriate parties to be involved, what issues will be addressed, sequencing of offers, and time horizon) provide opportunities for a mediator to push conflicting parties toward settlement. Such factors come under the rubric of heresthetic:

> It is true that people win politically because they have induced other people to join them in alliances and coalitions. But the winners induce by more than rhetorical attraction. Typically they win because they have set up the situation in such a way that other people will want to join them—or will feel forced by circumstances to join them—even without any persuasion at all. And this is what heresthetic is about: structuring the world so you can win. (Riker 1986, ix)

Much of what I have discussed above focuses on the role of third-party mediation as a positive factor in bringing about settlement of revolutionary conflict. It is appropriate, however, to focus on those aspects of mediation that may *limit* the potential of settling conflict.

First, it is important to realize that mediators are not disinterested actors in the settlement process. As Touval and Zartman (1985) point out, "It is reasonable to assume that mediators are no less motivated by self-interest than by humanitarian impulses. To some extent, then, the mediator is a player in the pot of relations surrounding a conflict, and has some interest in the outcome (or else it would not mediate)." The results of any settlement must please the mediator as well as the players involved: what the mediator feels is an acceptable solution places limits on what an acceptable solution will be for the conflict. And a mediator's acceptable solution may not coincide with one or both of the actors involved.

Beyond interests in a settlement, mediators bring other baggage as well. They have preconceptions of the actors involved; they have varying degrees of experience in dealing with a specific situation; they have differing degrees of leverage; they have larger reputations that may affect how the actors involved view the mediator's goals and interests; and indeed, the mediator's concerns about reputation may prevent him or her from possible actions or choices.

## *Ripeness and Mediation*

William Zartman (1983, 1985) has developed a theory of conflict mediation that is derived from the concepts of bargaining, alternatives, and problem solving. According to Zartman, the key to understanding the resolution of intense conflict is the notion of "ripeness," that is, moments at which crises are highly conducive to resolution by an outside actor. He seeks "to develop some guidelines for positive intervention" and maintains that it is important to distinguish when conflicts are best left untouched from the times that outsiders can play an effective mediating role. Zartman's theory of effective mediation consists of two elements: first, a situation of ripeness that lends itself to possible mediation and, second, a series of injunctions for mediators to follow to resolve the conflict.

A crisis is ripe when (1) there exists a situation of deadlock and deadline, (2) "unilateral solutions are blocked and joint solutions become conceivable," and (3) the party that previously had the upper hand in the conflict has slipped and the underdog has gained in strength. Each side perceives that it is unable to win the conflict by itself and that such a state of affairs will last into the indefinite future with each side still possessing the ability to make the other hurt. At the same time, each party perceives "a moment when things will significantly get worse if they have not gotten better in ways that negotiation seeks to define" (Zartman 1983, 353). Zartman describes such conditions as "a mutually hurting stalemate." The challenge for an outside actor lies in presenting "an alternative to the conflicting parties that attains some of the goals of their first tracks [unilateral preferences] while eliminating or reconciling the more conflictual elements" (Zartman 1983, 354).

For Zartman, the presence of a mutually beneficial settlement is not enough to prompt parties to forgo the search for unilateral alternatives. Ripeness must be triggered by a moment that prompts a decision to escalate or deescalate. It is a sense of crisis that drives parties in conflict to reevaluate their search for victory. Zartman warns, however, that parties in conflict who are able to ride out a crisis often become much less amenable to negotiation.

Zartman counsels that potential mediators can work to effect settlement of conflict by creating the perception of a ripe moment among the combatants. Leverage comes from various sources, including military and economic punishments and rewards, but primarily it "comes from their [mediators'] ability to construct a perception of a better outcome for both parties other than the one at the end of the plateau or the first track, not from any dominant relationship that allows them pull strings or puppets." A mediator must convince the parties that their unilateral alternatives are blocked and present them with "an outcome that has something for everyone." To push the parties to settlement, the mediator should impose deadlines on the participants to create "a sense of urgency." Finally, since a rough symmetry is required for a hurting stalemate, a mediator might have to go so far as to provide military aid to one of the parties to reinforce the conflict.

I am convinced that the concept of ripeness should be a cornerstone to a theory of effective mediation. A major goal of this study is to try to refine and improve Zartman's concept. As a first cut, however, Zartman provides us with a set of indicators to look for in our cases of mediation in Zimbabwe: a sense of a hurting stalemate, a sense of a moment in the future that will worsen if negotiations fail, a sense that the tide of combat has changed, the mediators' need for leverage, the use of deadlines, and the development of a joint settlement that will address the minimal needs of the parties.

## Toward Refining Ripeness

A first step toward strengthening Zartman's concept is to call into question his implicit conception of the main antagonists as unitary actors that perceive or calculate the gains and losses of combat, negotiation, and surrender in terms of the government or insurgency as a whole. Although twice in his book *Ripe For Resolution* Zartman acknowledges that internal politics is a factor in conflict resolution, for the most part he treats the parties as if the organizations as a whole had perceptions of stalemate or deadlock or urgency. This is similar to many treatments of parties in warfare as single rational actors. But for rationality to reside within organizations and determine its best course depends on rather problematic assumptions. Pfeffer points out, for example, that the ability of an organization to make rational decisions requires a high degree of solidarity, consensus, and unanimity on dimensions of values, goals, and preferences. But, "once consensus is lost, once disagreement about preferences, technology, and management philosophy emerge, it is very hard to restore the kind of shared perspective and solidarity which is necessary to operate under the rational model" (1981, 32). While often acknowledging that the combatants rarely meet these attributes ascribed to them, scholars seldom examine the implications of organizations being coalitions composed of factions and individuals.[12]

In terms of mediation of conflict, the two views of actors in conflict lead to different assumptions about the ripeness of conflict for resolution and how a third party can assist its termination. In Zartman's analysis, the proper cue is a perception of deadlock and deadline. The alternative view states that questions about the "objective" military situation are intensely political and depend on bargaining within the parties. Ripeness in this consideration can be a function of internal changes: the emergence of new leaders, the consolidation of a divided leadership, or the division of a government that was previously unified in its war aims.[13]

Under Zartman's assumption, a mediator uses leverage on the parties in conflict. Under the second assumption, a mediator might choose to assist factions within parties to strengthen their hands in a negotiation. The mediator can attempt to identify those leaders who favor settlement and those who oppose settlement and can attempt to strengthen the former and isolate the latter. This, however, is a very delicate process. If important leaders are frozen out of the negotiating process, they may have the ability to ensure that a settlement will not succeed. Moreover, outside attempts to aid soft-liners may backfire and weaken their position (Mitchell 1981, 284–286).

Factional politics and the fact that some individuals will not compromise under any circumstance place changes internal to the parties at the fore of conflict resolution. Echoing Zartman's analysis of escalation as a decision point that mediators can take advantage of, it is clear that the fear that the conflict could reach a point where settlement is closed off should prompt moderate factions in both groups to reveal their true intent. A mediator, in addition to the suggestions made by Zartman and those that stem from the politics within the parties, must act as a conveyor of information about player-types. A mediator must also decide if there are individuals who will not accept settlement and then carve out a solution that isolates them.

Finally, mediators themselves are seldom unitary actors and can be beset with the same factional problems that are observed in the antagonists. The ability of a mediator to speak with one voice is usually crucial in bringing parties to agreement. Unilateral initiatives by individuals acting on behalf of the mediator can prove disastrous to creating the coalitions necessary for settlement. The same holds true for carrots offered and sticks threatened: the receiver of the message must believe that the promises of the mediator are credible. If messages are contradictory because of disunity in the mediation effort, uncertainty is increased as to the mediator's intention. Moreover, disunity within the mediator can lead to the parties in conflict attempting to play off factions to increase the likelihood of a settlement that favors them.

## The Research Design of the Book

To arrive at a better understanding of the success and failure of negotiations under conditions of civil war, I use in this book the method of structured, focused comparison to study four different episodes of mediated negotiation between insurgents and the government of Rhodesia. I will briefly discuss my choice of cases and the general questions that structure the analysis of the cases.

Structured, focused comparison is a method for gaining maximum theoretical utility from case studies.[14] It is particularly useful for the research objective here, where the number of instances of negotiated settlement in revolutionary situations is small but the number of possible relevant theoretical variables is large. The comparison of cases is aided when the researcher can hold some factors constant among the cases. In addition to the insight that strict comparison can provide, the researcher can bolster the yield of the comparison by using what George (1983a) refers to as process tracing: the use of evidence that tells a story that meets the rigorous standards of historical scholarship. In this way, the reader can judge whether the historical explanation "fits" with the explanation suggested by the contrast and comparison of important explanatory variables.

For my purposes here, I want to compare a case of successful mediated termination of civil war with cases of unsuccessful mediated termination. Although most attempts to settle civil war through negotiation have failed, the 1979 Lancaster House agreement on Zimbabwe stands as a striking success. It is a particularly attractive case for those interested in generating insights into failure and success, because it follows a series of failures to mediate an end to the conflict, which can be treated as subcases. Chapters 2 through 5 examine the following attempts to negotiate a settlement to the Zimbabwean revolution: (1) the 1974–1975 détente exercise of Kenneth Kaunda and John Vorster that led to the failed Victoria Falls conference between Ian Smith and black nationalists in August 1975; (2) the 1976 attempt by Henry Kissinger to bring an end to the conflict that led to the failed Geneva conference of October to December 1976, chaired by Ivor Richard as representative of the British government; (3) the ill-fated efforts of David Owen and Cyrus Vance in 1977–1978 to put forward proposals to end the conflict and bring the actors to an all-parties conference to settle; and (4) the successful 1979 Lancaster House Constitutional Conference on Rhodesia, chaired by Lord Carrington on behalf of the British government.

By comparing these four attempts to end the civil war in Zimbabwe, one can hold some variables constant over the subcases and therefore highlight important differences among the attempts. Moreover, because it is also a single case, one can study process variables such as learning, changes in actor preferences, and coalition formation among the different parties. The cases are also useful in that they contain instances where the war could have escalated into a larger conflict but did not. This provides important evidence for examining escalation as an alternative for parties in intense conflict.

In choosing a case study, one will confront disadvantages and advantages to the case. In the Zimbabwean case, what I lose in possible noncomparability to experiences of other societies, I gain in sharpness of focus, subcase comparability, and the opportunity to see the whole process over a variety of mediating efforts. For meeting the rigors of process tracing, the case is also advantageous. Although the case has lasted long enough to judge it a stable success, it is still recent enough that many of the key participants on all sides of the struggle are still around and willing to tell their stories. I have also been fortunate to find many invaluable primary documents in different archives.

To get the maximum theoretical value from a comparison of cases, it is necessary to develop a set of general questions to ask of each case. Before turning to the case studies, I would like to summarize the specific theoretical issues that I want to address in the book. Having done so, I will present various questions that need be answered in each case in order to develop an ordered bank of data for contributing to our understanding about negotiations in civil wars and the role that mediation plays in the resolution of such conflict.

First, I want to investigate how third-party mediation can contribute to the resolution of civil wars. I start with the work of William Zartman, who argues that there is a condition in conflict that approximates ripeness or a situation in which mediation can play a positive role in resolving crises. He contends that the crucial components of ripeness involve the antagonists' perceptions about the course of the conflict and their alternatives to combat: Is the war a hurting stalemate? Is there a time in the future when the conflict will worsen seriously if not resolved by negotiation? Are the fortunes of the players changing, so the party that was previously an underdog is now gaining in power relative to the stronger party? Does there exist a solution through which the players can meet their minimal demands through negotiation? A major goal of this study is to try to refine and improve Zartman's concept.

Second, I want to investigate the relationship between politics internal to groups and the ripeness of conflicts for resolution.

Organizations in such intense conflict as civil war are rarely unified in their evaluations of the conflict or their perceptions of the opponent. There may exist factions that desire settlement, while others demand a fight to the finish. Such issues may get enmeshed with an individual leader's calculations about his or her power within the group and pose individual risks to pursuing peace. Thus, I am interested in changes within groups and their effect on the likelihood of settlement: Are the parties consolidated in such a way that there is a consensual evaluation about the course of the war? Are there important differences within the party concerning the conflict? In what way do interparty negotiations affect politics within the parties? Such questions, if examined in a comparative light, may suggest that ripeness can be a function of changes within actors.

Third, I want to understand how a mediator can transform a conflict that is ripe for resolution into a conflict that is fully resolved. In keeping with the focus of this study on bargaining and negotiation, I emphasize leverage, problem solving, political skill and tactical manipulation, and the ability to create alternatives and to build coalitions. Is it possible for a mediator to create "ripeness" in a conflict? Can changes of mediator or changes within the mediator lead to "ripeness"?

Fourth, I want to examine the processes of learning and control of information that tie the mediator to changes in the actors' perceptions of the conflict, to changes internal to the warring parties, and to changes within the mediator over strategy and leverage.

These goals demand that in each case study I ask the following questions:

1. Who are the main actors? What are their goals? What are their perceptions about their adversaries and the course of the conflict?

2. What is the goal of the mediator? What is his or her strategy? What leverage does the mediator intend to use? What are the mediators' perceptions about the parties in the conflict? What information does the mediator have about the goals and reputations of the antagonists? What is the mediator's reputation among the warring parties? Has the mediator had the chance to learn from other episodes of negotiations? What lessons does she or he carry into the new mediation effort? Does the mediator have a conception of a possible settlement?

3. Do the actors perceive the situation to be a hurting stalemate? Do they perceive a moment in the future where they will be worse off if negotiation fails? Has there been a noticeable recent reversal of fortunes among the players? Have they reached some kind of bargaining parity?

4. Are the players internally unified in their evaluation of the course of the conflict? Are the players internally consolidated behind a leader who has a reservoir of authority to draw on to make decisions?

Does the group speak with one voice? Does a change in leadership coincide with a change in group position?

5. Is the mediator able to update her or his information in order to be more efficacious? Is the mediator able to manipulate information in order to move the parties toward settlement? Are there limits to the mediator's ability to solve the conflict? Are the goals of the mediator in conflict with those of the antagonists? Is the mediator unified in her or his attempts to resolve the conflict?

In the next four chapters I turn to the specific cases of negotiation in the Zimbabwean civil war. I have structured the chapters as follows: (1) an examination of the mediators—their reasons for getting involved and their strategy for settlement; (2) a look at politics within the actors in conflict; (3) the narrative of the mediation and negotiation; and (4) a review of the broader strategic context in which the negotiations took place. At the end of Chapters 2, 3, and 4, I discuss the failure of the negotiations in terms laid out in this chapter—ripeness, leverage, alternatives, politics within the groups, the use of strategy and tactics of the mediator, the problem solving of the mediator, and the limits that the mediator brought to the conflict. In Chapter 5, I describe the successful Lancaster House settlement of the Zimbabwean civil war. In Chapter 6 I describe the reasons for British success at Lancaster House and compare and contrast the four mediation attempts. And in the final chapter, I draw on the case material to strengthen and refine the notion of ripeness in civil war negotiation.

My material for the case studies stems from the following sources: (1) books and articles; (2) primary documents, including the minutes of the Lancaster House conference, from the National Archives in Zimbabwe and the Hoover Institution Archives in Stanford, California; (3) newspaper articles and primary documents on the Zimbabwean revolution that have been gathered into a seven-volume compendium by Baumhogger (1984); and (4) personal interviews with many of the main participants, some of whom requested anonymity.

## Notes

1. De Reuck (1984) argues, "A totally irresolvable conflict would presumably imply a literally inevitable future in which adaptation was absolutely impossible. Some changes certainly seem inexorable and adaptation sometimes seems inconceivable, but that is a different thing altogether from denying in principle the possibility of alternative outcomes or learning to solve the problems of legitimate accommodation."

2. Diamond (1987) has incisively reviewed Horowitz's encyclopedic work, pointing out that the psychological identity component of ethnic conflict is often manipulated by elites for their own power or gain. When I was in Zimbabwe, I asked Joshua Nkomo, considered the leader of the Ndebele

people, about the conflict between Shona and Ndebele in Zimbabwe. His response was revealing: "There is no conflict between the peoples of Zimbabwe. It is something that we leaders create" (Nkomo 1987, interview with author).

3. In Table 1.1, I have included the following conflicts that are not on Singer and Small's list of civil wars: Algeria, the German revolution of 1919, Malaysia, Korea, Mozambique, Angola, and Ireland. The following wars on Singer and Small's list do not appear in Table 1.1: China 1913, China 1914, China 1928, China 1935, Burma 1950–1953, and China's cultural revolution of 1968. I have treated the Chinese cases after 1927 as one case of a civil war: China 1927 to 1949. I did not include Burma since sporadic fighting has continued since 1953. I have omitted the cultural revolution because of the confusion surrounding the case.

4. Although Cyprus today is not in a state of civil war, the agreement that was reached in 1964 was violated a number of times, leading to Cyprus's partition.

5. Pillar classified the following as negotiated settlements of civil war: Laos, 1962; Laos, 1973; Jordan, 1970; Yemen, 1970; Lebanon, 1975–1976; and Zimbabwe, 1980. The only wars that he and I have in common are Yemen and Zimbabwe. I omitted the two Laotian settlements, Lebanon, and Jordan because of their instability and the inability of the settlement to terminate the conflict. For reasons he does not spell out, he fails to include Lebanon 1958, Sudan, the Dominican Republic, Honduras, Uruguay, and Mexico, all of which are listed in Singer and Small's Correlates of War project that Pillar and I used for compiling our lists.

6. Readers can judge for themselves the likelihood of a compromise agreement between Peruvian authorities and Guzman; see Shakespeare (1988). In the case of Khomeini, Sick (1985) points out that many analysts of Iranian politics dismissed the Ayatollah's commitment to total Islamic transformation of Iran. While Sick argues after the fact that in Khomeini's writings and speeches there was plenty of evidence that demonstrated Khomeini's uncompromising character, Sick misses a crucial point. The rhetoric of all purportedly revolutionary leaders calls for complete transformation; it is still a judgement call on what the individual may do in a negotiating situation. In the Zimbabwe example, for instance, the rhetoric of Joshua Nkomo and his party, ZAPU, was not qualitatively different from the rhetoric of Robert Mugabe and ZANU. Yet, throughout the revolution there was the perception that while Nkomo may be pragmatic, Mugabe was an ideological radical who would not compromise on any position. In the end, Mugabe's true character was revealed to be pragmatic.

For a similar perceptual problem, see the discussion of Rothchild (1987, 87–90) on the difference between pragmatic perception and essentialist perception in ethnic conflict.

7. In the judgment of John Service, U.S. diplomat assigned to the Dixie Mission in Yenan, the CCP was sincere in its wishes for a rapprochement with the Guomindang in 1944 (Service 1974). For an examination of U.S. mediation in the Chinese civil war, see Levine (1979).

8. Observe the parallel to the problem of appeasement in the 1930s.

9. The dilemmas of revolutionary betrayal form the plots of three great novels: *Man's Fate* by André Malraux, *Germany 1918—A People Betrayed* by Alfred Doblin, and *To Bury Our Fathers* by Sergio Ramírez.

10. This is an extremely problematic assumption; see Gutman (1988).

11. This discussion relies on Smoke (1977), Bar-Simon-Tov (1980), and Schelling (1966).

12. Thomas Schelling's work is exemplary of this point. Working from a game theoretic perspective that treats organizations as unitary, rational actors, he admits that "for working out the incentive structure of a threat, its communication requirements and its mechanism, analogies with individuals are helpful, but they are counterproductive if they make us forget that a government does not reach a decision in the same way as an individual in a government. Collective decision depends on the internal politics and bureaucracy of government, on the chain of command and on lines of communication, on party structures and pressure groups, as well as on individual values and careers" (Schelling 1966, 86).

13. As Schelling (1966, 85–86) points out, "To coerce an individual it may be enough to persuade him to change his mind; to coerce a government it may not be necessary, but it also may not be sufficient, to cause individuals to change their minds. What may be required is some change in the complexion of the government itself, in the authority, prestige, or bargaining power of particular individuals or factions or parties, some shift in executive or legislative leadership."

14. George and McKeown (1985) provide an excellent overview of the potential usefulness of case studies for theory development.

# 2

# The Vorster-Kaunda Détente Exercise: "Talking Without Negotiating"

*One learns a lot about people by merely studying what they do not want to know. Everybody doesn't want to know something or other.* —Dambudzo Marechera

In this chapter I will describe the historical background to the Zimbabwean civil war and recount in detail the first attempt to mediate a settlement between black leaders and the white government of Ian Smith. The attempt, which took place in 1974 and 1975, was fostered by Kenneth Kaunda, the president of Zambia, and John Vorster, the prime minister of South Africa. Although the effort ultimately failed, it was to become an important blueprint for subsequent tries to bring a peaceful resolution to the war in Rhodesia.[1] I will first provide a historical and cultural capsule of the conflict in Rhodesia, then describe the strategy employed by the unlikely team of mediators and the results of that strategy, and, finally, analyze the failure of those regional leaders to bring peace to Zimbabwe.

## Historical Background

The "self-governing" colony of Southern Rhodesia was a hybrid possession of the British Empire, somewhat akin to Bernard DeVoto's description of Texas—half horse and half alligator. Nominally under the control of the British, it was de facto ruled by its white settlers. Southern Rhodesia was very much the product of its namesake, Cecil Rhodes, who once said that if it had been in his power, he would have "colonized the stars." Rhodes, through force and chicanery against the territory's African inhabitants, had established a foothold there in the late 1800s. Rhodes's British South African Company had consolidated its rule there through a charter granted by Britain. A key turning point in the country's history took place in 1922 when its white settlers were given the opportunity to vote on the future of their new home. Their choices were to continue under the charter, join the Union of South

Africa, or opt for self-government.

The majority of whites chose self-government in 1923. Now formally annexed to Britain, but with power devolved to its white settlers, Rhodesia achieved the anomaly status of "self-governing" colony:

> Under the constitution of 1923, a Crown-appointed governor acted on the advice of Rhodesian ministers except in regard to certain legislation—for example, legislation pertaining to discrimination against the "indigenous population," over which the British government retained a right of veto. As Sir Roy Welensky put it [in 1967]: "The British government has never had the power unless they were prepared to use the sword. They have never had the power to force anything on Rhodesia." (O'Meara 1975, 7)

For most of its history, a white minority that never amounted to more than 5 percent of the population ruled over and systematically oppressed the black majority in Southern Rhodesia. In the early 1960s, Britain began pulling out of its African colonial possessions and gradually turning over power to the African populations. The devolution of power had come earlier and deeper in Rhodesia than in other British colonies, so for decades white settler self-government had become well entrenched. When formal British decolonization began to accelerate, the white minority government led by Prime Minister Ian Smith rebelled against the threat of British pressures for majority rule and unilaterally declared its independence (UDI) from Britain in 1965.[2]

In the years following 1965, a guerrilla war erupted against the white government. The various liberation movements, however, were split by ethnic and ideological divisions. The three important actors were two parties with military strength—ZANU (Zimbabwe African National Union), founded by Ndabaningi Sithole and eventually led by Robert Mugabe, and ZAPU (Zimbabwe African People's Union), led by Joshua Nkomo—and a political party with a wide constituency—the ANC (African National Council), eventually led by Bishop Abel Muzorewa.

In the early stages of UDI, Britain sought to negotiate with the Rhodesians on the terms of formal decolonization. Twice, in 1966 and 1967, in talks on the battleships *Tiger* and *Fearless,* British officials and Ian Smith failed to gain agreement on the question of independence. The British position, opposed bitterly by the white Rhodesians, was labeled NIBMAR (no independence before majority African rule).

In 1971, an agreement was reached between Sir Alec Douglas Home and Ian Smith that was to lead to the formal independence of Rhodesia—an agreement that put the likelihood of majority rule into the twenty-first century. The British, however, stipulated that the agreement had to pass a test of support from the black population of Rhodesia. To investigate the acceptability of the proposals, the British formed the Pearce Commission, which was responsible for canvassing African opinion on the agreements. This marked the first time that ordinary blacks in Rhodesia were consulted regarding the future independence of their country. Since most of the black nationalist leaders (Nkomo, Sithole, Mugabe, and countless others) were in prison or in exile, the task of organizing opposition to the proposals fell on the shoulders of Abel Muzorewa, a United Methodist bishop. The opposition campaign was a stunning success: the Pearce Commission reported that the overwhelming majority of Zimbabweans opposed the terms of the agreement, thereby sinking the Smith-Home pact.

If at this point Muzorewa had retired from the spotlight, he would have been a national figure commanding respect and honor for his work against the British–Rhodesian pact. Muzorewa, however, flushed with victory and intoxicated by his new-found political leadership, tried to seize the moment and negotiate a settlement with Smith. He spent the next ten months, head to head with Smith, negotiating, cajoling, pressing the Rhodesian leader for concessions. Ten months of negotiation gained six more seats for blacks in a white-dominated legislature and a program that might yield majority rule in forty years. When the bishop took these terms to the leadership of the ANC for ratification, his ten months of work were dismissed in less than ten minutes (Meredith 1979). Muzorewa's first negotiating experience squandered much of the political capital he had gained from the campaign against Smith-Home and provided him with a reputation as a terribly unskilled negotiator who could be exploited in the future.

Muzorewa's failure coincided with a change in the contest between blacks and whites in Rhodesia. The guerrilla war that had begun in 1965 had taken little toll on white Rhodesia until 1972. At the end of that year, ZANLA (ZANU's army—the Zimbabwe National Liberation Army), using sanctuary in neighboring Mozambique, began implementing a strategy based on the politicization of the countryside and hit-and-run terrorist tactics against "soft" targets such as schools and farms. The decision to intensify the war against the Rhodesian government posed a real security threat for the whites, and two factors contributed to change the military situation in favor of the revolutionaries. First, the collapse of the Portuguese authorities in Mozambique in 1974–1975 opened a 600-mile-long sanctuary for Zimbabwean guerrillas. Second, the draconian antiterrorist activities of the white security forces drove tens of thousands of rural Zimbabweans into refugee status across the border in Mozambique.[3] These refugees provided a pool of young and willing prospective guerrilla fighters against the white regime. Many in the aftermath of Muzorewa's failure to gain majority rule from Smith concluded: "Whites must be led down the garden path to the place of slaughter. Morality does not come into it" (Zvobgo, quoted in Flower 1987, 126).

Rhodesia's geography and the pattern of white settlement in the country produced a way of life and a regime susceptible to guerrilla war. The most recent census at the time (1969) showed a European population of 228,296 and an African population of approximately 5.4 million. Although Rhodesia was a country of about 153,000 square miles (roughly the size of Montana), a little over 71 percent of the European population (163,182) lived in the four cities in Rhodesia with populations over 45,000 (Salisbury, Bulawayo, Umtali, and Gwelo).[4] Salisbury alone contained 42 percent of the European sector. Another 31,000 Europeans lived in small towns and villages, which left approximately 33,500 Europeans in spread-out farming areas far removed from urban centers and other farms. The 1969 census put the number of Europeans who were "economically active . . . in agriculture, livestock production, and hunting" at 7,396 (Rhodesia, Central Statistical Office 1971). The amount of farming lands that were apportioned to Europeans in 1969 for farming amounted to 45 million acres (Bowman 1973, 12), or about 6,100 acres per farming European. Each isolated farm, not easily defended, became a target for the guerrillas.

Although the agricultural sector employed less than 4 percent of the European population, it was crucial for Rhodesia's economy. In 1975, for example, agriculture accounted for a little under 11.5 percent of the gross domestic product (Rhodesia, Ministry of Finance 1975). Much of Rhodesia's agricultural crop was tobacco for export, bundled in disguised crates and shipped to a network of intermediaries, all in a vast charade to beat international sanctions that were imposed in 1965 and 1968. While the Rhodesian government publicly maintained a stoic indifference toward such sanctions, the Rhodesian business community was reeling from their effects (Minter and Schmidt 1988, 220–225).

Other aspects of Rhodesia's demographic profile stand out: 85,000 Europeans were either under the age of fifteen or over the age of sixty— too young or too old to fight in a guerrilla war. The Rhodesian army did not use women for combat duty, which meant that its recruiting pool was somewhere around 60,000 to 70,000 white men. Eventually, the Rhodesian armed forces drew on the African population for their fight, but nonetheless all European males aged eighteen to sixty were subject to draft by the end of the war in 1980. As the war continued and more and more males were called and recalled to duty, the economy suffered tremendously because of the loss of skilled white labor and management.

At the end of 1972, however, only a few within Rhodesia's intelligence and military command understood the full implications of a counterinsurgency war against black guerrillas. The war against the guerrillas from 1965 to 1972 had been successful, but it had also bred overconfidence within the Smith government (Flower 1987, 112). The opening up of the Mozambican front and the change in black strategy had turned the military situation around. Ken Flower, head of intelligence under Smith, writes about that time as a transformation from "a winning position . . . [to] the stage of the 'no-win' war, which lasted from December 1972 to 1976" (Flower 1987, 119). From 1972 on, a serious split emerged within the Rhodesian government over the nature and severity of the guerrilla threat. Intelligence professionals like Flower argued for the need for political settlement, while politicians within the Smith regime—often relying on erroneous comforting reports provided by the Ministry of the Interior—believed that the war was winnable (Flower 1987, 25). In the middle between the two groups was the Rhodesian military, which needed the experience of combat to sway it from Smith's point of view. Few of these splits, however, were evident to those outside the government. To its own citizens and to the world outside, the Rhodesian government seemed a bastion of unity.

After the Pearce Commission had ruled that the Home-Smith agreement was not approved by most Zimbabweans, the British sought to wash their hands of the affair. Three times they had negotiated with Ian Smith, and three times their efforts had come to naught. Smith had developed almost a mythical reputation among the British for his negotiating style. Lord Home, for example, described his experiences dealing with Smith as follows:

> Negotiating with him was a very different thing from anything I had done before. You had to repeat yourself a lot. He was a very difficult man to pin down and keep pinned down to a particular point, a very slow negotiator. When you made an arrangement with him or thought you'd got an arrangement, you would find on reassembling that he'd found some qualifications. And so it went on, a long, slogging, difficult process. (Quoted in Lapping 1985, 491)

Lord Blake put it more bluntly: "For Ian Smith negotiation was not a matter of compromise, but of wearing down one's opponent till he concedes all the points at issue" (Blake 1977, 362). Smith, himself, described his delaying tactics as "pulling the wool over the eyes of the British" (*Times*, May 8, 1978). Robert Matthews, a political scientist, refers to Smith as a master of "talking without negotiating" (Matthews 1978).

Whereas Smith and others felt little need for give and take with Britain, this was not so concerning Rhodesia's relations with South Africa. Smith was an enormously popular figure with many white South Africans but was disdained by South African leaders because of his obstinacy in the face of their advice. When Smith was contemplating UDI, Hendrik Verwoerd, then prime minister of South Africa, had counseled against such a course. When John Vorster replaced Verwoerd, he referred to Rhodesia as "the Achilles heel of Southern Africa" and urged Smith to reach some kind of settlement. Incidents between Rhodesian forces and ZIPRA (ZAPU's army) near the South African border in 1967 had prompted Vorster to provide the Rhodesians with 2,000 paramilitary police, helicopters, and pilots. More important, South Africa was Rhodesia's economic lifeline to the outside world for military supplies and equipment, food, and oil. By 1976 a Rhodesian intelligence briefing admitted that "Rhodesia is totally dependent upon South Africa for military and economic survival" (Flower 1987, 132). Smith thus had to walk a very taut line in his battle to thwart majority rule. He could try to appeal over the heads of the South African leaders directly to their followers for support, but doing so risked alienating "the only leaders who could pressurize us" (Smith 1987, interview with author).

By 1974, the abyss between whites and blacks in Rhodesia was as great as the divide between Ian Smith and the British. Southern Rhodesia's 1923 constitution, unlike that of South Africa, committed its peoples to a "color blind" franchise (O'Meara 1975, 8). Property and educational requirements, however, prevented almost all blacks from political participation. In the 1950s, a few whites, most of them members of families that had lived in Rhodesia since the 1920s, attempted to include blacks in the political process through a gradual reform of the election roll. This movement ended abruptly in the late 1950s as whites who had emigrated to Rhodesia during the post–World War II years came to dominate white politics. Such whites, who formed the nucleus of the racial supremacist Rhodesian Front, would find their leader in the person of Ian Smith. Smith and the Rhodesian Front dominated white politics in Rhodesia from the early 1960s on. One study estimated that white liberals who opposed Smith never constituted more than 20 percent of the electorate (Hancock 1984).

The influence of new whites coming to Rhodesia cannot be underestimated. Most of the Europeans in Rhodesia were newcomers and, unlike their Afrikaner compatriots south of the border, could not claim the legitimation of "being African, too." Moreover, the experience of the Afrikaners over three centuries provided the basis for the formation of the Afrikaans identity myth (Thompson 1986). The Rhodesian identity had to be created for most in a compressed amount of time, perhaps thirty years. In the 1969 census, for example, the number of non-Rhodesian-born whites to Rhodesian-born was 130,613 to 92,934. When those whites under the age of twenty are subtracted from each category, giving us white adults eligible to vote, the numbers become even more dramatic: 115,362 European adults born outside of Rhodesia to only 29,785 European adults born in Rhodesia. Of those not born in Rhodesia, 49,585 came from South Africa, 52,468 came from the United Kingdom, and another 10,000 more or so came from various former crown colonies that had achieved independence (Rhodesia, Central Statistical Office 1971).

The whites extended their disenfranchisement of Africans to social and economic affairs. The most important resource to the people of Rhodesia was arable land, which from the beginning of the twentieth century had gradually come under the possession of the small European population. In 1930, the Land Apportionment Act legally segregated the holding of land by giving Europeans the right to purchase in the most desirable agricultural regions. The remainder of the land was distributed to Africans. Ten percent of the land was set aside for those Africans with the resources and desire to compete in Rhodesia's Darwinian economic environment of the 1930s. The remaining 90 percent of African land was committed to communal farming in areas called the Tribal Trust lands.

This system of land rights was further codified in 1969 with the passage of the Land Tenure Act. The act, which Rhodesian Front members waved as a banner of their racial enlightenment, "equally" divided the land in Rhodesia into 45 million acres for blacks and 45 million acres for whites. Given the discrepancy in farming populations between the two groups, this "equal" distribution provided the average white farmer 6,100 acres compared to 7 acres for the average African farmer. This again tells only part of the story, for the richest, most fertile land was distributed to the whites, and the African was left parcels of arid, barren soil (Austin 1975).

The inequality in land holdings mirrored other important discrepancies between blacks and whites in Rhodesia in terms of jobs, wealth, health services, government expenditure on students, and access to education. In most cases, such inequalities were reinforced through laws and sanctions designed to deprive the black population of basic human rights. Far from seeing the system they had constructed as an affront to human dignity, most Rhodesians saw their relationship with the Africans as a "partnership" between "the black horse and the white rider" (Godfrey Huggins quoted in O'Meara 1975).[5]

The white community, self-contained amidst an ocean of blacks, forged a worldview that denied the intelligence and humanity of the African people. Most whites knew blacks only in the context of master and servant. This distance between whites and blacks was difficult to traverse even for the liberal Rhodesian white who made an effort. Harkness Holderness, a white who had fought for black political participation in the 1950s, describes this distance:

> We felt we had begun to establish a powerful bond of trust with Africans who would in various ways have a significant place in the politics of the future, and that we were now able to see and understand what the picture looked like seen through their eyes—at any rate while we were with them, and however it might fade when we were not. And it was a striking phenomenon: that it did tend to fade almost as soon as you got back into the white orbit. And that in turn was evidence of another phenomenon: that it was quite impossible to explain what the picture was like to a fellow white, at second hand. The only way for him to see it was by being in first hand contact with them. (Holderness 1985, 93)

The black leaders of the time often felt estranged from those white liberals who worked for change. Ndabaningi Sithole, one of the founding leaders of Zimbabwean nationalism, wrote in 1959:

> Most European liberals, I discovered, while in full sympathy with the miserable lot of the African people, approached the problem as one of the white man ruling the African justly, not one of Africans taking over from the whites. The latter was our approach. They wanted to see the black man treated justly as a human being. They wanted him to receive a fair economic reward based on merit and qualifications, and not on the colour of his skin. They wanted to see the African allowed to use public facilities like anybody else. They wanted to see universal education provided for the African child and a host of other improvements made for the African. But they had serious reservations on an African take-over. They did not subscribe to "one man, one vote." (Sithole 1968, 33)

To complete the story of social and political chasms in Rhodesia in the early 1970s, it is necessary to look as well at the splits among the black leaders who were fighting for Zimbabwe. Such splits were mostly muted until the early 1960s, when disputes over the capabilities and strategies of the leaders led to public fighting between the supporters of Joshua Nkomo, who went on to found ZAPU, and the supporters of Ndabaningi Sithole, Robert Mugabe, and Herbert Chitepo, who led ZANU. The split originated over the ability of Nkomo to lead the nationalist movement, but more layers of difference were added. Nkomo, although always stressing the national character of ZAPU, found his strength in the areas around Bulawayo in Matabeleland, where a minority ethnic group that constituted 15 percent of Zimbabwe's population—the Ndebele—lived. Later, ideological, strategic, and logistical differences would also emerge: ZANU chose a guerrilla strategy and aligned itself to China and, locally, to Mozambique, while ZAPU downplayed guerrilla tactics, received arms, training, and advice from the Soviet Union, and based itself in Zambia. The political parties proliferated in the early 1970s as ZANU splintered into different wings, one backing Sithole and one supporting Robert Mugabe.

Confusion was added when Bishop Muzorewa formed the African National Council, an umbrella group within Rhodesia, to fight the Smith-Home agreement in 1972.

The various black partners (or rivals, depending on the particular day) posed a problem for any potential mediator. Regional leaders such as Kenneth Kaunda, president of Zambia, and Julius Nyerere, president of Tanzania, often found themselves exasperated at what Masipula Sithole labeled "struggles within the struggle" (M. Sithole 1977). When unity was achieved briefly in 1974, Sithole (brother of Ndabaningi Sithole) eloquently described the coalition of the different nationalist factions:

> We must state at this point that the said declaration of unity united sheep, foxes, hyenas, and leopards. The sad assumption was that the four would realize that they had many things in common: They were animals and their common enemy in the bush was the lion. All that was needed for unity was to bring them around a table, sign a piece of paper singing *"Ishe Komborera Afrika!"* (Lord Save Africa), and all would be well. Yet we know that the interests of leopards, hyenas, foxes, and sheep do not necessarily coincide, even given their common fear of the lion. (M. Sithole, 108)

The ability of the nationalists to cooperate was put to its biggest test in 1974. That year, prompted by the collapse of the Portuguese colonial empire in Southern Africa, John Vorster, the prime minister of South Africa, made it known that he was willing to work with any interested party toward a peaceful settlement to the Rhodesian conflict. Kenneth Kaunda, president of Zambia—the state bordering Rhodesia to the northwest that had been hurt tremendously by the war—responded favorably to Vorster's offer and set in motion the most dramatic, far-reaching attempt to that point to bring all of the parties in the war to the bargaining table.[6] The strategy of this so-called détente exercise was simple. South Africa would use its power to persuade the Smith government to negotiate a transition to majority rule, and Zambia, with the assistance of the other "Front Line States" (at that time Tanzania and Botswana, and shortly to include Mozambique and later Angola), would impose unity on the various nationalist parties to create a single voice to speak for the black majority in Rhodesia. The attempt to reach a settlement lasted the better part of a year and ended in a failed conference at Victoria Falls in August 1975.

## The *"Détente Scenario"*

In early October 1974, Mark Chona, Kaunda's personal secretary; Marquard DeVilliers, a South African businessman; and General Hendrik van den Bergh, head of the South African Bureau of State Security, produced a document entitled "Towards the Summit: An Approach to Peaceful Change in Southern Africa," which was the basis of the mediation plan. Although the document concerned the region as a whole, it contained specific policy recommendations for Rhodesia. The document formed the basis of an agreement between Vorster and Kaunda on the need to bring about a negotiated settlement in Rhodesia by using their respective powers to pressure the various parties to the negotiating table.

As described by David Martin and Phyllis Johnson, Zambia presented Vorster with a set of conditions to be met concerning Rhodesia:

> These laid down that he advise Smith "that a political solution is most desirable and very urgent," that he not interfere in Rhodesian internal affairs, that he withdraw his security personnel and equipment from Rhodesia, that he declare that a negotiated settlement was in Rhodesia's best interests, and that he be against any further escalation of the war in Mozambique or tension in the area. All these conditions were supposed to be met by the end of November, with the South African government ensuring that the Rhodesian government moved quickly towards a constitutional conference by implementing the following six points:
>
> a. Releasing all political detainees and prisoners since their voice is both credible and final in any negotiations. In this connection Mr. Joshua Nkomo, Rev. Ndabaningi Sithole and their Lieutenants command tremendous influence and will for a long time remain the voice of reason;
>
> b. Lifting the ban on ZAPU and ZANU and the restrictions of movements on leaders so that they participate fully and constructively in the search for a just political solution as an alternative to the current armed struggle;
>
> c. Suspend [sic] political trials and revoke death sentences for political offenders;
>
> d. Suspend [sic] all politically discriminatory legislation;
>
> e. Gearing the SAG [South African Government] administration to help defuse racial tension and create a political climate for the acceptance of the proposal of the constitutional conference representing ZAPU and ZANU, the Rhodesian Front and other political parties in Rhodesia under British chairmanship. In these circumstances the current armed struggle will be replaced by a new spirit of cooperation and racial harmony which is the foundation for political stability and therefore justifying withdrawal of the South African security forces;
>
> f. SAG to make it clear that they will support any legally constituted Government irrespective of its racial composition in Rhodesia." ("Towards the Summit . . . ," quoted in Martin and Johnson 1981, 140–141)

In return, "Zambia 'and friends' would publicly welcome these moves and they would 'use their influence to ensure that ZANU and ZAPU desist from armed struggle and engage in the mechanics for finding a political solution in Rhodesia'" (Martin and Johnson 1981, 141, quoting "Towards the Summit . .").

Although there is no written record of a discussion between the two governments about the kind of constitutional and transitional arrangements they thought might be appropriate for Rhodesia, Martin Meredith, among others, states that Vorster had agreed with the Zambians on "the framework for a new political structure in Rhodesia to be used as basis for negotiations: a five-year transition period to majority rule; a common voters' roll based on a qualified franchise; and the elevation of Africans to senior posts in the Cabinet and the civil service" (Meredith 1980, 154).[7]

Five years as an appropriate transition period was the common reference point at that time. Smith, for instance, sent a telex to Kaunda on December 3, 1974, that said that he was "concerned over reports said to be emanating from African leaders who went to Lusaka for discussions with the four presidents. The reports indicate that these leaders are expecting majority rule to be attained within five years, or the life of one parliament." The telex urged Kaunda to make clear to those leaders "that he would be prepared to consider variations of the present franchise, provided there was no lowering of standards" (Martin and Johnson 1981, 152). The message to Kaunda brought a swift rebuke from Vorster, but the question of whether a specific plan had been agreed to by Zambia and South Africa remains open.

Support for a positive answer to the question comes from two sources unlikely to agree on anything during that time: Robert Mugabe and Des Frost, chairman of Ian Smith's ruling Rhodesian Front party. Mugabe, in a report on December 17, 1974 to the Catholic Commission for Justice and Peace in Rhodesia, gave ZANU's understanding of the détente process and their opinions about it. Mugabe contends there had been discussion of a formula for the transition, but it was based on the impetus of Vorster:

> Voster [*sic*] asked that two Rhodesian representatives be sent for and the attorney General and the Secretary of the cabinet came. It transpired that a five year transitional period seemed acceptable to the Rhodesian Government. Next Voster [*sic*] discussed the franchise and a common voters' roll; to the latter he had no objection. It was agreed that completed primary education with one year of further education should be the minimum; the one year of further education could be an education of any kind, academic or otherwise. No additional qualifications should be imposed on the voters. All further details were to be left to a constitutional conference. Kaunda accepted this. It is estimated that this would bring 200,000 to 300,000 Africans on the voters' roll and this would mean that majority rule would become a possibility during the five year transitional period. Smith agreed to these suggestions, in principle, but reserved some alternatives for the

constitutional conference. (Mugabe 1974, 1)

On the same day that Mugabe made his report (which was not made public until February 25, 1975), Ian Smith, when asked of rumors about such a plan between Vorster and Kaunda, tactfully replied: "I believe that South Africa and Zambia are now on record as saying recently that it was up to the Rhodesians themselves to determine their future and that outsiders would refrain from interference. I believe it highly unlikely that either Zambia or South Africa would be party to trying to put over a plan along these lines." Des Frost, however, was a touch less diplomatic. While dismissing such plans as unrealistic, he said, "Let's be honest. This was something that the South Africans started" (Keesing's, 26912).

The initiative between South Africa and Zambia began in *public* in a well-orchestrated campaign that started October 23, 1974, when John Vorster addressed his Senate with the following words: "Southern Africa is at the crossroads and has to choose now between peace and escalating conflict. . . . The price of confrontation would be high, too high for Southern Africa." Appealing to the new leaders of Mozambique, he emphasized the sizeable economic ties between their country and South Africa, the need for peace and order to prevail between them, and the fact that "it was in the highest economic interest" that Mozambique continue its dealings with South Africa. Turning to Rhodesia, Vorster threw the weight of South Africa's support behind an early constitutional settlement, emphasizing, "Now is the time for all who have influence to bring it to bear to find a durable solution so that internal and external relations can be normalized." Vorster concluded by stating that "South Africa considers herself to be part of the African continent and wishes to develop peaceful relations and cooperation with Black African states" (Keesing's, 26909).

Three days later, at a ceremony celebrating Zambia's tenth anniversary of independence (attended by two South African dignitaries—Harry Oppenheimer, chairman of the Anglo-American Corporation and DeBeers Consolidated Mines, and Sir Richard Loyt, vice-chancellor of the University of Cape Town), Kenneth Kaunda welcomed Vorster's remarks as "the voice of reason for which Africa and the rest of the world have waited." He called "upon South Africa to withdraw its forces from Rhodesia and to make a choice between 'the road to peace and development' or 'an escalation of conflict in Southern Africa.'" Amidst Kaunda's plea for a just settlement to the Rhodesian conflict are the words, "African countries will not take up arms and fight against South Africa. The people of South Africa will face the primary task of shaping their own destiny" (Keesing's, 26909).

To any astute observer it is clear that the basis of a quid pro quo was developing. In exchange for South Africa's complicity in bringing a settlement in Rhodesia, Zambia (and presumably the other countries of Southern Africa would fall in line) would in effect recognize South Africa's whites as "African" and pledge noninterference in their efforts to deal with their problems as they saw fit. Vorster, on October 28, responded to Kaunda's speech by welcoming "any initiative which could lead to the de-escalation of conflict in Southern Africa. Anybody who wishes to co-operate towards this aim will find that I am ready for such co-operation. It would seem that the President of Zambia is agreeable to such an action and I welcome it" (Keesing's, 26909).

Vorster's détente approach to the crisis in Southern Africa was highly controversial. Throughout the détente exercise, Vorster faced tough opposition within his government, especially from his military. From 1974 to 1976, two antagonistic approaches to the events in Southern Africa competed for power. The first was détente, backed by Vorster, van den Bergh, and the Foreign Ministry, especially Brand Fourie and R. F. Botha (no relation to P. W. Botha). The second was what came to be known later as the forward strategy, which countenanced no moderation toward "communist-backed terrorism," lumped together all of the revolutionary movements in Southern Africa into this category, and preached an aggressive counterrevolutionary interventionist policy. The approach was mainly associated with the then minister of defense and future prime minister, P. W. Botha, and the chief of South African Defence Forces, Gen. Magnus Malan. The current dominance of the military in South African politics can be traced to this time, as Botha and Malan took a hard line toward events in Angola, Mozambique, and Rhodesia in opposition to Vorster's détente policy.[8]

This split profoundly affected South Africa's policy in the region. Although it would take South Africa's intervention in Angola at the end of 1975 and the conduct of their operations there to reflect a government in disarray and profound conflict about aims and methods (Grundy 1986, 88-92), the split emerged early on with Botha's opposition to Vorster's moderate line toward FRELIMO's revolutionary triumph in Mozambique in 1974:

> P. W. Botha, as Minister of Defense, took an opposing position and sought to support counterrevolutionary guerrillas trying to unseat President Machel. At the same time that Vorster had agreed to assist with the repair of Mozambique's railways and harbors, according to Dr. Eschel Rhoodie, Botha secretly ordered MIS (military intelligence services) to supply extensive quantities of arms and ammunition to guerrillas operating from a base near Komatipoort. When General van den Bergh learned of this he sent men to Nelspruit and Komatipoort to immobilize the equipment being transported to Mozambique. (Grundy 1986, 89)[9]

The effects of this schism would spill over to South Africa's conduct in Rhodesia later.

## The Evolution of Terms

During the détente era, the mediators, Kaunda and Vorster, seemed to be groping for a solution to the Rhodesian conflict. In the original détente scenario for Rhodesia there is no suggestion of a cease-fire prior to negotiations, nor is there any stipulation that preconditions could not be set before negotiations started. Yet, as will become apparent, this was how the mediation framework evolved—a framework that proved to be totally unconducive to serious negotiations between the parties. To understand how it came into being, one must look to the first reactions of the nationalists and Smith concerning any possible negotiations, and how the mediators composed the terms of the settlement as they went along.

During this time, public utterances of the ANC and Smith tended to focus on the role of Britain in any proposed talks. On November 4, Smith, in a television interview, "expressed the view that the British Government wanted an agreement to be reached between Black and White Rhodesians and he did not see that 'the British Government can play any part in that.'" Smith also emphasized that he would not sit at a negotiating table with the two banned African nationalist organizations—ZAPU and ZANU—partly because of the "heinous crimes they had committed against the African people." Two days later Dr. Gordon Chavunduka, the secretary-general of the ANC, replied that "any constitutional conference would have to include Britain, because she still had a 'responsibility' towards Rhodesia" (Keesing's, 26909).

South Africa's position on this issue was much closer to Smith's demand and became a part of the package deal with Zambia. South Africa insisted that it was for the Rhodesians to work out Rhodesia's problems, a signal that South Africa did not intend to participate during the meetings but would watch from the sidelines and pressure the parties when talks threatened to become completely deadlocked. It was also an implicit signal to Great Britain that South Africa did not think it appropriate that the British be a party to the negotiations except at the conclusion, when, both parties having reached agreement, it would be Britain's duty to grant Rhodesia legal independence. This suited Great Britain fine, for its experiences dealing with the renegade Smith regime had led it to seek any excuse to avoid having to assert itself with regard to its former colony.[10]

Although this issue was easy for the South Africans to resolve, they were worried that both sides might make other demands that could derail the talks. In particular, they were alarmed by Smith's statements about refusing to meet with members of ZANU and ZAPU. If Smith remained adamant, then the talks would be a nonstarter, for Vorster had agreed with Zambia that ZANU and ZAPU were appropriate participants to the talks.

Vorster, a week after the public speeches ushering in the détente era, flew to Salisbury and pressured Smith into freeing the leaders of the nationalist movements so that they could travel to Lusaka and meet with Kaunda and the other Front Line presidents. Vorster emphasized that if the problems of Rhodesia were to be solved by black and white Rhodesians, it was necessary to include all at the negotiating table. Although Smith had no qualms about meeting Muzorewa and the ANC, he was loath to talk with the other nationalists, whom he branded as terrorists. Beyond the question of his personal antagonism toward these individuals was a larger question of how to sell to his own political constituency talks with people whom he had vilified as murderers of women and children, and with whom he said he would never negotiate. Later, Smith was to claim that "as a *quid pro quo* for their release, it was agreed that terrorism in Rhodesia would cease immediately, while the released detainees would be permitted to engage in normal political activities" (Smith statement at trial of N. Sithole, March 24, 1975; Keesing's, 27086). His demand, therefore, was that there be "a cessation of terrorism" before a constitutional conference could be convened. It is important to note that Smith did not say a cease-fire, but rather that terrorism would cease immediately. Vorster could sell the former to Kaunda but not the latter, and so informed the Zambians that a cease-fire would be a key to the mediation efforts.

For Vorster and Kaunda this was not foreign to the spirit of the mediation plan they had envisaged. Kaunda felt that this could be thrust upon the nationalists if there was a quid pro quo of the release of all political detainees inside Rhodesia. Within the scenario worked out by Chona, DeVilliers, and van der Bergh, there is the seed of a notion of stopping the war as a precondition to talks; after all, Zambia "and friends" promised "to use their influence to ensure that ZANU and ZAPU desist from armed struggle and engage in the mechanics for finding a political solution in Rhodesia." Moreover, Mozambican president Samora Machel later recalled that when he and the other Front Line leaders met to work out the specific demands that they would make of Vorster, it was understood that Vorster was seeking a "paralysation" of the war (Martin and Johnson 1981, 145).

A phrase that keeps recurring in South African communiqués and Rhodesian messages is "a constitutional conference to be convened *without preconditions.*" We can only speculate that this stemmed from a demand made by Smith, albeit a demand Vorster would see as totally within reason. Given subsequent wranglings between the main antagonists, this can only be seen as code for no demand that Smith accept majority rule or commit himself to one person–one vote before the start of negotiations. If Vorster broached the subject of majority rule in five years to Smith, the Rhodesian prime minister could quote to the South African Vorster's own words that "Rhodesia's problems were for Rhodesians to figure out." Smith could say "in principle, majority rule in five years, provided that proper standards are maintained, is reasonable, but I think it is really something we should work out among ourselves. Of course what we will not countenance is a wholesale turning over of power straight away" (Keesing's, 26909). Armed with an agreement in principle that Smith would negotiate if no preconditions were set, and also believing that an immediate handing of power to the blacks would create the chaos he was seeking to avoid, Vorster could present those conditions as part of the détente process.

Thus, by default the détente exercise came to revolve around an effort to get all parties concerned to engage in a cease-fire and for the Smith government to release all political detainees within Rhodesia. This accomplished, the blacks and whites would be expected to sit down and work out procedures for the establishment of majority rule. As it turned out, the stipulations of (1) the "elimination of terrorism" (Smith) or a cease-fire (Kaunda, Vorster, et al.) and (2) "no preconditions for negotiation" were stakes driven into the heart of the mediation effort.

## *The Front Line States, the Nationalists, and Unity*

When Kaunda and the Front Line presidents (now including Samora Machel of Mozambique) met with the nationalist leaders, it became obvious that the détente exercise was more problematic than had been expected. Kaunda had badly misread the chances for a meaningful unity among the black parties and had totally underestimated the intransigence of one of the parties (ZANU) with regard to any proposed negotiations. While he can be accused of näiveté on the first account,[11] his ignorance of the second is partly understandable. While I don't wish to emulate the "little did Marie Antoinette know as she donned her powdered wig" approach to history (as Arthur Stinchcombe calls it), nonetheless events going on within ZANU at the time had a powerful impact on the course of the talks.

On November 8, with Smith's permission, Joshua Nkomo, leader of ZAPU, was released from detention and flown to Lusaka to meet with Muzorewa, Kaunda, Machel, Nyerere, and Seretse Khama, the president of Botswana. The Front Line presidents also requested that Ndabaningi Sithole, as leader of ZANU, make the trip. Unbeknownst to the presidents, however, only days before their request, Sithole had been removed from his leadership position by other ZANU executives acting on their own initiative in prison.[12] In his stead, the ZANU leadership in prison sent Robert Mugabe and Moton Malianga, with Mugabe to act as spokesman for ZANU. Upon arriving in Lusaka, the pair was met with hostility and suspicion by the Front Line presidents, with Machel going so far as to accuse Mugabe of taking part in a "coup" (Martin and Johnson 1981, 150). Nyerere told Mugabe that Sithole was the leader of ZANU. The Front Line presidents kept Mugabe and Malianga detained at their hotel and did not allow them to meet with Herbert Chitepo, the ZANU leader in exile. The next morning, Mugabe and Malianga were sent back to Rhodesia with a command to send Sithole in their place.

The purpose of the meeting on November 8 was to bring the various parties up to date on the détente exercise and to urge them to unite under one umbrella organization. The Front Line presidents told these leaders that because of Vorster's efforts they believed that Smith was ready to concede to majority rule. They argued that if he did so, many lives would be saved and therefore it was worth the effort to test Smith's intentions. Nyerere and Kaunda also assured them that if the talks failed, the nationalists would still receive support for the armed struggle. Both Nkomo and Muzorewa were behind the plan, but the presidents thought it best that Sithole agree on behalf of ZANU, because they did not believe that Mugabe truly represented ZANU and its army.

The Front Line presidents' hostile reaction to Mugabe becomes totally understandable when one considers what happened the following week. Sithole arrived in Lusaka with Maurice Nyagumbo, who was under orders from the ZANU leadership to make it clear that Sithole could speak only as a private citizen and not on behalf of ZANU. Nyagumbo was allowed to meet with Chitepo, Josiah Tongogara (the commander-in-chief of ZANLA, ZANU's army), and two members of ZANU's Revolutionary Council (called the "Dare"), John Mataure, and Mukudzei Mudzi. Upon hearing Nyagumbo's news, the leaders in exile reacted with disbelief and horror (not too strong a word, because the Executive Council's decision spelled doom for ZANLA operations in Zambia and Tanzania). Only Nyagumbo's account of the meeting can do justice to the confrontation:

> I accused the President (Kaunda) for stampeding ZANU into joining or uniting with ZAPU in an endeavour to save his useless friend Nkomo. I told him that ZANU viewed the situation with grave concern. . . . I accused the President of trying to impose leadership on us. I told him that Rev. Sithole was in Zambia as a private individual.
> . . .
> Herbert Chitepo was sobbing like a small child. . . . Mataure, Tongogara and Mudzi . . . all shed tears with shouts of "You have succeeded in betraying not only ourselves but also those who have died in the struggle." The whole theme was very emotional and my

reaction to it at that stage was that we were not going to change our minds just because they, the Revolutionary Council, did not approve of the decision taken by the Executive in prison . . . (later) Tongogara "said that they were prepared to concede to the decision of the Executive but that the Executive should now tell them where to go with all the wounded who were in Zambia and where to train all our people now in the Tanzania training camps." [Chitepo told Nyagumbo that his actions were giving Kaunda the excuse he had long wanted for throwing ZANU] "not only from Zambian soil but also from Tanzania and Mozambique." . . .

I finally conceded. . . . I assured the four men of the Dare that I would convince the Executive in prison because of the danger they had outlined was to be faced by the nation as a whole. [Nyagumbo was further rebuked by Nyerere and Machel. The latter] minced no words as to what he was going to do with us if we had maintained our decision; he was going to order the arrest of our two thousand five hundred fighting men . . . in Mozambique. I must admit that President Machel was the only man who succeeded in intimidating me. (Nyagumbo quoted in Ranger 1980, 76–77; the words in brackets are Ranger's)

Nyagumbo returned to prison and informed the leadership that Sithole could be removed by a vote of the Central Committee. Until that time, however, Sithole would be considered ZANU's leader. The Executive Council in prison acceded to the demands of the Front Line presidents but believed that the whole attempt would be unproductive. Nyagumbo wrote to Terrence Ranger at the time, "To us it sounded very tricky . . . both Vorster and Smith wanted a breathing space and we did not think that the 'Freedom Fighters' had yet made the necessary impact" (Nyagumbo to Ranger, November 30, 1974, quoted in Ranger 1980, 77).

Despite the objections of ZANU, the Front Line presidents were able to forge a fragile unity. On December 8, it was announced that the parties of ZANU, ZAPU, FROLIZI (a small splinter party in exile led by James Chikerema), and the ANC had merged under the umbrella of the ANC. Muzorewa was chosen as head, because none of the other leaders could countenance Nkomo or Sithole in charge. The most important point of compromise that made the unity possible was an agreement to continue the armed struggle. The marriage was not made in heaven: Muzorewa was particularly bitter about ZAPU and ZANU continuing to plan strategy away from the ANC and at the public attacks on Muzorewa broadcast by ZANU from Lusaka. One, in particular, boasted that "if both Mr. Ian Smith and Bishop Muzorewa were put before me, I would choose to shoot Muzorewa first before I shoot Ian Smith" (Muzorewa 1978, 148).

The odd party to the unity talks was ZANU. Neither its political leaders within the country nor those in exile wanted to unite with the other parties or stifle the armed struggle. Chitepo at the time explained to his ZANU comrades that "we were coerced, but we want to get out of it. We had no choice. Even Nyerere forced us. They want a settlement but we don't believe one is possible" (Mubako 1987, interview with author). On a flight from Dar es Salaam, Chitepo told a reporter that "there will be no talks, no negotiations, no discussions involving our movement until Mr. Smith recognizes the right to immediate majority rule. . . . Until we hear that man, the rebel leader of the rebel regime, speak those words our war goes on and it will continue until we have liberated every acre of our country" (Martin and Johnson 1981, 151). The guerrilla army was especially wary of moderating combat precisely at the time it was enjoying its best success and was clearly having something to show for it. As for Sithole, even if he personally wanted a settlement—and at times in the past he had displayed a willingness to negotiate[13]—his shaky position within ZANU demanded that he take as hard a line as possible. He was in no position to take risks with an accommodating line.[14]

As to those ZANU leaders who had overthrown Sithole, their attitude was anger and mistrust. Robert Mugabe, in his report to the Catholic Commission on Peace and Justice, expressed his bewilderment that Kaunda could undertake such negotiations with South Africa: "We wondered how he, a man dedicated to Pan-Africanism and to our national course, could now hobnob with our enemy, Voster [*sic*]. We think that Voster [*sic*] understands only the language of the bullet!" Moreover, Mugabe mentioned what certainly ran through the minds of all ZANU members when he questioned Kaunda's motives: "We wondered whether Zambia's economic situation could have caused this change in Kaunda, whether he preferred the route to Beira [through Rhodesia] over that to Dar es Salaam. Also Zambia needs South African goods. So we did not trust Kaunda, especially not since he is a friend of Nkomo and trying to raise him to be our equal" (Mugabe 1974, 2).

Mugabe's account also underscores ZANU's feeling of being railroaded into the unity agreement and talks with Smith. The ZANU leaders told Sithole to tell Kaunda "to take us back to QueQue [the prison where they had been detained for ten years]; we had not asked for the talks and the time was not yet ripe." When Nkomo disbanded ZAPU to join the ANC, "we did not mind because we thought that without us the rest would be toothless. Sithole reported this to the three presidents and they were alarmed and called in our whole executive" (Mugabe 1974, 4). At this point Nyerere threatened ZANU to form a common approach, which the Executive Council agreed to do. But the whole unity question threatened to fall apart over the wording of its proclamation. Nkomo insisted that the memo read "the former ZANU and the former ZAPU," to signify that a fusion of the groups had taken place. The reaction of all parties concerned provides a depth of insight to the issue:

> Sithole objected that not a fusion but only a united front had been agreed on. Nyerere then became very angry and threatened to walk out, but Seretse Kama [sic] restrained him. Nyerere asked Muzorewa what he thought about it and Muzorewa said that he took it that a merger had occurred. So said Kaunda and Seretse. ZANU therefore refused to sign. ZANU again obstructed unity. Nyerere called in all three delegations and we met in the first open session.
> Nyerere attacked both ZANU and ZAPU: "ZAPU is mutopo [eternal]! ZAPU is in my blood! What is this creature called ZAPU? ZANU is a military machinery. What is this creature called ZANU?" He scolded us and then Kaunda spoke and attacked us still more viciously, calling us treacherous, criminal, selfish and not taking the interest of our people to heart. If we did not comply, he would no longer entertain our military presence in Zambia. Only Seretse Kama [sic] said anything soothing, but his advice was to heed what had been said so far. Nyerere again attacked us and asked for a response. (Mugabe 1974, 4)

It is small wonder that Mugabe, when asked about the motives of Kaunda and Nyerere, replied, "We are suspicious of these" (Mugabe 1974, 6).

Although ZANU publicly committed themselves to the negotiating process, nothing was further from the minds of many in the party. One of the most hard-line members of the ZANU prison Executive Council, Edgar Tekere, seven months after Mugabe's report wrote in a letter:

> Right from the time we left detention in December we spared no time at all in going out to the people to speak nothing else but violence and urge people to join our military. We did not mince our words and did not care who listened in house to house meetings across the country . . . we ignored the whole talk about talks, denounced the whole concept of talks at every platform offered and worked hard to ensure that such talks do not really start because we saw them as nothing else but a trick to defuse our military effort without a ghost of a prospect for *majority rule* now . . . In the meantime Nkomo was getting himself into all sorts of secret deals with the whites and he and Muzorewa were actually sweating to kill the war effort. We ourselves could see that we were making a terrific impact on the minds of the people. (Tekere to Didymus Mutasa, July 22, 1975, quoted in Ranger 1985, 268–269)

Finally, apart from the crisis within the political leadership of ZANU at the time, there was also a severe crisis concerning the military leadership. On December 7, the day before the unity agreement was announced, Thomas Nhari, a commander in ZANLA (ZANU's army), traveled to Lusaka and kidnapped a number of ZANU people, including Tongogara's wife and children. The rebellion by Nhari, which had some support from the guerrillas, was to lead to the deaths of more than 100 soldiers and cadres who supported him, including John Mataure, a member of the Revolutionary Council. The causes of the rebellion have been attributed to anger on the part of some of the ZANU guerrillas over inferior weaponry they were receiving from China, to a belief that the current leadership was not providing the supplies they needed, and (the most divisive aspect) to an ethnic factional dispute between members of the Manyika and Karanga subgroups of the Shona people of Zimbabwe. In fact, Nhari was a paid agent of Smith's government, an integral part of the Salisbury regime's attempt to split the nationalists from within (Flower 1987, 146).

## Breakthrough and Breakdown

The first meetings between officials of the Rhodesian government and the Front Line presidents took place on December 6, 1974. The meeting ended "in apparent deadlock over a demand made on the African side for 'immediate majority rule in Rhodesia,' which was deemed unacceptable by the Smith regime" (Keesing's, 26910). In a statement released on December 7, the Rhodesian prime minister's office said that during the talks the Rhodesians had stipulated, "First, that there should be a cessation of terrorism in accordance with the Prime Minister's frequently stated principle that he would only be prepared to discuss constitutional issues with those who undertook to work constitutionally and within the law. Secondly, that any constitutional conference would have to accept that there would be no lowering of standards." The statement went on to say that their representatives had been "informed that there would be no cessation of terrorism unless it was agreed that a precondition of the constitutional conference was that it would be on the basis of immediate majority rule," a proposal unacceptable to the Rhodesian government (ARB, 3467).

South Africa's response to these developments is informative. Emphasizing that Rhodesia had "adopted a very realistic and reasonable attitude and throughout fulfilled its obligations in terms of its commitments," and that "Zambia as well as the other parties also made an honest attempt to find a solution and made a full contribution to this end," South Africa blamed the breakup on "the new demand at the end of the proceedings. This demand was in total conflict with the spirit, intent and result of the agreement up to this point. Rhodesia cannot therefore be blamed for the failure of the negotiations." South Africa then warned that "unless the other parties return to the basis and method of approach which was agreed upon before the deadlock on Friday, it must be assumed that agreement cannot be reached." The release concluded that South Africa would continue to work to bring all parties to the conference table and if it failed, "The alternative is too ghastly to contemplate" (ARB, 3468).

What should be emphasized here are two phrases: (1) a demand, "in total conflict with the spirit, intent and result of the agreement up to this point" and (2) a "return to the basis and method of approach which was agreed upon before the deadlock on Friday." South Africa was communicating that South Africa and Zambia had established ground rules for the negotiations, which did not include a demand for immediate majority rule. Only if this is so can it be emphasized that Rhodesia had been "reasonable" to that point.

South Africa then pressured Rhodesia back to the negotiating table in Lusaka, and Kaunda made sure that demands for immediate majority rule were ruled out of order. On December 11, Smith announced that a constitutional conference would be held, and that "on an assurance that there would be a cease-fire in the 'terrorist' war, all Black political detainees in Rhodesia would be released" (ARB, 3468).

Muzorewa was to write later that Smith had made up this deal: "During the talks . . . Ian Smith tried to create the mirage of agreement where it did not exist"—referring to the nationalists' supposed commitment to stop terrorism in exchange for release of detainees (Muzorewa 1978, 144). In part this is correct; the nationalists had not acceded to any such agreement. Furthermore, they were to allege at a later date that there existed a cease-fire agreement that they refused to sign in December, precisely because it was on Smith's terms and would provide advantage to his forces.

In part, however, Muzorewa is incorrect that Smith fabricated the deal. Vorster commented the next day that "Smith and his government had proved beyond all doubt that they were not only prepared to make their contribution towards peace in southern Africa, but through their actions they had manifestly confirmed it." He added that, "if the negotiations ahead are conducted by all parties in the same spirit, it is reasonable to expect that success will be achieved. The stage has now been reached where it is appropriate for all States and organizations outside Rhodesia not to interfere in this matter and to leave it to the white and black people of Rhodesia to find the final solution to their problems without interference." In conclusion, Vorster reiterated his pledge to withdraw South African police from Rhodesia "as soon as it is clear that terrorism had ended" (ARB, 3470).

The government of Botswana also praised Smith and the deal. And in a remarkable statement, the *Times* of Zambia called Smith "the man of the hour in white southern Africa," and noted that "it did take some heroism for him to do what he has done."

## The Deal Bogs Down

Within days, statements by Smith, Muzorewa, and Sithole derailed the negotiation process. Muzorewa, in a short interview in the *Rhodesia Herald* on December 12, used the phrase "on the basis of majority rule" four times in describing the necessary conditions for gaining independence. Muzorewa also stated the nationalist stance on the cease-fire: none until a firm date had been announced for the conference. Upon questioning from reporters, however, Muzorewa backed off, saying there was no contradiction between his position on the cease-fire and what Smith had said. This was an unfortunate error because it gave the appearance of nationalist acceptance of Smith's announcement.[15] Sithole was more forthright with the press the next day: "There is no way we can reach an accommodation with the Rhodesian Government, because the Rhodesian Government is dedicated to minority rule." If roundtable talks were to occur, they would have to involve "a neutral venue and a neutral chairman." When asked about the details of the cease-fire, Sithole responded, "I don't know. I have no ideas whatever on that one" (ARB, 3472).

The extent of Smith's "conversion" was delimited in an interview on December 15. Smith stated that although he believed in majority rule, if it meant "the counting of heads like the counting of sheep then, of course, I am opposed to that." When queried about "speculation that what he really had in mind was a parity in Government and majority rule in about five years," Smith replied, "I can assure you that those thoughts have never entered my mind and I don't believe they ever will." On the details of the proposed conference, he professed a belief that it would take some time before it could take place—"January, maybe February," and discussed for the first time a demand that would prove to be a sticking point for the negotiations for the next year: "I can think of no more neutral ground than Rhodesia, quite frankly, and I would be surprised if there were real, genuine Rhodesians who would go so far as to say that a vital conference such as this, which is going to determine the future of our country, should be held outside Rhodesia." Smith concluded, "We have got to bring the African in more. . . . If I found Africans of ability and merit I would be prepared to bring them in and give them a chance. Because of the extremists we have not had a chance to try this" (ARB, 3472).[16]

On the same day, Robert Mugabe, upon his release from prison, said, "We want immediate majority rule accepted as a fact, but we will deal with the mechanics after the fact has been accepted." He candidly admitted that "the negotiation exercise has been forced on ZANU," but that they would do their utmost to make it work. The next day Jason

Moyo, chairman of ZAPU at the time, said "that his organization's military units had been ordered 'to cool it provided the Rhodesian forces do the same, but there is no truce.'" He added that majority rule was "'not negotiable,' but 'we can talk about the methods of transferring power from the White minority' and he would support Bishop Muzorewa's demand that the constitutional conference should be held in Britain" (Keesing's, 26912).

The peace process became bogged down for three reasons. First, there was no agreement about the terms and conditions of the cease-fire. Second, the nationalists were angered by the attempts to eliminate the violence without eliminating the reasons for the violence. Many blacks had concluded that only armed struggle would make Smith capitulate to majority rule. Until Smith conceded, the guerrillas did not want to relinquish pressure on the white regime. Third, the process became embroiled in an infinite regress of each side waiting to take the first steps in carrying out this undefined exchange, and when no exchange took place, blaming the other for not carrying out its terms.

What is remarkable, given the ambiguities of the proposed agreement, and its apparent nonstarter status, was that this framework was never called into question. For example, on January 14, after a trip to Southern Africa, British prime minister James Callaghan told Parliament: "Unless our efforts in this direction are to be wasted, there are two essential requirements. First, early progress must be made towards securing the observance of all the provisions of the agreement worked out in Lusaka last month. . . . Second, to keep the momentum going in order to pave the way for a successful constitutional conference, the now united ANC and Mr. Smith should undertake direct exploratory talks" (ARB, 3506).

## Developments from January to April

How did each side interpret the Lusaka "agreement"? The Smith government began the release of some political detainees in the middle of December. Rhodesian airplanes also dropped leaflets into guerrilla areas telling the combatants that the war was over and that they had to turn in their weapons and surrender or leave the country. Many guerrillas reacted angrily to this "apparent betrayal by Zimbabwean leaders" and "adopted the slogan, 'Down with détente'" (Muzorewa 1978, 144). On the guerrilla side, the cease-fire was never honored. In the first month of the "agreement," violence continued, including the killing of six South African policemen in combat.

On January 9, 1975, Desmond Lardner-Burke, the Rhodesian minister of justice and law and order, declared that the further release of political detainees would be halted because African leaders had failed to stop hostilities. He added that violence "in some areas had in fact increased," and accused the guerrilla leadership of urging the "terrorists" to continue "the struggle." Moreover, Lardner-Burke charged that the nationalists were taking advantage of the situation by sending more troops into the country (Keesing's, 27083).

This prompted a quick rebuke from the ANC. James Chikerema, on January 10, stated that a formal cease-fire would come into being only when a firm date had been set for the constitutional conference. He accused the Smith government of not honoring the Lusaka agreement: "His soldiers went into our areas, so they were killed. Each time they drop leaflets on us we will shoot down the planes" (ARB, 3508). Two days later, the ANC Central Committee voted not to attend any conference with Smith until he had carried out the terms of the "Lusaka Agreement." They accused Smith of "a flagrant violation of the terms of the ceasefire" by ordering the guerrillas to surrender or leave the country: "A ceasefire means no more than stopping to shoot and to advance beyond the lines where the respective forces are found. It does not mean surrender" (ARB, 3507–3508).

The Rhodesian government, on January 18, "rejected the ANC's view that a ceasefire meant an end to the shooting rather than a surrender of arms, and moreover stated that the shooting had not stopped. . . . The Rhodesian Government emphasized that there had been no signed documents as a result of the Lusaka discussions and that Rhodesia had 'made it perfectly clear' that its conditions for a constitutional conference were total cessation of 'terrorism,' which meant either surrender to the security forces or total withdrawal from the country by the 'terrorists'" (Keesing's, 27083).

South Africa and Zambia were quick to react to the war being waged in the press. In South Africa, the media, which had been very critical of Smith in the preceding week, once again lambasted him. *Die Transvaler*, the Nationalist party organ in the Transvaal, stated that "it is lamentable that in Rhodesia double-talk, vagueness and evasion on this critical matter should cloud Black-White relations, and that at the cost of the entire southern Africa" (Keesing's, 27084). Behind the scenes, the South African government announced that it was sending its minister of the interior and information, Dr. Connie Mulder, to Salisbury for a "vital" visit. On the nationalist side, Kaunda had two officers of the ANC accompany him to the town of Mbala, Zambia, on January 18, to talk with Nyerere and Machel. Reports in the press speculated that the meeting was an attempt "to resolve the ceasefire confusion." Subsequently, Edson Sithole[17] (one of Muzorewa's aides), Robert Mugabe, and three other ANC officials met with Ian Smith's cabinet secretary, Jack Gaylord, and two other government officials in Salisbury on January 20 and discussed possible arrangements for the constitutional conference. The next afternoon, the South African government announced that the "vital" visit of Mulder had been canceled because of "discussions yesterday in Salisbury between Rhodesian Government officials and the ANC, and recent developments as well as additional information just received" (ARB, 3502).

That same day, Ndabaningi Sithole was interviewed and asked to spell out his position on the constitutional talks. He felt that progress could be made "if Mr. Smith was prepared to think in terms of majority rule in three to five years." It seemed to him, however, that all Smith wanted was "to legalize the unilateral declaration of independence." Sithole underlined that a slow transition was acceptable to the nationalists provided that the principle of majority rule was accepted. Sithole also enunciated the risks of taking such a conciliatory line at that time: "Most African people, I find, take the view that constitutional talks will not yield the desired results. They accuse us, their leaders, of going back to our practice of the 1960s, when we used to talk a lot to Great Britain and the United Nations. All those talks resulted in nothing. The African people feel very strongly that the solution is to be found on the battlefield" (Keesing's, 27084).

Another push to get the warring parties together took place at the beginning of February. Two Rhodesian government officials flew to Lusaka on February 4 for talks with the Zambian government. The next day in Salisbury Smith met with Muzorewa, Sithole, Nkomo, and two of Muzorewa's assistants, Gabellah and Chavunduka, to discuss technical details of a conference, in particular a venue and chair. During the period February 6–8, these same ANC officials met with the Front Line presidents in Dar es Salaam and Lusaka. These meetings were described as "stormy" as Kaunda expressed his anger at ZANU's intransigence and Nyerere emphasized the need for accommodation (Meredith 1980, 172–173). The presidents were said to have urged the nationalists, especially ZANU, to observe the cease-fire. On February 9, the South African foreign minister and secretary for foreign affairs traveled to Lusaka to meet with members of the ANC and the foreign ministers of Zambia, Tanzania, and Botswana. At that time, the ANC asked the South Africans to hasten their withdrawal from Rhodesia as a sign of good intentions. On February 11, the Rhodesian government announced that South Africa had withdrawn some of its police from forward positions in the Zambezi valley in response to "undertakings from the Zambian Government about guerrilla infiltrations across the river" (ARB, 3537).

At that time, John Vorster still felt confident that some settlement could be reached. In Monrovia for secret talks with Liberia's president, William Tolbert, he went so far as to tell Tolbert, "If there are no preconditions and if violence stops [in Rhodesia] I can guarantee that a solution can be found." He also assured Tolbert he was preparing to "withdraw SA forces from Rhodesia as soon as violence had ended" (transcript of conversation leaked by Liberian government, quoted in Legum 1975, A40).

On February 12, Smith once again met with Muzorewa, Nkomo, and Sithole. According to Martin Meredith:

> The fundamental differences over majority rule precluded any real progress, and the nagging dispute over continued guerrilla activity meant that even further contacts were in jeopardy. In a two-week period in February, the government listed twenty incidents including murder, mortar attacks and ambushes. The government attributed the blame to Sithole, asserting that he had never accepted the idea of détente or the ceasefire. It seemed plausible to Smith that if Sithole could be removed, the more militant elements among the nationalists, principally ZANU supporters, could be isolated, and thus leave Smith to deal with moderate nationalists like Nkomo. (Meredith 1980, 174)

Prompted by the publication of the Mugabe Report to the Catholic Commission on Peace and Justice, both sides went public on February 25 on the lack of progress in the talks. The government stridently maintained that Smith had never considered majority rule in five years; indeed "a well placed source close to the government asserted that Rhodesia would never be handed over to majority rule—not next year, not in five years, not in ten years, not at all." In an interview with the *Rhodesia Herald*, a spokesman for the Smith government made public part of their strategy for splitting the nationalists. Stating that "if militant nationalists are going to persist in the totally impossible demands that have been made public so far, there is no hope whatever of reaching an agreement with those people." The source went on, "If the more moderate elements are prepared to reach an accord which seeks an outlet for responsible political aspirations—within their own areas on a provincial basis—there is every hope that accord can be reached" (ARB, 3538).

A spokesman for the ANC immediately rejected this position and refuted rumors that there were elements who would accept such a compromise. Elliot Gabellah made it clear that majority rule was the only acceptable basis for a settlement, and that the talks had bogged down because of disagreements concerning where the constitutional conference would take place and whether the ANC would accept an offer by Smith to guarantee the safety of ANC leaders who would have to negotiate if the conference were inside Rhodesia.

A week later, the ANC's National Executive Committee met to decide whether to continue talks with Smith. The meeting brought to the fore tensions that had been under the surface during the previous two and a half months. Young ZANU supporters at the meeting called for the ouster of Nkomo and a rejection of a moderate line. After the meeting, Bishop Muzorewa told some reporters that the ANC was "a very united organization." Sithole said, "Although the ANC is united in its goal of achieving majority rule, there are differences over tactics: ZANU. . . supports direct confrontation on the battlefield" (Keesing's, 27085).

Sithole was arrested by the Smith government on March 3 on charges that he was plotting to assassinate other ANC leaders, a complete fabrication on the part of the Rhodesians.[18] Muzorewa quickly stated that all talks would be off until Sithole was released. Nkomo, however, disagreed and argued that talks should continue, emphasizing that this was an old tactic of the whites to imprison leaders during negotiations and that this should not affect them. Mugabe, at a separate press conference, echoed Muzorewa's stand and flatly condemned the Smith government for "shattering the so-called détente." Mugabe went on to accuse some within the ANC of having shown their support for an agreement "based on provincialization and continued white domination" and that therefore the arrest of Sithole did not surprise ZANU. Finally, in one of the most telling remarks made by one of the nationalists, Edson Sithole, the publicity secretary for the ANC and one of Muzorewa's aides, charged the Smith regime with committing "a terrible blunder: No ANC leader could continue talking to the Government without exposing himself as a moderate and in support of the Government's action." It is telling because of the implication that there was a moderate line within the ANC that might seek a settlement on different terms than the hard-liners.

The South African government reacted swiftly and put heavy pressure on the Rhodesians over the arrest. On March 10, the South African minister of police announced that all South African police in Rhodesia were being withdrawn to base areas and would not partake in active duty. The announcement followed a speech by General Peter Walls, commander of Rhodesian armed services, who, after informing the press of the South African action, warned South Africa that it "has a moral obligation to help Rhodesia if detente breaks down." The *Guardian* reported on elements within Rhodesia who "take the view that if the Rhodesian settlement talks fail—and with them détente in Southern Africa—Mr. Vorster will nevertheless have to continue to help Rhodesia to fight the guerrilla war. In this way South Africa, instead of making peace with its black neighbors, would be drawn into a potential mini-Vietnam in Southern Africa" (ARB, 3569).

The Rhodesian government had originally announced that Sithole's trial would be held in private, but after Smith met Vorster in Cape Town

on March 16 and 17, the decision was changed. The public pronounce-
ments from the meeting once again reiterated that South African police
would be withdrawn as soon as the cease-fire was in place and added
that "the position of the detained African nationalist whose case is at
present under the personal consideration of the Rhodesian Attorney-
General was also discussed." It was alleged that Vorster had also "told
Mr. Smith that even in the event of an all-out nationalist war against the
Salisbury regime, South Africa might confine its role to a rescue
operation for a beleaguered white population in Rhodesia" (*Sunday
Tribune*, Johannesburg, quoted in ARB, 3571).

The next day, a car bomb planted by Rhodesian agents killed
Herbert Chitepo, the ZANU party leader in exile. Allegations ran wild:
some blamed the Rhodesian Special Branch, some blamed factional
warfare within ZANU, some even blamed the Zambian government.
The Zambians, fearing that some would take seriously accusations of
their involvement, went overboard. They arrested Tongogara and some
of his lieutenants and charged them with the murder.

Chitepo's death and the actions taken by the Zambian government
would destroy ZANU's war effort for the year, lead to irreparable splits
within ZANU, and prompt ZANU's rejection of Kaunda as a sponsor.
It would also embolden Smith's government not to settle. A writer for
the *Times* (London) commented at the time, "Neither Mr. Smith nor Mr.
Vorster know whether ZANU, after Chitepo's death, could with the aid
of FRELIMO, really mount an effort in Rhodesia that would force
Rhodesians to think in terms of a precise timetable for handing over
power. Both, though for different reasons, are probably inclined to wait
and see just how much muscle the Africans can develop in the coming
months, both before and after Mozambique's independence in June"
(ARB, 3570).

On April 3, Dr. Hilgard Muller, the South African foreign minister,
traveled to Salisbury to meet Smith. The next day, Smith released
Sithole from prison so that he could attend an Organization of African
Unity (OAU) summit with Nkomo and Muzorewa, "as a request from
Bishop Muzorewa, supported by the four northern Presidents and the
South African Government." Smith added, "I must tell you that this is
not a decision to which the Rhodesian Government readily agreed.
However, we were assured that to do so would significantly assist the
cause of détente." While white Rhodesians were outraged at the
violation of their sovereignty, a much more important reaction was
registered by Robert Mugabe. According to what he told his biographers,
the arrest of Sithole and then his subsequent release were the last straws
in his cooperation with the détente exercise: "Mugabe was not just
suspicious of the peacemakers, he was positively contemptuous. Smith,

and Vorster, were simply leading Nkomo, Muzorewa and Sithole into a sell-out of the Africans" (Smith and Simpson 1981, 78).

## *From April to August: The Prelude to Victoria Falls*

The months between April and August saw a number of important developments: (1) responses to actions taken by Zambia over Chitepo's murder; (2) continued squabbling between Smith and the ANC over necessary conditions for a cease-fire, leading finally to Smith's willingness on May 22 to hold a conference without conditions; (3) continued pressure on Rhodesia by Vorster, including the final withdrawal of South African police in August; and (4) interorganizational warfare within the ANC as ZANU and ZAPU continued to fight within Rhodesia and in the guerrilla camps outside the country, amidst charges by the ANC leadership that Joshua Nkomo had entered into secret talks with Ian Smith.

After the OAU summit in April, the Front Line presidents tried to strengthen the hand of the nationalists by pledging new resources to building the liberation army, including providing new training camps in Mozambique and Tanzania. The presidents also attempted to force the armies of ZANU and ZAPU to merge, in the belief that having separate armies weakened the struggle against Smith. Kaunda forced soldiers from both armies to be herded together in camps within Zambia, leading to armed battles within the camps and Zimbabwean guerrillas killing each other. Zambian troops that were called in "to provide order" exchanged fire with ZANU guerrillas, killing eleven and sparking accusations on both sides as to responsibility.

Relations between Zambia and most of ZANU had deteriorated completely. In the wake of the Chitepo assassination, Zambia arrested hundreds of ZANU supporters and surrounded their army bases in Zambia. The Zambian government closed the offices of ZANU and ZAPU in Lusaka and declared them to be illegal organizations. Most important, Zambia arrested Tongogara and other ZANLA military commanders and charged them with the death of Chitepo. In an effort to show that the Zambians were not involved with the killing, they tortured the accused ZANU leaders to extract confessions from them. They also set up an international panel to investigate the killings, which found on the basis of Zambian police evidence that Tongogara had ordered the assassination. He was later found not guilty when the judges trying his case established that the two witnesses who formed the basis of the accusation against him had given their confessions under severe duress: their stories had been beaten out of them.

Anyone in ZANU faced a stark choice during that period: whether or not to believe the Zambian government and support the charges against Tongogara. The Zambians stated that the motive was tribal politics: the death of Chitepo was the climax of a bloody feud among Karanga and Manyika, warring subtribes within ZANU. During the period preceding the murder of Chitepo, there had been fighting within ZANU when the Nhari faction (mostly all Manyikas) tried to wrestle military leadership from Tongogara. There were rumors that Chitepo had been implicated in the Nhari rebellion; whether he was or was not, he was vulnerable to the charge because he was the only remaining Manyika in the ZANU leadership.

Ndabaningi Sithole chose to believe Kaunda and the Zambians. Mugabe and others stood by Tongogara, with Mugabe going so far as to blame Kaunda for involvement in the assassination as a way of forcing détente down the throats of ZANU. The split had reverberations down to the armed camps. Each company of guerrillas had to decide whom to believe and whom to support for leadership. But such a problem did not exist for the waves of new recruits who were leaving Rhodesia during that time. The estimated 12,000 new volunteers that Mugabe and Edgar Tekere brought with them from Rhodesia into Mozambique were firmly against Sithole and Kaunda.

Within the ANC, another split was developing as Nkomo attempted to wrestle the leadership from Muzorewa. In June 1975, while Sithole and Muzorewa were outside of Rhodesia, Nkomo called for a meeting of the ANC Congress, where he attempted to wrest its leadership from Muzorewa. The attempt failed and the congress turned violent: ZANU and ZAPU supporters attacked each other and Rhodesian police opened fire on both, killing five men. Leaders of the ANC blamed Nkomo for holding the congress and charged him with secretly entering talks with Ian Smith. Nkomo's position was not helped when Smith, in a television interview in June, described Nkomo as "a strong personality with qualities of leadership."

In this context, talks about talks continued between the ANC and Smith. The first direct meetings since Sithole's arrest were held on May 22, 1975. During the meeting, Smith offered to drop any preconditions for holding a constitutional conference, including a cease-fire. He told reporters afterwards that he put an ultimatum to the nationalists: "We either agree to hold a conference or we say it is off and give reasons why." He also threatened to hold talks with other black groups, as he had evidence "of a growing feeling among responsible Africans that the ANC is not measuring up to its task" (ARB, 3636).

The next meeting between the two sides came on June 12 and also ended in deadlock. The dispute concerned the venue of the conference. The nationalists demanded that it be held outside Rhodesia to ensure the safety of its leaders from arrest or detention within Rhodesia. Smith responded that it would be impossible, as "he could not afford the time to attend a lengthy conference outside Rhodesia." For the next month and a half Muzorewa issued statements urging Smith to hold a conference and threatening to increase the intensity of the war (ARB, 3668).

On July 31, South Africa announced that all South African police would be out of Rhodesia, leaving a "defense gap which will have to be filled by the redeployment of Rhodesia's own defence troops." On August 1, Smith told his House of Assembly in Salisbury, "I am prepared to go outside of the country for a full constitutional conference but preliminary negotiations would have to take place inside the country." He also mentioned that he had set in motion "arrangements . . . to seek an internal agreement with other groups and organizations more truly representative of genuine African opinion."

Vorster's decision to withdraw the police from Rhodesia met opposition from the hard-liners in South Africa:

> Immediately after the reported withdrawal of SAP (South African Police) units from Rhodesia in 1975, Dr. Rhoodie has maintained that Botha arranged for 500 troops to be airlifted from Waterkloof Air Force Base to Rhodesia to help Ian Smith's security forces combat the Patriotic Front [*sic*] fighters. This coincided precisely with Vorster's assurances that South Africa was no longer directly involved in the Zimbabwean war. Again, at the eleventh hour, General van den Bergh told Vorster about Botha's designs and foiled Botha's plans. (Grundy 1986, 91)

On August 8 and 9, Smith and three cabinet members traveled to Pretoria for talks with Vorster and Mark Chona, who was "acting on behalf of the Governments of Botswana, Mozambique, Tanzania and Zambia and for the ANC." A joint press release issued simultaneously from Lusaka and Pretoria made public the contents of the "Pretoria Agreement" between Smith and Vorster. The agreement called for a meeting between the Rhodesian government and the ANC to take place no later than August 25 at Victoria Falls, the purpose of which was "to give the parties the opportunity to publicly express their genuine desire to negotiate an acceptable settlement." After the conference, the parties would "discuss proposals for a settlement in committee or committees within Rhodesia." The parties would then "meet again in formal conference anywhere decided upon to ratify the committee proposals which have been agreed upon." The release concluded by saying that "the South African Government and the Governments of Botswana, Mozambique, Tanzania, and Zambia, respectively, hereby express their willingness to ensure that this agreement is implemented by the two parties involved." One part of the agreement, however, was not made public; on the draft of the agreement was written at the bottom, "It stands to reason if we wanted to succeed there must be no infiltration of terrorists. This part not to go into the document as it will complicate matters. Mr. Smith gave the assurance that there will be no new detentions while the Committee stage is in progress" (draft of the agreement, in Baumhogger 1984, 7).

Smith explained to his House of Assembly that the Victoria Falls meeting was to be "no more than a signing ceremony," which "might not last more than 30 minutes." He emphasized the provision of the agreement whereby any committee talks would take place in Rhodesia, a provision, he noted, that had the ANC's approval. He was asked about amnesty for ANC leaders and responded that this had been "discussed in Pretoria, and an amicable agreement was arrived at which has been accepted by all parties." On August 14, in an address to the nation, Smith stressed that the agreement was signed not only by Vorster and himself, but also by a representative of the Zambian government acting on behalf of the ANC.

There was a problem, however. The agreement stipulated that the tough negotiating—the committee work—would take place within Rhodesia. And although Smith's guarantee at Pretoria that no new detentions would take place during the talks might have satisfied Mark Chona, it did not satisfy some members of the ANC—most notably Ndabaningi Sithole and James Chikerema. What has not been written about this episode is that there was one element of the ANC that certainly would not postpone the talks because of this issue: Nkomo. He more than anyone would benefit from the agreement as stipulated. He was the only leader at the time who was active inside Rhodesia and had already established a reputation as a reasonable leader with Smith. He had the least to fear about the talks being held inside Rhodesia.[19]

Muzorewa made public his unwillingness to attend "a serious constitutional conference for only 30 minutes," and disassociated the ANC from a willingness to hold meetings within Rhodesia. Nonetheless, he led the ANC delegation to the preliminary talks scheduled for Victoria Falls. His twelve-person delegation included Sithole, Nkomo, and Chikerema and a support group of thirteen political and legal advisers. Smith took with him four cabinet members but, significantly, no legal adviser.

On August 26, 1975, a South African train ambled onto the bridge that spans the gorge at Victoria Falls and stopped so that the middle car of the train saddled the point that marks the border between Zambia and Rhodesia. From the Zambian side of the bridge entered Muzorewa, Nkomo, and Sithole. From the Rhodesian side Smith and the Rhodesian delegation boarded the train, which sat hundreds of feet above the waters of the Zambezi River. Making their way through the train, the adversaries met at a table halfway and proceeded to have the first formal talks on ending the ten-year-old civil war. The meeting lasted fourteen hours, of which no more than 150 minutes were spent with each side directly addressing each other (Meredith 1980, 192).

The meeting was a nonstarter: Muzorewa demanded majority rule and Smith refused, referring to the Pretoria agreement. Muzorewa demanded amnesty for ANC leaders who would be negotiating inside Rhodesia and Smith refused, referring to the Pretoria agreement. Within private session, the ANC argued among themselves about whether amnesty was part of the Pretoria agreement, and six of them contended that it was not.

During the evening sessions, the ANC hammered out an eight-point document to present to Smith that included a provision for immunity for the ANC negotiators. Smith refused to budge. The meeting adjourned near midnight, not to be reopened the next day.

## The Aftermath of Victoria Falls

In the aftermath of the Victoria Falls conference, the fragile threads of unity that held together the ANC tore irreparably.  On September 2, Sithole established another in the long list of acronyms that plagues any student of Zimbabwean politics: the ZLC, or the Zimbabwe Liberation Council, which was to act as the leadership of the ANC's exile wing. Sithole had announced that he had been elected chairman and that the leadership would consist of Chikerema and George Nyandoro of FROLIZI, two ZANU officials who had been associated with the Nhari rebellion—Noel Mukono and Simpson Mutambanengwe—and four members of ZAPU, who subsequently denounced the council and refused to have anything to do with it.  The decision was to prove disastrous for Sithole.  First, it marked the final break between most of the guerrillas in ZANU and Sithole, because they had no respect for Mukono and Mutambanengwe and felt that Sithole had acted solely out of nepotism.  Second, the decision gave Nkomo the opportunity to sever his connections with Sithole and to attempt to reach a settlement with Smith on his own.

Nkomo acted quickly to take advantage of the situation and called for an executive meeting of the ANC inside Rhodesia that week. Nkomo's followers, who were in the majority, voted to hold leadership elections on September 28.  On September 11, in Lusaka, Bishop Muzorewa publicly expelled Nkomo from the ANC. The internal fights exasperated Kaunda and prompted the Zambian government to announce that the bishop could not make decisions for parties within Rhodesia while he was in Zambia.  The announcement also triggered fighting between ZANU and ZAPU troops that were stationed together in Zambia; a small number of ZANU and Zambian soldiers were killed.

The Front Line presidents attempted to act as peacemakers among the nationalists. In a meeting of the antagonists and the four presidents, Kaunda asked each side to reconsider its actions. Muzorewa refused to budge on readmitting Nkomo to the ANC. Jason Moyo, on behalf of Nkomo, refused to cancel the plans for elections on September 28. Kaunda said later, "In the end, we had no choice but to say: 'Look in this case then, we can't help you. . . . We have done everything possible; we have released you from jail and so on. But now you are not willing to co-operate. You want to go your separate ways. Well, we support whoever wants to fight for independence under majority rule'" (Meredith 1980, 200; the above section draws on his book, 198–201).

The split between these factions had far-reaching implications for the attitudes of the Front Line presidents. First, there was unfinished business: infighting among the nationalists had given Smith the chance he needed to weasel out of the Victoria talks. In the immediate aftermath of the talks, the public statements by Zambia were optimistic, indicating that agreement had been close and that talks were still a real possibility. Although Tanzania and Mozambique had lost patience with the détente exercise at that point, Zambia was willing to try one last time, and Nyerere and Machel acceded to Kaunda.[20] Kaunda made it clear to Nkomo that Smith was to be tried one last time: Would he commit to majority rule or not? (Masarurwa 1987, interview with author; ZAPU Delegate B. 1987, interview with author.)[21]

Throughout the months leading up to Victoria Falls, Smith had been wooing Nkomo to enter talks with him. After his release from detention, Nkomo had argued a much more conciliatory line than Sithole and had considered Muzorewa's leadership inept. But as long as he remained part of a coalition with them, he did not defect. As late as August 30, Nkomo had publicly stated that "the ANC will not attend any talks without its full negotiating team. . . . The delegation must be the same that was on the bridge" (ARB, 3742). With the split between the parties finalized on September 28, Nkomo was elected chairman of the ANC within Rhodesia and subsequently accepted Smith's offer in October to hold talks.

A second implication of the failure at Victoria Falls was that both Nyerere and Machel clearly favored an intensifying of the war effort. They had reached an impasse over trying to create some unity among the various factions and so chose a new tack: to sift through the claims of legitimacy of the various factions and find those leaders who were seen as genuine representatives of the military. In the case of ZIPRA (ZAPU's army), it was easy: Nkomo was firmly in control. In the case of ZANLA, no less than Sithole, Muzorewa, and Chikerema were claiming leadership of the guerrillas.

Nyerere and Machel's task was made easier in November 1975,

when ZANLA commanders at Mgagao base camp addressed a letter to Machel and Nyerere[22] stating that Muzorewa, Sithole, and Chikerema were totally discredited:

> These three have proved to be completely hopeless and ineffective as leaders of the Zimbabwe revolution. Ever since the Unity Accord was signed on 7-12-74 these men have done nothing to promote the struggle for liberation of Zimbabwe, but on the other hand, they have done everything to hamper the struggle through their power struggle. . . . An executive member who has been outstanding is Robert Mugabe. He has demonstrated this by defying the rigours of guerrilla life in the jungles of Mozambique. Since we respect him most, in all our dealings with the ANC leadership, he is the only person who can act as middle man. We will not accept any direct discussions with any of the three leading members of the ANC we have described above. We can only talk through Robert Mugabe to them." ("Mgagao Declaration," in Baumhogger 1984, 27)

The wording of the declaration is instructive: the guerrillas were rejecting the triumvirate of Sithole, Muzorewa, and Chikerema as leaders, but this did not imply that Mugabe was seen as their new leader. Rather, he was to be trusted as a middleman or, as he was referred to throughout 1976, "a spokesman."

As 1975 was drawing to an end, the civil war that broke out at independence in Angola had a forceful influence on the Front Line presidents. The civil war among the fighting nationalist parties there deeply disturbed the region's black leaders and they wanted to avoid a repetition of that in Rhodesia. The presidents forced the merging of ZIPRA and ZANLA camps, which proved a recipe for disaster. At that time, Machel and Nyerere also discussed the development of "a third force," composed of young military commanders from ZIPRA and ZANLA. The presidents' disgust with the political machinations of Sithole, Muzorewa, and Nkomo prompted a willingness to abandon the founders of Zimbabwean nationalism—if leadership could emerge from the guerrillas themselves.

## Analyzing the Failure of "Détente"

The détente episode underscores the problematic nature of ripeness as an analytical concept. In late 1974, factors loomed large enough to have made for a "ripe moment" to resolve the conflict. Within the region the collapse of the Portuguese empire in Mozambique forced the rethinking of previously straightjacketed beliefs about the necessity and desirability of a negotiated settlement in Rhodesia (Middlemas 1975, 281–308). White Rhodesians had not foreseen that such a total collapse of a colonial authority could happen. Great unease circulated through the military: the Portuguese with an army much larger than Rhodesia's had been unable to defeat the FRELIMO guerrillas. Six hundred miles of Rhodesia's eastern border would be open as a penetration route for ZANLA. Coupled with a new infiltration by ZIPRA troops from Botswana to the southwest, Rhodesia faced their capabilities being stretched to their limits. In the words of Moorcraft and McLaughlin (1982, 84), "Rarely has the strategic initiative passed so swiftly and so decisively to guerrilla forces."

The effects were felt immediately: net inflow of new residents in 1974 dropped to its lowest point since 1965. Although more residents entered the country than exited during 1974 as a whole, this was not true for the last three months of that year. Militarily, the country's armed forces were advising settlement in the belief that the war was unwinnable (Lapping 1985; Flower 1987, interview with author). Economically, Rhodesia anticipated the possible closing of its border with Mozambique and the shutting off of trade routes that carried between 60 and 80 percent of their exports (Martin and Johnson 1981, 225). The Rhodesian economy, which to that point had weathered international sanctions, was reeling from the effects of OPEC and the quadrupling of oil prices (Moorcraft and McLaughlin 1982, 160). Finally, combined with the abrupt decolonization of Mozambique were the initiatives of John Vorster and Kenneth Kaunda, which in terms of surprise rival that of Anwar Sadat's peace initiative to Israel. White Rhodesia faced not only the specter of an intensified guerrilla war, but the possible abandonment of their biggest supporter.

If South Africa had been willing to force Smith to accept the principle of majority rule at that point and had moved quickly to seal an agreement, the outcome could have been different. Barring such an acceptance by Smith, the nationalists, however, would not negotiate. The events of late 1974 that had so thoroughly called into question Rhodesian resolve and commitment had emboldened the guerrillas. The fighting wing of the nationalist movement could see the fruits of their struggle and could anticipate their situation getting only better, thanks to events in Mozambique. This is not to say that they were unwilling to negotiate: a large section of the nationalist movement desired a settlement, and the guerrillas themselves did not want to fight a war for the sake of fighting a war. What the guerrillas understood better than most, however, was that Smith wanted an end to the war, but not genuine majority rule. They perceived accurately that Smith was not ready to negotiate in good faith, and therefore the guerrillas did not want to let go of the pressure that had begun to shake the foundations of Rhodesian confidence.

This relates to a different component of ripeness: the swaying of tides in conflict. As mentioned in Chapter 1, Zartman suggests that ripeness often coincides with a moment where an underdog begins to rise and the more powerful begins to decline. December 1974 was such a moment. The reactions of each side to their change of fortunes is educational. For white Rhodesia the effects were neither simple nor one-directional. The shock of the fall of Mozambique and the surprise of Vorster's initiative clearly sobered some Rhodesians to the desirability of a settlement. But it was precisely the suddenness of the defeat of their white neighbor to the east that increased white fear of the unknown in Rhodesia and prevented the Rhodesian government from taking bold steps that would have been necessary for a negotiated settlement.

A ripe moment, according to Zartman, has to be seized by a mediator. Vorster thought he was doing just that. What Vorster didn't seem to understand at the time is that ripeness is an ephemeral thing, which can vanish overnight. In ideological terms, and for his own domestic political reasons, Vorster was close to Smith on the question of maintaining standards in any transition—he in effect counseled caution to the parties: "Don't make preconditions now, have a conference and work things out there." Vorster was as frightened as Smith by "immediate majority rule" and therefore saw Smith as utterly reasonable in refusing to accept such a demand. This points to an important fact about mediation: that it is the third party that defines who is being reasonable in making a demand or holding out against a concession.

It would be incorrect to say that Smith did not make concessions. Within his constrained world view, within the ideological strictures of white Rhodesia, and compared to his previous actions, Smith took steps toward settlement in November and December 1974. He was compelled to free the nationalist leaders from detention and to talk directly with them. Smith thought of himself as eminently reasonable, and *given the discourse of the détente exercise as defined by Vorster and to a certain extent Kaunda,* he was found to be reasonable. He was successful in putting the onus of blame on the black nationalists in the early parts of the exercise, therein buying him time, which also lessened the feeling of possible impending collapse. And to those who see the failure of this episode as the result of Smith's chicanery and ability to circumvent meaningful negotiations, one has to remember that it was the Front Line presidents who established unity among the black nationalists as a sine qua non of the negotiations, and that Kaunda himself went along with Vorster's go-slow, no preconditions for talks, cease-fire framework. The truth of the matter is that an important power of third parties is that they define what is "reasonable" both in the course of how they plan the negotiations and in how they react to the demands of the participants and the participants' refusals to make concessions. The agreed-upon framework called for a cease-fire before direct talks. Such an arrangement was not called into question by the mediators; it was never seen as unnatural or unreasonable, so the first party to object to such an arrangement was, by definition, unreasonable. On the matter of "no preconditions," when certain quarters demanded as a precondition for direct talks a concession by Smith of immediate majority rule, Smith, by the rules of the game, could cry, "Unfair!" and the referees, Vorster *and Kaunda*, would have to whistle a foul.

The moment passed. As 1975 progressed, things did not seem so utterly bleak for the Rhodesians as they had in November and December 1974. Three things undid the power of the ripe moment. First, a temporary side effect of the collapse of white Mozambique and Angola was an increase in immigration to Rhodesia during 1975. The year proved a boom for Rhodesia in that category. Second, the disunity and splits among the nationalists emboldened the Rhodesians to exploit those splits and drive a wedge between the parties, thus making negotiations unlikely. The coup de grâce, which one ZANU member (Mubako 1987, interview with author) acknowledges as the Rhodesians' most stunningly successful strike of the war, was the assassination of Chitepo. Because the Zambian government overreacted, the assassination utterly destroyed the ZANLA war effort in 1975, leading to the third factor. Militarily, 1975 seemed utterly serene because of the disorganization of the guerrillas caused by the decapitation of their leadership. It would set back the nationalist military effort at least a year and would also lead ZANLA to foreclose any negotiations with the Smith regime. ZANLA had no interest in the proceedings of Victoria Falls, for in the words of one of their leaders, "We were interested in regrouping the war effort" (Mubako 1987, interview with author).

Finally, the episode suggests that although a ripe moment may lead actors to settlement, a ripe moment that passes may embolden the antagonists in the conflict, a point made by Zartman. The effect of a crisis event may at first startle an actor to rethink the desirability of continuing the conflict: the prospect that the future holds an "alternative too ghastly to contemplate" may force the actor to make concessions. But if the numbing effect wears off, and the ghastly consequences have not materialized, the actor may become more emboldened than ever in refusing to compromise. The behavior of Smith in 1974 and 1975 has to be seen in that light. The fall of Mozambique was a trigger event that sent shock waves through the white military and business communities. Smith was forced to make concessions, but he did not end the conflict. When time passed and the dire straits predicted in 1974 did not occur in 1975, Smith became even more set against compromise. It then would take a reintensification of pressure to force him back to the negotiating table.

The détente exercise failed because of five reasons outlined in Chapter 1. First and foremost, many in the Rhodesian government, especially Ian Smith, did not feel that the military situation was unwinnable. Second, Smith believed that he had alternatives to conceding to a settlement that would forfeit white control: he believed that there were blacks who would negotiate an agreement that would preserve white domination. Third, the goals of the mediators, Kaunda and Vorster, placed limits on achieving a settlement. Fourth, the disunity among the nationalists and, in particular, within ZANU meant that internal political considerations were more important than the negotiations with Smith. Finally, the attempt at mediation lacked a problem-solving component that would have made any settlement possible.

For Rhodesia, the objective military situation in 1974 and 1975 looked containable, although the indicators did not all run in one direction. The government's analysis of the security situation consisted of a number of different strands, which when woven together produced a composite picture not unfavorable to the Salisbury regime. A new front had been opened by ZIPRA along the Zambian border, and Rhodesian intelligence estimated that at the end of 1974 there were between 300 and 400 armed guerrillas inside Rhodesia (Cilliers 1985, 21). This was of little concern to the security forces whose "morale was high and [whose] prospects seemed better than a mere twelve months previously." This high morale was produced by a high kill ratio of nearly ten guerrillas for every one security force member lost, a ratio deemed necessary to quell the threat (Cilliers 1985, 21). The military leadership was concerned, however, with ZANLA's change in strategy to a Chinese-style campaign that emphasized the politicization of the rural masses and with ZANLA's effectiveness in carrying out that strategy from the Mozambican border. Whereas previous guerrilla actions, all taking place along the Zambezi River, had never been a problem—"we knew who they were, where they were coming, and we eliminated them" (Flower 1987, interview with author)—the Smith forces began to find that their intelligence had dried up in the ZANLA regions (Flower 1987, interview with author; Martin and Johnson 1981, 146). Moreover, the security forces were aware that the population along the Mozambican border was excited over the emergence of ZANLA in the region (Cilliers 1985, 20).

This awareness of ZANLA's new effectiveness was to lead to a split within the Rhodesian military over how the war should be run and how one evaluated whether one was winning or losing. One side maintained, as Ken Flower put it, "that this was not a war that could be won by improving efficiency" (Flower 1987, interview with author). Some within the military cautioned Smith to begin a serious search for a political settlement.

We can say, then, that Rhodesian military performance was good but that concern was growing about ZANLA's support. Concern was offset in part by the security forces' knowledge of struggles within ZANU, and the grave problems those struggles posed for continuing guerrilla effectiveness. And although the Portuguese colonial administration in Mozambique had been overturned by FRELIMO in 1974, the implications of the new regime on the border were not felt until early 1976. Ian Smith did not see the conflict as one where the white government was heading for elimination.

A second point raised in Chapter 1 concerns alternatives. Smith believed that he did not have to reach a settlement that would concede majority rule, because he believed that there were blacks who would negotiate for less than that. There were two aspects of this belief. First, Smith wanted a settlement with one of the recognized black leaders, because he felt that their reputations *internationally* would produce recognition for his regime. Smith, however, wanted to dictate the terms of the settlement and not forfeit white control. In many respects, black disunity played into Smith's belief as he was able to pry individual leaders away from the others in the attempt to entice them into agreement. The responsibility here rests squarely on the shoulders of those black leaders who entered into bilateral talks with him. As a U.S. diplomat said at the time, "Part of the difficulty in persuading Smith to leave the arena was that he always managed to find a new dancing partner" (Martin and Johnson 1981, 227).

The other aspect of Smith's desire for a settlement with blacks on his own terms is that he believed that he didn't need the nationalist leaders to get one. In fact, he didn't believe they represented black opinion within Rhodesia and that if left to his own devices he could find "responsible" blacks who agreed with him. In what would prove to be a continuing theme throughout the years under consideration here (and ironically up to the present, as demonstrated by his wealth of remarks from 1980 to 1987 attesting to his continued belief in knowing what blacks really want in Zimbabwe), Smith dismissed the various liberation movements as having no support among the blacks within Rhodesia; they were to him terrorists solely dependent on external aid for their struggle. Smith repeatedly claimed that he really knew what blacks wanted within Rhodesia and that he would find "responsible" leaders who really spoke for the masses and would negotiate a settlement with them that solved their "problem," as he put it.

This incredible ideological self-deception would prove to be a recurring stumbling block to serious negotiations. The extent of Smith's ignorance of the hearts and minds of blacks within Rhodesia was staggering. In 1972, just hours before the first major guerrilla strike within the country, and only months after the African population had overwhelmingly rejected the Smith-Home proposals and displayed both defiance and a willingness to continue suffering rather than accept a settlement on Smith's terms, Smith announced:

> I have been taken to task in certain quarters for describing our Africans as the happiest Africans in the world, but nobody has yet been able to tell me where there are Africans who are happier—or, for that matter, better off—than in Rhodesia. . . . The reasons for this relaxed racial climate which we enjoy here are many. First and foremost is the nature of the people who make up our country. The Africans of Rhodesia are by nature unaggressive, and they have an instinctive leaning towards a peaceful communal life. They have a highly developed sense of humour—which is an essential ingredient of happy race relations—and they have an appreciation of the security, both for themselves and their families, which flows from a stable and orderly system of government. (Martin and Johnson 1981, 1)

The arrogance in assuming to know the nature of a people; the ignorance in assuming that passivity induced by powerlessness, fear, and coercion implies consent and appreciation; and the paternalism inherent in referring to the blacks in Rhodesia as "our Africans" combined to produce a coherent yet utterly false understanding of the underlying reality. David Caute has captured this element of the white Rhodesian worldview in the most elegant prose:

> Our subject is, in fact, a collective state of mind; more particularly the extraordinary mental manoeuvres by which pillage is termed responsible government, repression becomes law and order, usurpation is called authority, violence is lauded as restraint; the peculiar indignation, the outrage, the sense of ingratitude, experienced by the conquerors when the dispossessed natives attempt to recover by force what was taken so recently from them by force. Our subject is the myths, evasions, legends, reifications and strategies of false consciousness; the bones, nerves and flesh of an ideology. (Caute 1983, 32)

That Smith did not take seriously the liberation movement and actively foresaw an alternative solution with other "responsible" blacks, and that such views powerfully affected his unwillingness to negotiate at Victoria Falls, can be seen from this interview given five days after the conference:

> Q. You have said: We have never had a policy to hand over to any black majority government, and as far as I am concerned we never will have. The ANC on their side, even at Victoria Falls, I gathered from you, talked almost immediately of majority rule now. Can these two standpoints ever be reconciled?

A. I must repeat to you that you would be amazed at the number of black Rhodesians who tell me that the last thing they ever want in Rhodesia is black majority rule. And I think this is where our strength lies. I honestly believe that more black Rhodesians support me than support Bishop Muzorewa.

Q. Is there any way of testing that sort of thing by a referendum or any other method?

A. Well, it is very difficult when you face up to the fact that the majority of the black people are inarticulate. They do not really understand our system of politics.

Q. Mr. Smith, for nearly 10 years now you have been leading a country in which there are 22 Africans for every one white man. Do you believe your government's actions are making life more secure for the white man in Rhodesia?

A. Yes, with all sincerity I can assure you this is a matter which receives great consideration as far as I am concerned. And I believe this is the position mainly because of the number of black Rhodesians who agree with me. I have got enough sense to realize that I have got to bring all my people together. I have got to have the support of black as well as white Rhodesians. You would be surprised at the number of black Rhodesians who say the last thing they want is black majority rule in Rhodesia. They believe we have got to work together. The white man needs the black man and vice versa, and I do say to you in complete honesty and sincerity I believe the majority of black Rhodesians as well as the majority of white Rhodesians support me in my policy. (Interview in Baumhogger 1984, 11–12).

A little over a month later, Smith would raise the hackles of the South African government and press by insinuating that "if we had not embarked on this particular détente exercise we would by now have achieved a settlement in Rhodesia" (in Baumhogger 1984, 13).[23]

South Africa as one of the mediators of the exercise was well aware of Smith's intransigence and the Rhodesian confidence that Smith's army could eliminate the liberation movement. At a meeting earlier in the year between cabinet officials of the two countries, a Rhodesian official had shocked the South Africans by querying why they were so concerned, because, "We can handle the munts" (a derogatory term for blacks) (Legum 1975, A47). To deal with this, South Africa was prepared to apply massive pressure to force Smith to negotiate in good faith. It is at this point in the analysis that the disunity of the liberation movements plays another key role. If we recall in Chapter 1 that what the mediator views as an acceptable settlement places limits on the mediation effort, it is easy to understand why South Africa failed to exert its leverage on Smith. The acceptable settlement for South Africa was majority rule that would lead to a moderate, stable regime as its neighbor to the north. The disunity among the blacks, and Smith's active persuasion, convinced South Africa that to undercut Rhodesia at that particular point would most likely produce a black-against-black violent confrontation, endemic instability, and violence against whites. Moreover, Vorster had to be very careful about how far to push Smith, for fear of domestic backlash among white hard-liners in South Africa. One important lesson that emerges from this episode is that if a party in conflict is being pressured by a mediator to enter a settlement the party doesn't like, that party may be able to neutralize the mediator's leverage by appealing to forces internal to the mediator, such as public opinion or important elites within government.

The other mediator, Kenneth Kaunda, also brought with him baggage that placed limits on the settlement effort. His need for ending the war drove the Zambian government to produce a negotiating body that was divorced from the guerrillas who were bearing the brunt of the fighting at that time. When faced with guerrilla intransigence on negotiation and a leadership that felt similarly, the answer of the Front Line presidents was to identify Sithole as the leader for ZANU at a time when he had lost much of his authority. Furthermore, since Kaunda was tied to Nkomo and preferred him to the other nationalist leaders, it created intense suspicions about Kaunda's motives among ZANU people. In their attempts to enforce unity, Zambia intensified disunity between the two guerrilla armies, ultimately driving ZANU out of Zambia into Mozambique and Tanzania. Only when Samora Machel joined the picture was there an actor that could pressure ZANU on settlement questions.

A fourth factor contributing to the failure of détente concerns the lack of a problem-solving component to the exercise. This prompts a counterfactual question: If the blacks at Victoria Falls were unified, and South Africa had compelled Smith to "cry uncle," could a peaceful settlement have been reached at that point? I believe not. There was no real plan by the mediators, no sense of a just solution, only an inchoate assumption that unity and pressure would suffice to get the participants to hammer out an accord. What is striking is the lack of statements concerning the substantive issues that were at stake and how they could be resolved: how to monitor a cease-fire, how to integrate revolutionary and state armed forces, what kind of constitution to have, what guarantees and agreements were appropriate, what date was feasible for a change in government. Presumably, the parties involved were somehow to define all of the relevant issues and reach agreement on the many details, with little assistance other than a threat to negotiate hanging over their heads. If one contemplates how far apart the parties were on the simple issue of accepting majority rule, one should then think of the potential differences on a constitution, cease-fire, and election. The lack of a possible solution at the core of the mediation effort would have been a recipe for tendentiousness and recrimination between the blacks and whites and among the blacks themselves. There would be multiple opportunities for any party to wreck such a negotiation if they so desired, and many did so desire.

To continue the counterfactual, even if unity had been attained among the blacks, were the most important participants in the conflict—the guerrillas—represented? Before Sithole's ouster by other ZANU founders, ZANLA considered Sithole its leader. The recruitment of new soldiers into the guerrilla camps in early 1975 brought huge numbers into the ZANLA fold who backed Mugabe. Within ZANLA there was a general impatience with negotiations: most of the guerrillas believed that Smith had to be brought to his knees through force before Africans could win their rights in Zimbabwe. Could Sithole really deliver the ZANLA constituency after being passed over in favor of the more militant Mugabe? Could the military aspects of a settlement be worked out without the close cooperation of the guerrillas who opposed Sithole? Could any leader representing the guerrillas negotiate a settlement at that time? This brings us back to the issue of ripeness and illustrates that for a conflict to be ripe for resolution depends on properties internal to the parties concerned: Is each contending party consolidated in such a way that its leaders can seek a settlement with the other party? Do the risks of negotiation endanger any leader's position?

In the aftermath of the talks, four consequences loomed large. First, there were prices to be paid for those nationalists who entered negotiations and failed. Muzorewa and Sithole were soundly rejected by the military leaders of the ZANLA guerrillas. Second, failed negotiations, in conjunction with the loss of support for Muzorewa and Sithole, strengthened the hand of Mugabe, who did not want a negotiated settlement. Third, the failed negotiations prompted an intensification of the armed struggle. The failure of Smith to bargain in good faith strengthened those who saw a deeper, more violent conflict as the only way of winning independence. As predicted from our earlier discussions, when joint solutions fail, the search for unilateral alternatives intensifies. Finally, the cease-fire was shown to be a counterproductive preliminary to a settlement. Both sides used the lull in the fighting to strengthen themselves in anticipation of the renewal of fighting. Both sides accused the other of benefiting from the cease-fire, thus reinforcing a belief that neither side wanted peace.[24]

## Notes

1. In this book I use Rhodesia and Zimbabwe interchangeably for the period before independence in 1980. When referring to the inhabitants of the

country, I consistently refer to whites as Rhodesians and blacks as Zimbabweans.

2. A detailed history of Rhodesian politics before 1972 can be found in Bowman (1973), O'Meara (1975), and Blake (1977).

3. The United Nations High Commission for Refugees estimated that in 1976 alone 10,000 to 14,000 Zimbabweans crossed into Botswana, while 35,000 fled to Mozambique. In early 1977, there were an estimated 50,000 refugees in camps in Mozambique (International Defence and Aid Fund 1977, 7, 60). One author claims that at the end of the war in January 1980, there were 300,000 Zimbabwean refugees in Mozambique, Botswana, and Zambia, with half of that total from Mozambique alone (Thompson 1985, 9–70).

4. After independence many of the names and spellings from the colonial era were changed. These four cities are known today as Harare, Bulawayo, Mutare, and Gweru.

5. Godfrey Huggins, or Lord Malverne, was prime minister of Southern Rhodesia from 1932 to 1952.

6. For a discussion of Kaunda and Vorster's embrace of a peaceful settlement in Southern Africa, see Anglin (1975) and Jeeves (1975). Vorster's policy was part of his larger vision of South Africa as a dominant regional power in coalition with "moderate" black states in the region (Geldenhuys 1984). Many readers of earlier drafts of this book expressed surprise at South Africa's willingness to seek a settlement to the conflict in Rhodesia based on majority rule. A passage from Flower's autobiography describes the reasoning of Hendrik van den Bergh, the head of BOSS (the South African intelligence agency): "Time and again in the ensuing years van den Bergh asked me to convey a message from Vorster to Smith to the effect that South Africa was anxious to get the Rhodesian question settled before they were forced into a settlement over South West Africa, and that Smith would be in a less favourable position if he continued to procrastinate while South West Africa became Namibia. I remember van den Bergh saying there were only 40,000 whites of Afrikaner stock in Rhodesia compared with 75,000 in South West Africa, which meant that Rhodesia's future was of less importance to South Africa than the future of South West Africa. In any event, he was adamant that Rhodesia's destiny must differ from that of South Africa or South West Africa, for Rhodesia had opted out of their future in 1922, and he maintained that whereas the separation of the races was entrenched in South Africa's national policy, the RF's pursuit of apartheid in Rhodesia was 'an embarrassing anachronism'" (Flower 1987, 157).

7. Martin and Johnson contend that "Kaunda and Vorster had agreed on a new qualified franchise of six years' primary education plus one further year's education; this would bring enough new African voters to the electoral roll to bring a majority rule parliament after five years of the life of one parliament" (Martin and Johnson 1981, 153). Later in the book, while making the same point, the authors present a slightly different version: "South Africa had in fact put forward a plan which included a common roll based on a qualified franchise: the franchise was seven years' primary education plus one further year of education" (p.192). They cite as their sources stories published in the *Guardian* and the *Times* of December 17, 1974, and an interview with Tom McNally, who had served as James Callaghan's political adviser and had traveled to Southern Africa at that time. In Joshua Nkomo's autobiography, he also writes, "It seemed that Prime Minister Vorster might be able to

persuade Smith to agree to a formula by which the fighting in Zimbabwe would be stopped and we would get real majority rule within five years" (Nkomo 1984, 153). Ken Flower claims that Vorster had told him that these terms were drummed up by the Zambians, but that he found them "reasonable."

8. As Kenneth Grundy argues, "Crucial to the maintenance of the South African regime is the necessity to devise a coordinated, holistic, counterrevolutionary strategy. It is the mark of the present government, although it by no means originated when P. W. Botha replaced J. B. Vorster as Prime Minister, that a more conscious, concerted and systematic effort is being made to integrate various mechanisms of white control to produce a counterrevolutionary package more rationalized and efficient than at any time before. P. W. Botha and his most trusted associates, particularly General Magnus Malan, had sought to fashion such a strategy during Botha's tenure as Minister of Defence in the Vorster government" (Grundy 1986, 17–18).

9. Flower also writes of this period that within the South African government, "almost everyone [was] denigrating almost everyone else." An especially heated rivalry had developed between BOSS and Military Intelligence, with each organization producing drastically different analyses of threats in Southern Africa. At one point, Flower was alarmed by van den Bergh's plea "to commit to the wastepaper basket all reports received from their Military Intelligence" (Flower 1987, 154–156).

10. Evidence for this position can be seen in British Foreign Office explanations for Foreign Secretary James Callaghan's trip to Southern Africa, which began December 31, 1974. In a statement to the press, the British Foreign Office said "that the Foreign Secretary intended simply to examine with African leaders in what way Britain could be of use in helping to find a solution to the Rhodesian 'problem.' Britain preferred merely to 'keep in touch' with the African initiatives.... The British government still recognized its legal and constitutional responsibility regarding Rhodesia, but did not want to take the initiative on new moves" (ARB, 3504).

11. Smith, however, can be accused of no such thing. When Mark Chona arrived in Salisbury on December 8 to fetch Nkomo and Sithole, Smith wagged a finger at him and said, "If you can achieve unity, you can come back here and cut off this finger."

12. Six of the top leaders of ZANU were held in detention together at QueQue prison. While in prison, they managed to function as the Executive Committee of ZANU. The day-to-day leadership of the struggle was in the hands of Herbert Chitepo in Lusaka, Josiah Tongogara, chief of staff of ZANLA, and the Revolutionary Council. There are two main alternative explanations for the removal of Sithole. The removers contend that Sithole had renounced publicly the use of violence for the struggle in order to save himself from further punishment and therefore had to be reprimanded. Sithole argues that the split was simply a product of ethnic hostilities and rivalries directed at him because he came from a minority (the Ndau people).

13. See Sithole's letters to the Pearce Commission of 1972 in Nyangoni and Nyandoro (1977).

14. Even so, it should be emphasized that accounts of the period state that Sithole and Mugabe signaled that they would accept a three- to five-year transition to majority rule if the principle of majority rule was accepted by Smith. What neither of them would accept was a curtailment of the war effort before such an acceptance.

15. Muzorewa, although blaming Smith for creating a mirage of an agreement, certainly contributed to that mirage by his waffling that day. An alternative explanation is that factions of the new ANC did accept the Smith terms and were willing to initiate an immediate cease-fire. At one point Muzorewa writes, "Smith constantly referred to the 'cessation of hostilities' as a precondition to any constitutional talks. We ·‒‒‒‒ ‒‒‒‒ it was the guerrilla incursions into Rhodesia (Zimbabwe) which had forced Smith to want to talk with us as political leaders. *All the former ZANU members amongst us* were adamant in refusing to allow our negotiations to hinge upon a 'ceasefire' or 'cessation of hostilities'" (Muzorewa 1978, 146; emphasis added). An interesting specification: Does this imply that there were other parties in the ANC that were less stringent on such a position?

16. Smith's remark here should be put into its proper context: (1) Smith and the Rhodesian Front had not shown any inclination to that point to bring blacks into leadership positions—in fact their whole raison d'être was to prevent racial progress; (2) cosmetic slow change had been rejected twice by blacks in the two years preceding Smith's remarks, so it is unclear why they would accept it then; and (3) at the time of Smith's remarks, only two Rhodesian Front cabinet ministers had publicly entertained the possibility of bringing blacks into the cabinet.

17. Edson Sithole, although a part of Muzorewa's camp, was Ndabaningi Sithole's cousin.

18. Charges by the Rhodesians were subsequently dropped and replaced with terrorism and murder charges based on Sithole's leadership of an organization "which has been and is responsible for terrorism in Rhodesia." He was also charged with obstructing the settlement talks and undermining the Lusaka agreement. One of the more bizarre evidential twists was provided by Derek Robinson, commander of the Special Branch of the Rhodesian Police. At the trial, Robinson testified that "during a visit to Lusaka in February when Mr. Sithole had met the late Mr. Chitepo, there was no evidence that he had given any orders to halt the guerrilla war"!

19. Colin Legum argues that this stipulation torpedoed the talks from the beginning, for it was something the ANC could not accept and Chona had not received their approval (Legum 1975). While the latter is true—this was another example of the Zambians accepting something on the part of the nationalists without their full approval—the former is only partially correct. What I suspect happened is that Sithole and Chikerema were adamantly against any meetings within Rhodesia, Muzorewa leaned that way but was waffling, and Nkomo did not care and served to benefit if the meetings took place in Rhodesia. On August 13, Muzorewa announced that Smith had given "a solemn undertaking that, while negotiations are in progress, the ANC leaders in Rhodesia will be completely free to consult with their colleagues outside Rhodesia," which was good enough for Muzorewa. One can imagine the two senior revolutionaries, Chikerema and Sithole, bridling at others negotiating for them within Rhodesia with only the guarantee that they may be consulted at some point. On August 15, Muzorewa flip-flopped: "We reject completely the holding of a committee or committees within Rhodesia." Smith responded by saying in essence that if the ANC wanted to back out on the written agreement, that was their business, but the failure would lie with them. Smith added that it would be out of the question that Sithole and Chikerema would be granted amnesty (ARB, 3738–3739).

20. Nyerere described his skepticism toward Nkomo meeting Smith for further talks: "So silly Smith is not a fool either. He knows Vorster has played all his cards and Vorster is in danger of being accused that he is selling out the white people . . . all those pressures were there, Smith played his cards very well until all those pressures were completely gone.

"Now I am told Joshua Nkomo can sit down with him. He thinks things are going on very well. I don't believe this now. When all these pressures are not there my friend Joshua can now sit down with Smith. Smith sitting there, Joshua sitting here and Smith just hands over power to Joshua. No pressure. No threat from South Africa. No threat of guerrilla fighting. No threat of sanctions at all but somehow Smith now says to Joshua, when all these pressures have gone, 'Joshua now I am handing power over to you.' This is going to be the first miracle in the world! I have never heard a thing like that before" (quoted in Baumhogger 1984, 61).

21. My description of the Nkomo-Smith talks differs from that found in Meredith (1979) and Martin and Johnson (1981). In those books the impetus for the talks is attributed solely to Nkomo. The impression is given that Kaunda did not actively support Nkomo's attempted negotiations. Both books quote a statement, allegedly made by Kaunda to Nkomo, that was mentioned by Kaunda in an interview: "We can't take sides, but let me tell you Mr. Nkomo, that if you go ahead and achieve independence under majority rule, well and good. You are going to make the outside wing of the ANC irrelevant. On the other hand, if you don't pull it through, you are going to become irrelevant, and the relevant one is going to be Bishop Muzorewa's group and we, obviously, want to see independence come to Zimbabwe, whether it's through negotiations, or through fighting. So the decision's yours. If you win, then, of course, the whole of Africa is going to say Hallelujah. If you fail, the whole of Africa is going to condemn you" (Meredith 1979, 201).

In his autobiography, Nkomo states that during the period he was negotiating with Smith he was in close touch with Kaunda and Nyerere. In my interviews with two of Nkomo's top aides, they stated emphatically that the talks were welcomed by the Front Line presidents, especially Kaunda, who saw it as the best and final test of Smith's willingness to negotiate. Further evidence of this is that Kaunda sent a team of observers to the meetings between Smith and Nkomo.

If there is any disingenuousness here, I suspect that it is on the part of Kaunda, who was trying to maintain a public facade of neutrality toward Nkomo. As to Nyerere, I believe that he was genuinely ambivilant at first and was willing to go along with Kaunda and Nkomo but then got cold feet as the proposed talks became a reality. Martin and Johnson claim that "Nyerere warned Britain's Minister of State in the Foreign Office, David Ennals, in December 1975 that the guerrillas could be expected to reject any agreement they had not been a party to" (Martin and Johnson 1981, 227). This to my mind is evidence of learning on Nyerere's part, because until that time none of the Front Line presidents seemed concerned that the guerrillas might reject a political settlement reached on their behalf.

22. Significantly, the letter was not addressed to Kaunda, who was not trusted because of his role in the Tongogara trial and the perception among the guerrillas that he favored Nkomo.

23. According to Martin and Johnson, Smith's statement, aimed at the

white South African voters, absolutely outraged Vorster and poisoned the already shaky relationship between the two leaders.

24. For an argument suggesting that a cease-fire preliminary to war termination negotiations increases the likelihood of those negotiations failing, see Wittman (1979). For a critique of Wittman's article see Mitchell and Nicholson (1983).

# 3

# Henry Kissinger, Geneva, and "Lying to Both Sides"

*I wonder who's Kissinger now?* —William Kaufman

As 1976 began and the Smith-Nkomo talks were coming to their predicted barren end, the Rhodesian civil war came to the attention of a larger audience. The death throes of the Portuguese empire in Southern Africa set in motion a chain of events in Angola that forced all players in the region to reconsider the stakes involved in Rhodesia. Great Britain, which had handled the mediation efforts of Kaunda and Vorster the previous year with kid gloves, began to play a more active role in the resolution of the conflict. The United States belatedly "discovered" the liberation struggle there in April 1976 when Henry Kissinger toured Southern Africa and signaled U.S. desire to help reach a settlement in Rhodesia.

For South Africa and the Front Line States, Angola brought a new urgency to the Rhodesian problem. Vorster's previous interest in a settlement in Rhodesia had been based on his desire for a moderate "responsible" black regime that would not pose a threat to the white regime in Pretoria. The rapid escalation in Angola and the entry of Cuban troops added a new element to South Africa's concern: fear that a spillover of the war into Mozambique could lead to the involvement of Eastern bloc or Cuban troops in Rhodesia (Moorcraft and McLaughlin 1982, 34).

The South African intervention in Angola, however, also widened the split between John Vorster and P. W. Botha that had developed over the détente policy. In historical perspective, 1975 was a watershed in the growth of the South African Defence Forces in South African politics. One indicator of this is shown in Table 3.1, which indicates Pretoria's yearly military expenditures from 1958 to 1983. 1975 to 1976 marks the beginning of the rise of the hard-line forces in the South African government. Just as important as the increase in military expenditures were a series of administrative measures taken by P. W. Botha to streamline and centralize security planning (Grundy 1986; Frankel 1984; Rotberg 1985).

Table 3.1  South African Defense Expenditure, 1958–1983

| Financial Year | Rands[a] |
| --- | --- |
| 1958/59 | 36,000,000 |
| 1959/60 | 40,000,000 |
| 1960/61 | 44,000,000 |
| 1961/62 | 72,000,000 |
| 1962/63 | 129,000,000 |
| 1963/64 | 157,000,000 |
| 1964/65 | 210,000,000 |
| 1965/66 | 229,000,000 |
| 1966/67 | 255,000,000 |
| 1967/68 | 256,000,000 |
| 1968/69 | 254,000,000 |
| 1969/70 | 272,000,000 |
| 1970/71 | 329,000,000 |
| 1971/72 | 327,000,000 |
| 1972/73 | 358,000,000 |
| 1973/74 | 481,000,000 |
| 1974/75 | 692,000,000 |
| 1975/76 | 1,043,000,000 |
| 1976/77 | 1,408,000,000 |
| 1977/78 | 1,712,000,000 |
| 1978/79 | 1,759,000,000 |
| 1979/80 | 1,857,000,000 |
| 1980/81 | 1,970,000,000 |
| 1981/82[b] | 2,465,000,000 |
| 1982/83[b] | 2,668,000,000 |

*Source*: Philip H. Frankel, *Pretoria's Praetorians: Civil-Military Relations in South Africa* (Cambridge: Cambridge University Press, 1984), p. 72.
[a]All numbers rounded to the nearest million rand
[b]Estimated

The Angolan war also coalesced the leaders of Zambia, Mozambique, Tanzania, and Botswana around the desire for Africans to decide African problems.  The Front Line presidents had witnessed how quickly Southern Africa could become engulfed in the flames of superpower conflict. The intervention of foreign actors, the escalation of force and violence, and the loss of control by regional parties committed these leaders to arrest the growing use of the region as a battleground for the superpowers.

Such a commitment had implications for regional politics. It would necessarily drive a wedge through Kaunda's and Vorster's attempt to reach even a tacit understanding. After Victoria Falls, Kaunda, against the wishes of Nyerere and Machel, refused to abandon the search for a negotiated settlement. Kaunda also approved and perhaps even requested the South African intervention on UNITA's[1] behalf in Angola—a decision that put his relationship with the other Front Line presidents in jeopardy. When the MPLA took power and gained recognition from the OAU and when, subsequently, nothing came from Nkomo's efforts with Smith, Kaunda could afford to err no more. He made his peace with Nyerere and Machel and cast his lot behind a united approach to the region's problems.

For the United States, the international escalation of the Angolan war, coupled with the quick collapse of the Portuguese government there, led to a fundamental reassessment of U.S. policy toward Southern Africa. In the late 1960s, Henry Kissinger had been responsible for supporting the infamous "tar-baby" option, which foreclosed support for black liberation movements in the misguided belief that the white regimes were unassailable.[2] Even in the early 1970s, with the onslaught of revolutionary activities, the United States showed little interest in the black struggle for majority rule. Only after Angola had been transformed into an arena of superpower conflict, with the United States failing to gain "escalation dominance," did Kissinger take seriously the notion that his country had any interest in the independence movements and majority rule in the region.

## British and U.S. Initiatives

In February 1976, the Smith-Nkomo talks had reached an impasse and the war in Rhodesia began to heat up. On February 6, Ian Smith ordered an increased call-up of civilians for active military duty and informed the Rhodesian public that the fighting was now in a new and larger stage. Two days later in the Mozambican town of Quelimane, the Front Line presidents met and decided that talks were impotent for bringing about change in Zimbabwe and the armed struggle would have to increase. Kenneth Kaunda sent Mark Chona to London and Washington to inform the leaderships there of the explosive situation that prevailed in Southern Africa. On February 20, Ian Smith, in a public address, signaled his desire for the British government to "make a constructive and realistic effort to assist in our settlement." Having found that direct talks with blacks had not been fruitful for getting Smith's preferred settlement, the leader of the Rhodesian Front hoped to revert to direct bilateral talks with Britain. Clearly, Smith was angling for a return to the days of Tiger, Fearless, and Smith-Home, when Britain and white Rhodesia met to decide the future of blacks in the country.

The British sent Lord Greenhill to evaluate the situation and to judge the sincerity of Smith's approach. On March 2, Rhodesia struck at ZANLA guerrillas in Mozambique, prompting Machel to close his border with Rhodesia, trapping one-sixth of Rhodesia's rolling stock (worth 23 million British pounds) inside Mozambique (Martin and Johnson 1981, 226). Two weeks later, Nkomo and Smith announced what had been known for months, that their talks had broken down.[3] Nkomo threatened Smith with the consequences of all-out revolution. Smith countered that he had "listened for more than ten years to bragging about guerrilla plans. The fact is that when guerrillas entered Rhodesia by the hundred they were killed by the hundred. If in future they decide to come in by the thousand, they will be killed by the thousand" (Lapping 1985, 514). When asked about majority rule, Smith replied, "I don't believe in black majority rule ever in Rhodesia, not in a thousand years."

On March 22, James Callaghan, British foreign secretary, announced to Parliament the findings of Lord Greenhill's trip and proposed a new British policy toward Rhodesia. Callaghan began by stating that Smith's purpose in negotiations with Nkomo had been "to buy time in order to remove the pressures on him," and that the failure of the talks were due to Smith's "prevarications." He informed Parliament that Lord Greenhill's report had given no indication of Smith's willingness to come to grips with his problems and added that "he does not seem to realize that he no longer has much time to buy."

Callaghan then presented proposals to "help secure an orderly transfer of power in Rhodesia," based on consultations with the Front Line presidents:

> First, there must be prior agreement by all the principal parties to a number of preconditions. These are as follows: first, acceptance of the principle of majority rule; secondly, elections for majority rule to take place in eighteen months to two years; thirdly, agreement that there will be no independence before majority rule; fourthly, the negotiations must not be long drawn out. There would also need to be assurances that the transition to majority rule and to an independent Rhodesia would not be thwarted and would be orderly. If these preconditions were accepted, it would then become possible for the second stage to begin, namely the negotiation of the actual terms of a constitution for independence. ("Statement by J. Callaghan and Extract from the Following Debate in the British House of Commons, 22.3. 1976," in Baumhogger 1984, 78)

Callaghan made clear that Britain wanted a Rhodesia where both whites and blacks could work and prosper, and mentioned the possibility of development assistance and educational aid. He added that only when majority rule had been accepted and a deal worked out along the lines above would a lifting of sanctions be appropriate. The British foreign secretary also appealed over the head of the Rhodesian prime minister to the country's whites, telling them that Smith was leading them down "the path of destruction," and that Callaghan hoped other leaders might step forward who will "recognize the realities of the hour." In response to a question, Callaghan replied, "I do not know that I have much hope of persuading Mr. Smith, whose contradictory statements, even in the past three or four days, give little room for belief that it is possible to negotiate with him. I am not hopeful" (Callaghan, in Baumhogger 1984, 78).

At this stage, Henry Kissinger, smarting from Congress's rejection of his proxy war in Angola and looking at a situation ripe for further conflict in Southern Africa, began looking for opportunities to regain prestige for himself and for the United States. Kissinger decided to travel to Southern Africa to convince its leaders that the United States could play a positive role in the region and to work out a policy on Rhodesia, Namibia, and South Africa. Having been briefed about the Vorster/Kaunda line of attack on Rhodesia, Kissinger believed that with the added weight of the United States behind the process and his own abilities as a go-between, he could succeed where they had failed. He felt that he could best facilitate the process if he acted as an interlocutor rather than a mediator (Legum 1977, 129). As one observer notes, "He saw himself as bridging the gap that had opened between black and white leaders when their contacts were broken off after the Angolan episode" (Legum 1977, 129). In looking back in 1979 at his Rhodesian initiative, however, Kissinger added a different twist: his strategy was "to co-opt the program of moderate evolutionary reform, that is to say majority rule, and minority rights. At the same time we sought to create a kind of firebreak between those whose radicalism was geared to specific issues. We could meet the demands for majority rule; we never thought we could co-opt the ideological radicals; our goal was to isolate them" (interview in the *Washington Post*, July 3, 1979, in Martin and Johnson 1981, 235–236).[4]

In Lusaka, on April 27, 1976, Kissinger announced a new U.S. policy toward Southern Africa. Sent by President Ford "with a message of commitment and cooperation," Kissinger acknowledged, in his own way, that this new era in U.S. foreign policy might be considered by some to be cynical: "There is nothing to be gained in a debate about whether in the past America has neglected Africa or been insufficiently committed to African goals. . . . No good can come of mutual recrimination." Kissinger made clear that African problems were for Africans to solve: he did not bring prescriptions for their problems. Nor was he there "to set African against African, either among your governments or among factions of liberation movements." Kissinger expressed that the United States supported "self-determination, majority rule, equal rights and human dignity for all the peoples of Southern Africa—in the name of moral principle, international law and world peace."

With regard to Rhodesia, the secretary of state emphasized U.S. support for the Callaghan proposals; made clear to the Salisbury regime that they could not count on U.S. support; urged a rapid negotiated settlement; pledged financial support for Mozambique for applying sanctions against Rhodesia and offered help to any other neighboring nation that would do the same; promised the repeal of the Byrd amendment, which allowed the United States to import Rhodesian chrome in defiance of United Nations directives; proposed a fund that would help Rhodesian development after independence; and pledged U.S. assistance in the building of a Rhodesia where majority rule coexisted with the protection of minority rights. Kissinger concluded, "The United States is wholly committed to help bring about a rapid, just and African solution to the issue of Rhodesia" ("Address by H. Kissinger in Lusaka, 27.4.1976," in Baumhogger 1984, 91–92).

The talk handcuffed the Front Line States. As Meredith observes, "There were many in Africa who doubted the sincerity of this sudden U.S. commitment. But with those stated aims, Kissinger made it impossible for any black African leader to refuse to assist the American endeavor to bring about majority rule" (Meredith 1980, 222). Nyerere and Kaunda were willing to give Kissinger a chance but informed him that they would act as representatives of the black nationalists. Kissinger, in a press conference in September, said of the Lusaka meeting, "I agreed with the Presidents of the so-called frontline states . . . that a repetition of Angola should be avoided. By this we mean that the outside powers, and especially the superpowers should avoid direct contact with the so-called liberation movements; and to let the liberation movements be dealt with by the Black African states."

Smith reacted critically, denouncing the West for appeasing the communist threat in Southern Africa. Accusing Kissinger of "flagrant denial of the most fundamental principles of justice," he demanded the opportunity for Rhodesia to put their case to him. Playing to conservative audiences in Pretoria, London, and Washington, Smith stated that the Rhodesians had "no intention of allowing our country to degenerate into the sort of shambles which we see in Mozambique and Angola today." Smith then unveiled what he had been hinting at for some time: that he intended to bring in four traditional African chiefs into his cabinet. Such a move, Smith believed, proved beyond a doubt his commitment to a multiracial polity in Rhodesia. But it was also clear that it was not blacks he was seeking to convince but the world at large: "This presents us with the opportunity to prove conclusively to the outside world that it is the wish of the majority of Rhodesians, both black and white, to work constructively together amongst themselves in order to develop their country and promote their mutual wellbeing" (Baumhogger 1984, 94).

The move by Smith was trifling little and tragically late. It was a move that might have temporarily forestalled African protest in the 1950s, but even then one would have been skeptical. The move had no credibility as far as the nationalists were concerned and little credibility for ordinary Zimbabweans. But Smith's action was not aimed at them; it was aimed elsewhere. Would it play in Pretoria? Or in Washington? That the move gained guarded South African approval is apparent from an official commentary on Radio Johannesburg, which stated that it was "premature to write the move off as meaningless. . . . For Rhodesia, if not for the outside world, this is a new situation of major significance" (Baumhogger 1984, 95).

This was perhaps the only bit of encouragement Smith received from South Africa during this period. On May 14, in an interview with the *New York Times*, Eschel Rhoodie, South African secretary for information and a leader of the "détente" group, let Smith know in no uncertain terms that "military intervention by South Africa to uphold the Rhodesian Government is absolutely out of the question." He also added that "Mr. Smith would be making a mistake if he ridiculed the potential of the guerrillas operating across the Rhodesian frontier from training bases inside Mozambique" (*New York Times*, May 15, 1976, in Baumhogger 1984, 97). Rhoodie's remarks came two weeks after a public announcement by General Peter Walls, head of Rhodesian armed forces, that the Rhodesian security forces intended to launch an offensive into Mozambique to counter Zimbabwean guerrillas operating from there.

## Kissinger and Vorster

Kissinger put out feelers that he was willing to meet with Vorster in an effort to find common ground on the problems of the region. Kissinger's invitation could not be turned down. Although Vorster had responded in somewhat hostile terms to Kissinger's speech in Lusaka, the South African prime minister could take from the talk Kissinger's assurance that South Africa was part of Africa. Talks at the level Kissinger proposed had not occurred in thirty years, and such a meeting alone would accord legitimacy to the regime in Pretoria. With pitifully little to show for Vorster's moderate line in Southern Africa, Kissinger's offer could only strengthen the South African prime minister's hand against his own hard-liners. The two leaders agreed to meet in Germany on June 23 and 24.

In preparation for meeting Kissinger, Vorster kept up a steady, but low, level of pressure on Rhodesia. Until June 1976, South Africa had been paying half of Rhodesia's defense bill. Such assistance abruptly stopped and South Africa gave no signal whether they would continue such support for the upcoming year. Smith met Vorster ten days before his scheduled meeting in Germany. Amidst reports and allegations that the Rhodesian government was preventing their security forces from taking the war into Mozambique, the two leaders discussed "the security position in Southern Africa" and its ties with Kissinger's visit.

Little has been written on the June meeting between Kissinger and Vorster, except that the talks focused on Namibia and Rhodesia, and that Kissinger warned Vorster of an impending race war in South Africa. Kissinger put forth to Vorster U.S. desires to work with South Africa to reach settlements in Namibia and Rhodesia, which Christopher Coker (1986) describes as the beginning of America's "constructive engagement" policy. Vorster explained his relations with Smith and told Kissinger that movement was possible on majority rule there. The talks were adjourned with an agreement to follow up on them later in the year.

During the summer of 1976, the U.S. State Department worked closely with their British counterparts in searching for ideas for a Rhodesian settlement. Much of the discussion focused on the question of whether serious negotiations could occur with Ian Smith as one of the participants. The British position was an emphatic no. An aide to Callaghan adhered to the belief "that until you get rid of Smith you will not get a settlement because he's congenitally unable to settle. This is Smith's genius of course, the appearance of movement and momentum he can give to negotiations without conceding anything of substance" (Tom McNally, quoted in Martin and Johnson 1981, 239).

Indeed, Britain and the United States first looked to a settlement without Smith. In late August, Ted Rowlands, Britain's minister of state in the Foreign Office, traveled to Southern Africa to discuss with the Front Line presidents a plan whereby Smith would be ousted and a caretaker government formed to negotiate majority rule with the nationalists. Rowlands in an interview later said:

> I have to confirm that we were saying that we would get rid of Smith. . . . There were indications that the Kissinger-Vorster connection would work and produce an arrangement with a caretaker government. That was Kissinger's view, but he was keeping his options open as to whether Smith should be part of it. Britain was stressing that any arrangement must be minus Smith. (Rowlands, quoted in Martin and Johnson 1981, 240)

The Front Line presidents reacted in measured terms. Without more specific details, they felt, any comments would be premature.

## The Course of the War

Before going on to the details of Kissinger's mediation, it is necessary to review the military situation that existed at the time. For the whites of Rhodesia the war started in earnest in 1976. Whereas the effects of an independent Mozambique had before been hypothetical, Rhodesians now began to feel their sting. The added sanctuary for ZANU guerrillas operating from there meant that the war could be taken into larger parts of Rhodesia. The incredible exodus of tens of thousands of refugees provided vast numbers of new cadres to fight the war. At the beginning of 1976, Rhodesian intelligence estimated that in Mozambique there were approximately 15,000 ZANLA fighters in various stages of readiness (Cilliers 1985, 28). At the end of 1976, General Peter Walls estimated that 1,700 of those guerrillas had infiltrated inside Rhodesia (Gann and Henriksen 1981, 80).

ZAPU, which had stopped fighting during the Smith-Nkomo talks, began to infiltrate from Botswana. Throughout the war, ZANU did the bulk of the fighting and dying, and ZAPU kept most of its well-equipped, well-trained army in Zambia. This is not to say that they didn't have an effect, however. Whereas the Rhodesian counter-insurgency efforts had to be directed against ZANU, the Rhodesian security forces had to keep some of its forces pinned at the Zambian border in case of ZAPU attack.

For the three years 1973, 1974, and 1975 *combined*, 502 guerrillas, 63 security forces, and 317 civilians had been killed. In 1976 alone, the totals were 1,244 guerrillas, 112 security forces, and 548 civilians.[5] This, of course, does not tell the whole story. The numbers do not include those killed in Rhodesian external raids. Nor do the numbers convey the tangible effects on a way of living for those involved. For the black noncombatants in the rural areas, it meant a life torn between the repressive measures of the security forces—being herded into "protected villages," living with draconian curfews, having their life snuffed out on the slightest suspicion of aiding the guerrillas—and the random terror of the insurgents. For whites, those who counted in Smith's settlement calculus, the effects were differentiated. Most of the whites lived in the cities where the war was not fought, but they did have to fight in increasing numbers as more and more were called up. The most dramatic change in living conditions occurred for those who formed the backbone of the country's economy: the farmers who oversaw huge isolated tracts of land, who had to travel large distances to maintain their livelihood. In 1976, at least thirty members of farming families were killed. Each farm, miles from nowhere, became a target.

The year 1976 was the first year since 1966 that Rhodesia lost more whites to emigration than it gained through immigration. Table 3.2 shows the figures from 1964 to 1979. This outpouring of whites, mostly skilled and professional, struck at the center of the Rhodesian war effort, which relied on an "us vs. them" siege mentality and a "do or die against all odds" effort. When the "us" started to leave, the government took quick notice. In September 1976, strict currency allowances were established to attempt to stem the exit (Wilkinson 1980, 116–117).

Table 3.2  Net Immigration of Europeans into Rhodesia, 1964–1979

| Year | Net Immigration |
|------|-----------------|
| 1964 | –8,710 |
| 1965 | 2,280 |
| 1966 | –2,090 |
| 1967 | 2,050 |
| 1968 | 6,210 |
| 1969 | 5,040 |
| 1970 | 6,331 |
| 1971 | 9,407 |
| 1972 | 8,825 |
| 1973 | 1,682 |
| 1974 | 580 |
| 1975 | 1,928 |
| 1976 | –7,023 |
| 1977 | –10,908 |
| 1978 | –13,709 |
| 1979 | –9,557 |

*Source*: *Rhodesia Monthly Migration and Tourist Statistics For January 1980* (Salisbury: Central Statistical Office, 1980).

The war was putting severe strains on the Rhodesian economy. As mentioned earlier, the growth rate for 1977 was –7 percent. Direct defense expenditure had risen by 280 percent between 1972 and 1976. In 1976/77 23 percent of government expenditure was defense related (Cilliers 1985). Tourism had declined by more than half since 1972 (Wilkinson 1980, 116). Rhodesia's minister of finance, David Smith, had warned the prime minister early in 1976 that a settlement was needed by June 1977 (Martin and Johnson 1981, 248).

## The Prelude to Kissinger's Meeting with Smith

As Henry Kissinger and John Vorster prepared to meet on September 3 and 4, the heat was turned up considerably on Smith. What had been until then low-intensity pressure from South Africa became an all-out offensive. The turning point for Vorster was a Rhodesian raid on Nyadzonia in Mozambique on August 9, 1976. Striking at a refugee camp where ZANLA guerrillas were present, the Rhodesian forces slaughtered 1,200 people, including children. South Africa responded by blocking the flow of goods in and out of Rhodesia. By August 20, the choke points had created a logjam of nearly 50 million British pounds of Rhodesian goods inside South Africa, including 16,000 tons of Rhodesian citrus fruit for export that had to be buried (Caute 1983, 65). The South Africans cut off the money and supplies—especially ammunition, spare parts, and petrol—necessary for carrying out the war effort. On August 26, Vorster terminated "Operation Polo," the South African military helicopter assistance program. By withdrawing all helicopter pilots and technicians and twenty-six helicopters, the South Africans effectively cut Rhodesia's air force strike capacity in half (Moorcraft and McLaughlin 1982, 36).

The table was set for Kissinger and Vorster's meeting. On Namibia, Vorster rejected any negotiations with SWAPO (the South West Africa People's Organization). On Rhodesia, however, Vorster relayed to Kissinger that he thought he could deliver a commitment from Smith to majority rule. Further, he thought it best that Kissinger deliver the coup de grâce. Kissinger ruled out meeting Smith unless Vorster received a precommitment from Smith that he would accept majority rule. It was left that Vorster would bring Smith into tow while Kissinger further canvassed the Front Line presidents. With a shuttle trip to Southern Africa in mind, Kissinger sent a deputy to Tanzania who gained Nyerere's approval.

Kissinger left for Dar es Salaam on September 13. On board his plane, Kissinger confided, "Substantially Namibia is the easier problem, but procedurally the more difficult. Rhodesia is the other way round. It is easier to visualize a mechanism for Rhodesia." He admitted to being baffled by African emphasis on Namibia instead of Rhodesia. On the latter, Kissinger believed that "Nyerere had agreed to some of the details of the U.S./U.K. perception of how things might work, but he [Kissinger] was still afraid that if he failed to get a commitment from the whites the blacks might raise their demands." At that point he let it be known that South Africa had not committed itself to majority rule in Rhodesia on the basis of the British-American plan (from the notes of "a source close to Kissinger," in Legum 1977, A32).

In Tanzania, Kissinger met much skepticism from Nyerere. Nyerere harped on two points: (1) Kissinger should eliminate his references to the superpower aspects of Southern Africa and his use of anticommunist rhetoric, which emboldened Smith, and (2) Rhodesia was not ripe for settlement and therefore Kissinger should pressure South Africa on Namibia.[6] Nyerere is reported to have told Kissinger, "If you are saying you can convert Smith the chances are nil" (Martin and Johnson 1981, 249).

Kissinger informed Nyerere of the procedures for achieving majority rule in Rhodesia that were so easy to visualize. Kissinger envisioned that Smith would step down and a caretaker government with a black majority would be put into place, the same idea bandied about by Rowlands in August. Nyerere had no problems with that. Kissinger then suggested that in the interim there should be a Council of State, which would have a white majority. Nyerere rejected the proposal and proposed instead a "Chissano Government"—a transitional government similar to that in Mozambique—"where FRELIMO named the members and the Portuguese appointed a High Commissioner." An authoritative source quoted by Colin Legum states that "Kissinger seems to have accepted this formula, but said that Whitehall apparently preferred a council to a single person, though he was trying to dissuade them. Such a government would in fact be of a caretaker nature, and would include whites. It would probably reflect across-the-board interests rather than be strictly of the Chissano type" (Legum 1977, A33).

Kissinger traveled on to meet Kaunda in Zambia on September 16 and 17. Among the warnings that Kaunda passed on was that "Ian Smith is a very slippery fellow." Kaunda also wished him well and made it clear that if his effort came to naught, then violence would increase. At a press conference after his meeting with Kissinger on the seventeenth, Kaunda stated that what was desired from Smith was "a firm declaration by the rebel leader that he is now in favour of majority rule." Such a declaration would be followed by the British government stepping in to fulfill its legal obligations (*Zambia Daily Mail*, 18.9.1976, in Baumhogger 1984, 145). In an interview in October, Kaunda was to claim that during the visit "at no time . . . did Kissinger tell us the details of what he was going to tell Smith" ("Interview with President Kaunda," in Baumhogger 1984, 182).

On September 14, Vorster met Smith in Pretoria to apprise him of the situation. Although Vorster did not gain Smith's concession to majority rule at that point, the South African leader informed him that serious negotiations were set to take place soon and Smith should be prepared to make heavy concessions. According to Ken Flower, who was present at the meeting, Vorster presented Smith with the details of the Kissinger proposals and was told that these constituted Rhodesia's "last chance" (Flower 1987, 164–165).

As the talks with Kissinger began, Rhodesia's position was desperate. Military units in the field were forced to conserve on ammunition because of shortages (Meredith 1979), and Rhodesia faced equally severe economic problems. At a speech to the Rhodesian Front Congress on September 15, 1976, David Smith, the Rhodesian minister of finance, explained that "Rhodesia's foreign exchange reserves . . . had fallen alarmingly; without a substantial injection of soft loans, Rhodesia could not pay for the war, import the spare parts and new equipment industry needed, or cope with inflation." The urgency of the economic situation was "reflected in Rhodesian statistics six to nine months later. 1977 showed a negative growth rate of 7.8 per cent, by far the worst during the UDI years" (Martin and Johnson 1981, 248).

In a closed speech on October 7 to members of the Rhodesian Front, Ted Sutton-Pryce, a deputy minister in Ian Smith's office, described the prevailing situation at the time of the Pretoria talks in September. The text of the memorandum of the speech states:

> Vorster is the bad guy. The reason for the Rhodesian Front failure was due to pressure put on Rhodesia.
>
> United States 60m dollars exports are in the pipeline, rising to $100m by December. Without these exports moving, the government could not support an agricultural crop next year.
>
> Fifty percent of the Rhodesian defence bill was paid by South Africa until June. A reply has not been given since then as to whether they would support it for a further year. There had been a delay on war items for as long as two and a half years.
>
> The railway system is moving very few goods—reported congestion. The border was closed over the period of the Kissinger talks 1–4 days. Fuel supply down to 19.6 days. It is difficult to prove these facts as we cannot afford to antagonize South Africa by exposing her. The Prime Minister had considered appealing to the South African public over Vorster's head, but did not have enough time.
>
> Against this background they had no alternative but to accept the Kissinger package deal. ("Memorandum of Speech," in Baumhogger 1984, 202)

## Kissinger Meets Smith

Kissinger had confided to journalists on the trip that it was not his intention to dictate terms of settlement or forge binding agreements on the parties; rather, his goal was to make Smith concede to majority rule and then bring together all of the parties to hammer out an agreement under British supervision. But as has been shown, Kissinger did have settlement terms in mind when he traveled to Pretoria, and, moreover, they did not have the specific support of the African leaders in the region or the nationalist leaders they spoke for.

On September 19, 1976, Kissinger met with Ian Smith in Pretoria. In a meeting that was intended to last one hour, but instead went on for four, Kissinger pressured the Rhodesian prime minister to accept majority rule in Rhodesia. Kissinger attempted to shatter any illusions that Smith might have had about his position and the likelihood of U.S. help. Colin Legum describes the tightening of the screws on Smith:

> According to senior American officials, Kissinger conducted the meeting by putting three principal questions to Smith: (1) How do you think Rhodesia can be rescued now that you know you have lost the last two friends on whose help white Rhodesians had been counting— South Africa and the United States? (2) If things are going so badly now, where do you think you will be next March, if the fighting is stepped up? (3) And if you think that you will make it through next March, what about next year at this time? Kissinger then produced a summary of three sets of U.S. intelligence reports about Rhodesia's military position. . . . All three were in broad agreement; the only difference being their estimates of the time before Rhodesia's military and economic position finally collapsed. (Legum 1977, A35–A36)

Kissinger then told Smith that the proposals he brought with him were essentially British proposals and had been accepted by the Front Line States. He then gave them to Smith to read:

> 1. Rhodesia agrees to majority rule within two years.
> 2. Rhodesian representatives would meet immediately at a mutually agreed place with Black leaders to work out an interim Government until majority rule was implemented.
> 3. The interim Government would consist of a Council of State, half of whose members would be Black and half White, with a White chairman who would not have a casting vote.
> 4. All members will take an oath that they will work for rapid progress to majority rule.
> 5. The United Kingdom would enact enabling legislation for progress to majority rule. Rhodesia would also enact such legislation as may be necessary. (Proposals as presented in Flower 1987, 166–167)

Kissinger told Smith that under the circumstances this was the best deal that he could offer him. The U.S. secretary of state also added that the outcome of the election in the United States in November would have an effect on Rhodesia's position. Smith remembers Kissinger's line as inferring that if there was a new government in November, Rhodesia's position would worsen (Smith 1987, interview with author). Ken Flower maintains that Kissinger's words were stronger: "If the Republicans are not returned to office in November, the deal is off" (Flower 1987, interview with author).

Smith first asked whether the deal could say "responsible majority rule," which Kissinger refused. Later, Smith asked again and Kissinger replied that "where I'm from majority rule means one thing" (Flower 1987, interview with author). Smith asked if the ministries of Defense and Law and Order could remain in white control until independence.

Kissinger agreed that this was best and that, if need be, the Rhodesians should give the blacks a majority on the ruling council in exchange for those two ministries. After more haggling it was decided to drop the oath from the proposals. Kissinger then gave the details of an international trust fund to aid Rhodesia's independence (this paragraph relies on Flower 1987, 164–171; 303–307).

At that point, Kissinger left to meet with Kaunda in Zambia and Nyerere in Dar es Salaam. Smith returned to Salisbury to await word from Kissinger about Front Line acceptance of the deal. Kissinger presented the specific terms to Kaunda and Nkomo in Lusaka and was met with less than enthusiasm. Kaunda felt unable to comment until he had met with the other Front Line presidents. Nkomo stated that the proposals "were seriously flawed." Kissinger then went to Dar es Salaam where he met Nyerere, told him that Smith had agreed to majority rule, but did not tell him the details. In an ambiguously worded telegram, Kissinger signaled to Smith that he believed the Africans would accept the terms. On September 25, Smith announced on the radio to the Rhodesian people that a plan for majority rule had been accepted with the provisions discussed above.

As important as it is to understand the details of the negotiations, the formulas discussed, and the quid pro quos reached, one must also study the common understanding reached between Vorster, Smith, and Kissinger. What was the language that formed the context of their meetings and agreement? How did Smith and Vorster interpret U.S. motives, and how did Rhodesia fit into their plans? What common language existed for Kissinger to explain to Smith what needed to be done? How did South Africa portray its goals in Southern Africa to Smith? And how did Smith, in turn, understand South African initiatives? There has been much written about this meeting in terms of what was proposed, promised, counterproposed, and counterpromised, but what was the web of meaning that the participants shared?

Kissinger had made it plain that he wanted a settlement in Rhodesia. All cant about the morality and justice of majority rule aside, what mattered to Kissinger was the destabilizing situation in Southern Africa and the potential for further Soviet and Cuban involvement in the area. Smith had found this hopeful, in that the United States had finally awakened to the concerns of white Rhodesians. But what was so disappointing to Smith was that the U.S. and Rhodesian prescriptions for fighting the threat were so different. To Smith, the U.S. demand for majority rule in Rhodesia constituted appeasement to Soviet-backed terrorists. For Kissinger, majority rule that excluded the "ideologically radical" elements would be a firebreak against communist involvement. If he was committed to making a deal with Smith, Kissinger would have to square the two approaches. But since Vorster was going to do the squeezing of Smith, it would be left to Vorster to create a common understanding on U.S., South African, and Rhodesian aims and goals in Southern Africa.

This came at a particularly trying time for the racist regime in South Africa. Opinion in the South African government on Vorster's détente policy had always been divided, but with the loss in Angola, the deepening of the war in Rhodesia, and the Soweto riots at home, the intensity of opinion was at its peak. Vorster's "moderate Rhodesia" goal was at its riskiest and most controversial, and this would be its last chance. What Kissinger told Smith about the implications of the U.S. election in November were doubly true for South Africa: things would get worse. South African options were stark: either forge a settlement to its liking in Rhodesia and renew attempts at understanding with Zambia, or increase its support of Rhodesia and commit itself to underwriting that war and facing the consequences of a larger conflict.

On September 13, the day before Vorster met Smith in Pretoria, the South African prime minister announced that "if the peace initiatives in southern Africa fail, South Africa would ultimately have no option but to go into the breach; without U.S. support against communist expansionism both Western Europe and southern Africa will face a dark future" (Keesing's, 28042). At the meeting, Vorster and Smith discussed the South African prime minister's talks with Kissinger, and how Rhodesia fit into U.S. and South African plans. That evening after the talks, South African foreign minister Muller stated that the decision was up to Smith about U.S. efforts to bring about peaceful change in Southern Africa. He added, "If we and other African states are also prepared to throw in our full weight—and South Africa is prepared to do it—then I believe the peace offensive can succeed, and that Southern Africa in the future can also depend upon the support of the Free World against the Communist danger" (ARB, 4164).

The statements suggest an enemy (the communist danger), a community (the Free World) opposed to the enemy, and the support of the United States and some African states in moves (a peace offensive or initiative) *against* the enemy. A peace offensive makes sense only in considering a prize to be captured or perhaps an ally to be found. It is necessary to recall Kissinger's strategy of isolating what we will call the "pragmatic" blacks from the "radical" blacks. What was at stake was the redrawing of the lines of conflict in Southern Africa: an alliance between a Rhodesia ruled by whites and black "pragmatists" and those Front Line States who could live with South Africa versus the "ideological" radicals and their supporters. But who were the ideological blacks that Kissinger admittedly had written off? At the time, his description could only have been aimed at ZANU, Mugabe, and their most important patron, Machel. One could draw the conclusion that

Kissinger hoped that at a minimum Zambia would defect from the Front Line. At a maximum he hoped for Nyerere's acquiescence to such a plan.

In a secret document of the Rhodesian government of October 1976, the reasons for the U.S. initiative, *as Rhodesia understood them*, were described as follows:

> a. In the wake of the Communist gains in Mozambique and in Angola, the American authorities undertook a reappraisal of the strategic implications for the Western world in relation to its lifelines and its sources of raw materials.
> b. As a result of this initiative, a diplomatic/political formula was prepared to resolve the situation, the essential ingredients of which were:
> (i) establish moderate multi-racial government in Rhodesia and South West Africa;
> (ii) link the above with Zambia, Zaire, Malawi, SA, Botswana, Lesotho and Swaziland and create an anti-communist bloc;
> (iii) bolster the new block with substantial economic aid;
> (iv) make available military hardware to strengthen the capacity of the bloc to negate the Communist expansion plans.
> c. Since Rhodesia was regarded as the fulcrum of the whole plan, their main diplomatic effort was concentrated on this issue.
> d. As a result of shuttle diplomacy involving the UK, SA and the so-called "front-line" Presidents, firm proposals were tabled in Pretoria. ("Rhodesian Strategy," in Baumhogger 1984, 180)

One can argue that the Rhodesians really did not believe such a scenario, that this was simply a comforting interpretation as they attempted to weather the storm of majority rule. If so, then we would expect that Rhodesian security policies during that time would not be affected by this by-product of leaders' imaginations. Not so, however. The part of the document addressed toward security reads: "The agreement provides that terrorism will cease. It would be unrealistic to expect this to happen in any fixed time scale. *At best, the Zambian and Botswana fronts should stabilize.* The activity on *the Mozambique front will intensify* because any possibility of stability in the Rhodesian situation nullifies the Communist strategy." Later, a cryptic passage brings home in stark fashion what the Rhodesians believed was in store: "The black personalities who are likely to form a part of the interim government are expendable as far as the external militant forces are concerned. Their physical and political survival will depend upon continued cooperation with the white man" (Baumhogger 1984).

Much controversy has arisen over whether Kissinger promised Smith assistance if the agreement was squelched by the black nationalists. Again, this issue cannot be divorced from the context of the meeting. Smith stated in October that Kissinger had promised the

Rhodesians they would be stronger after accepting the package. Such an ambiguous statement could be interpreted any number of ways. Smith's conception of meeting with Kissinger assumed that Kissinger represented a return to the days of Tiger, Fearless, and Smith-Home, whereby white leaders of Rhodesia and elsewhere would decide the fate of the mass of blacks within the country. Smith believed that whether the blacks agreed or not, he had reached an agreement with Kissinger, which he expected Kissinger to carry out. For Smith, the agreement with Kissinger concerned the conditions for bringing Rhodesia to constitutional legality.

When I put the question of U.S. and British support to Smith, this belief became apparent. His answer is worth quoting at length:

Q. Did Kissinger promise you that you would get assistance if you accepted and this failed on the part of the nationalists?

A. Yes. There was no doubt that part of this was reconciliation and restoration of the position between ourselves and Britain and the rest of the Free World. They wanted to keep us as part of the Free World, we had always been part of the Free World, and there would be tremendous financial benefits and assistance that would flow.

Q. If the Patriotic Front and the other nationalists didn't go along with this?

A. Well, they had committed themselves to going along with it, according to Kissinger. And Vorster. Vorster told us at that time that he had very good contacts with these people and they were working with them and . . . Kissinger had extracted these bargains from them.

Q. But did Kissinger say to you that, if this fails because of the nationalists' part, say Nkomo, Muzorewa, Mugabe turned it down, "We won't forget the efforts you made"?

A. No. *There was no question of that happening.* The question was an agreement had been made—that providing we accepted, that would clinch the contract. Then the British government and the Americans and the rest of them gave an undertaking that they would proceed with it, that they would then legalize us. That's all that mattered. *It didn't matter two hoots whether Nkomo and company accepted it or not. They would have been irrelevant had we been legalized.* It was our unconstitutionality and the fact that Britain and the Free World were joining in with Russia and trying to undermine us. Once that ended, we had won, you see. We had no doubt in our minds that the whole thing would have been over then. Because these chaps didn't have the ability, the strength, the muscle, to do anything of any consequence to us without the support of Britain, the United States, and those countries. They were the ones who were imposing sanctions upon us. If sanctions were removed, the whole thing was over. (Smith 1987, interview with author; emphasis mine)

Kissinger's manner suggested that the framework and the proposals

were fixed. When Smith was presented with the demands and proposals
for majority rule, he assumed the negotiations were with Kissinger, and
not with the nationalists. When Smith made the demands that he did, he
was bargaining with Kissinger and Kissinger again did not dispel him
of the notion that he (Kissinger) was bargaining on the nationalists'
behalf. Smith and Vorster[7] believed Kissinger could bargain for the
nationalists. On both sides, the Kissinger-Smith talks represented a
return to the era when Africans were objects whose fate was determined
by the white man.

## *From Pretoria to Geneva*

It did not take long for any optimism springing from Kissinger's
mission to dissipate. The Front Line presidents immediately opposed
the package offered to Smith, saying that accepting it would be
tantamount to accepting the structures of racism and imperialism in that
country. Although they could not condone the specific details of the
agreement, they welcomed the acceptance of majority rule and looked
forward to the British convening a conference to hammer out the form
that it would take and the arrangements necessary to bring about the
transition. Smith, however, was adamant: It was a package deal—his
acceptance of majority rule was contingent on the conditions that
Kissinger had promised.

Kissinger's mission left the British in a severe bind. Given Smith's
acceptance of majority rule (however conditional it was), and the calls
of the Front Line presidents for Britain to therefore carry out its
colonial responsibility, the British felt compelled to hold formal
negotiations. On the other hand, no one in the British Foreign Office
felt that the negotiations had a chance of success. Nonetheless, Anthony
Crosland, the new British foreign secretary, announced that Britain
would chair a conference to negotiate the transitional arrangements to
majority rule for Zimbabwe. To ensure that all would attend, Crosland
and Kissinger announced that what Smith had agreed to was a basis for
discussion and negotiable.

Duplicity in this sordid affair was not left to Kissinger alone. In
Parliament, Anthony Crosland came under intense questioning by
Conservative members, including one Margaret Thatcher:

> *Mrs. Thatcher*: May I ask the Foreign Secretary again about the
> proposals put by Dr. Kissinger to Mr. Smith? It seems to me, from
> what the right hon. Gentleman has said, that he is now saying that the
> Foreign office was in error when it put out an official statement saying
> that Mr. Smith had accepted proposals put to him by Dr. Kissinger and
> those proposals represented an elaboration of the plan originally

advanced by the Prime Minister. Is that a correct statement, or was the right hon. Gentleman's office at fault?

*Mr. Crosland*: No, Sir, [*sic*] that was a correct statement, because all the proposals made in the course of this series of discussion, with not only Mr. Smith but the Black African presidents, were an enlargement of the Prime Minister's own statement of 22nd March. I am not authorised, obviously, to speak in detail on Dr. Kissinger's behalf. I repeat, however, what he said at a press conference at the end of September in New York. . . . He said that nothing had yet been settled regarding the composition of an interim Government or the allocation of Ministers. This is a matter which requires negotiation.

*Mrs. Thatcher*: What were the proposals that were accepted?

*Mr. Crosland*: The proposals that were accepted were what Mr. Smith set out in his six proposals. Dr. Kissinger had made it clear, and I have now made it clear, that these are in our view a useful basis of discussion. [HON. MEMBERS: "Oh."] They are a useful basis of discussion. I repeat the statement of Dr. Kissinger—that these are matters which require negotiation. But nevertheless they offer a useful basis for discussion. . . .

*Mr. Aitken*: Is the Foreign Secretary aware that his answers this afternoon give the impression that something fishy is taking place? Are we now to understand that nothing has been set down definitively in writing and that nothing has been signed, but that all we are talking about is a vague series of other people's proposals floating around between Mr. Smith and the African Governments? If that is the case, there could not be a worse basis for a serious conference and a serious agreement. ("Excerpts from a Debate in the British House of Commons Concerning the Proposed Geneva Conference, 12.10.1976," in Baumhogger 1984, 177–178)

The Front Line presidents, in anticipation of the conference, once again turned to the problem of unity. Following an appeal from the presidents, two ZAPU leaders, George Silundika and Jason Moyo, approached Robert Mugabe in the belief that a coalition between ZAPU and ZANU would be useful as a tactic at the negotiations. On September 29, the three leaders agreed to a pledge to form a united front against Smith. Mugabe was asked whether he would accept Muzorewa and replied that since they were all fighting for an independent Zimbabwe, Muzorewa could be included "only at the political level and not military level because he does not have an army" ("Reports on Unity Talks between ZANU and ZAPU in Lusaka, 28.–29.9.1976," in Baumhogger 1984, 162–163).

While teams from ZANU and ZAPU met in Maputo to hammer out the shape their unity would take, Nkomo and Muzorewa were together at a function in Gabarone, Botswana. Nkomo asked the bishop about joining the nationalist coalition. Muzorewa was terribly suspicious of Nkomo and postponed giving him an answer until Muzorewa returned to Rhodesia and met with his advisers. Upon returning to Salisbury on October 4, after nearly a year and a half in self-exile, Muzorewa was met by approximately 100,000 cheering Zimbabweans. At that point, Muzorewa, emboldened by the crowds, chose to ignore Nkomo's entreaties in what would be a turning point in the peace process.

On October 8, the same day that it was announced in London that the transitional conference would take place on October 25 in Geneva with Ivor Richard as chair, the Patriotic Front (PF) was formed between ZAPU and ZANU in Lusaka. The united front was a limited one: it did not include the merging of military operations and personnel, nor did it mean the loss of separate identities for the parties. The decision taken in Zambia simply amounted to an agreement to send a joint delegation to Geneva.

The Patriotic Front immediately set preconditions for their participation in the conference, including the release of all political prisoners, abolition of protected villages, and the lifting of the state of political emergency in Zimbabwe. They demanded that the talks should not be between the nationalists and the Smith regime, but rather between the nationalists and Great Britain as the responsible decolonizing power. Smith was welcome to attend, they offered, but only as an arm of the British government. Finally, the PF requested that the talks be slated to start two weeks after October 25, to give them proper time to prepare as a single team.[8] The British acceded to a three-day delay. The Front Line presidents subsequently urged the PF to attend without preconditions, and it accepted.

## Geneva

Britain's fundamental ambivilence toward about the conference was signaled in their choice of chairman. It was announced that the foreign secretary, Anthony Crosland, would not preside over the talks. In his stead, the unenviable task of running the conference would be given to Ivor Richard, the British ambassador to the United Nations—an appointment criticized by the nationalists. The opposition was not based on Richard's qualifications, but stemmed from the appearance that the British were not serious about the task ahead. The British replied that this was not the case and gave Richard ministerial status for the meetings.

Richard had been dealt a bad hand and knew it. As he later recalled,

> There was no kind of agreement among the parties before we got to Geneva, which is essential for such a conference. . . . We really had no clout attached to our role. . . . When we started the thing we didn't know if they [the Patriotic Front] wanted to talk. We had no idea what

was going to happen when they all turned up in Geneva. We didn't even know who was coming until the week before. If I recollect correctly, Sithole had only been invited the week before. God knows what was going to happen when they all turned up. We had to make rules about leaving guns outside, that kind of thing. So, it was all very much probing in the dark.

The trouble, you see, was that Kissinger of course believed or at least said he believed that he had got the Front Line States behind it, that they all had said, "Marvelous! Splendid! We all agree!" But by the time we got to Geneva there were qualifications from the Front Line States: enormous ones. They weren't endorsing a Kissinger deal, if indeed there was a deal by then; they were saying "Majority rule, yes, absolutely splendid: now then, we want one, two, three, four, five, six, seven, eight." So we had to get over that lot before we even got to the black nationalists from inside Zimbabwe itself, and I don't think Kissinger cleared any of it with them. . . . I don't see how you could have produced a settlement out of that mess. (Richard 1987, interview with author)

Richard's only hope in such a situation was to try to keep the parties at the negotiating table and hope that some points of agreement would emerge that could be built on:

My game plan? Keep it going. I thought I had two things on my side. One, the South Africans wanted a settlement and the new American administration would want a settlement. Two, I didn't think that the whites in Rhodesia would.really be prepared to face the war to the extent that they eventually did. I thought when brought to the precipice, when it looked as if the war was really going to intensify there would be enough common sense there to get some kind of settlement. . . . The only hope I had was to keep it going as long as I could, produce some kind of proposals that took into account a distillation of the different views and sell it to the Front Line States and South Africa. (Richard 1987, interview with author)

Richard did not realize that the Front Line presidents and South Africa were irreconcilable. On the eve of the Geneva conference, Smith still held out that the Kissinger package was nonnegotiable and that the package had to be accepted as the formula for the talks. Far from backing down on what had been their stance all along, the Rhodesians were positively emboldened. On October 31, three days after the talks began, Vorster publicly backed Smith's version and stated that only by sticking with the essentials of the Kissinger proposals could a settlement emerge. Sources reported that Vorster's speech was preceded by a meeting between Kissinger and R. Botha, South Africa's ambassador to the United States. The *Daily Telegraph* reported that "the interpretation placed on Mr. Vorster's carefully worded statement is that as long as Mr. Smith sticks to the terms of reference of his original statement, he can count on South African backing" (ARB, 4203).

Smith and the Rhodesian government's conversion to majority rule was purely tactical. A little over two weeks after Smith's acceptance of Kissinger's proposals, Ted Sutton-Pryce, Smith's deputy, outlined Rhodesian government long-term strategy:

> America cannot support Rhodesia with a white minority government because of world opinion. If there were an acceptable government in Rhodesia America would support this country with everything to combat communism except troops. . . .
>
> Kissinger deal: Set up an interim government and would have two years to sort out the constitution, after which majority rule. Not seen as one man one vote. America understands the problem better than the United Kingdom.
>
> Parliament would go into recess and not be dissolved. If the agreed constitution was not liked after two years, parliament would reject it.
>
> At worst we would be in a better position to fight the war than at present. We would have . . . two years trading on an open market. Revive the economy with two billion development fund. Two years to build up arms and war materials and the armed forces. The market for recruiting into the forces would be widened. ("Rhodesian Strategy Memorandum," in Baumhogger 1984, 202)

Smith knew that Kissinger's package hinged on Ford's election on November 3. If Kissinger stayed in office, Smith could hope for pressure to be put upon the blacks to take or leave the package. If the blacks did not accept, then Smith hoped that the Americans and British would institute the agreement, lift sanctions, and provide assistance for fighting the war. For Smith, the opening negotiations constituted a waiting game until the U.S. election. On November 3, Jimmy Carter defeated Gerald Ford to become the next president of the United States. On November 4, Ian Smith left Geneva to fly home to Salisbury, leaving his foreign minister, P. K. Van der Byl, in charge of the Rhodesian delegation.

A more ominous part of the Rhodesian strategy to prevent majority rule involved purposefully escalating the conflict. In October, South Africa had resumed the flow of supplies to Rhodesia. The Rhodesian military, which had previously planned a number of cross-border raids into Mozambique, were given the go-ahead for November. Smith and Van der Byl explained at briefings in Geneva the basis of their approach for the next three years. One confidant to their strategy wrote, "In their view, once Communist forces appeared in any numbers in Mozambique, South Africa would be compelled to enter the fighting on their side— and when that happened, the United States would follow. So the success of Smith's strategy depended on Mozambique and ZIPA [the joint forces of the Patriotic Front] bringing in the Communists—and the best chance of producing that result was for the Rhodesian troops to continue striking deep into Mozambique" (Legum 1977, A42). That

Smith wanted to escalate the conflict in the hopes of turning it into a wider conflagration was confirmed by Ken Flower, Smith's chief of intelligence at the time (Flower 1987, interview with author).

Although it is hard to imagine the United States intervening in Rhodesia during that period, it is useful to recall Nyerere's warnings to Kissinger that his continued use of anticommunist rhetoric and references to the Cuban and Soviet threat would embolden Smith. Even if Smith doubted whether the United States would really join the fray, he was more than eager to call South Africa's bluff. Knowing that Rhodesia had friends in the South African military, Smith decided once again to test Vorster's resolve and control over South Africa's Rhodesia policy.

If Smith was determined to cling to the Kissinger proposals, bide his time until the talks failed, and intensify the conflict in the hopes of bringing in outside help, what were the positions of the nationalists as Geneva began?

Robert Mugabe's patient work among the guerrillas in the camps in Mozambique had won him the imprimatur of Machel and Nyerere as the leader of ZANU. ZANU, however, was not a unified political and military force at the time. The political leaders of ZANU were firmly behind Mugabe. The military commanders just released from prison in Zambia—in particular, Tongogara, who was still commander-in-chief of the army—respected Mugabe and recognized him as their spokesman. Mugabe's command problem stemmed from the young military commanders in Mozambique under the leadership of twenty-eight-year-old Rex Nhongo, a tough guerrilla who had risen to the top command of ZANLA while Tongogara sat in a Zambian jail cell. Some under Nhongo's direction were solidly for Mugabe, some were ambivilent in their support for him, some were apprehensive of Tongogara's return, some wanted Tongogara as their leader, and some claimed allegiance to no politician. Simbi Mubako, Zimbabwe's first minister of justice, a Harvard-trained lawyer who was part of the ZANU legal team at Geneva and Lancaster House, described this period as Mugabe's consolidation of power (Mubako 1987, interview with author).

Mugabe was the only nationalist leader who had gained from the failure of Victoria Falls. His stand against negotiations with Smith and his call for continued armed struggle, combined with his conviction that Smith would never negotiate a fair settlement with the blacks of Zimbabwe, were the precise factors on which he built his bid for leadership of ZANU. Given that he was now in the global spotlight, any conciliation on his part would have been interpreted by the guerrillas as evidence that he was the same kind of leader they had rejected. This is not to say he would have been conciliatory if his political leadership was not in the balance; it is doubtful that at that historical moment any circumstance could have made him so. Mugabe made it clear that he was there only at the request of the Front Line presidents and that he believed there would be a settlement only when Smith was defeated on the battlefield.

Mugabe wore his radicalism on his sleeve throughout the conference. He focused on three demands in particular: (1) that a firm date be set for majority rule, preferably within a year of the conference; (2) that the transition period be irreversible in the sense of preventing the whites from reneging on the deal and resuming the fight in a stronger position; and (3) in keeping with this latter demand, that the white military be disarmed and replaced by ZIPA (the joint forces of ZANLA and ZIPRA)[9] during the interim period. These positions were nonnegotiable *at that time*, and the last really amounted to a demand for Rhodesia to surrender. Since Smith would never agree to such conditions, there was little chance of the conference succeeding, which did not bother ZANU. In fact, Mubako goes so far as to say that they wanted it to fail, because ZANU had not established itself sufficiently within the country and would be unlikely to emerge in a powerful position:

> We had not put enough military pressure on yet. We didn't believe Geneva would succeed, nor did we want it to succeed, because if it had, it would have been bad for ZANU. If Smith had said "let's go home and have elections," we would not have won. It was not in our interest to have a successful conference and go home and compete. Our demands were not met and we were happy they were not met. We could go back to the bush and increase the fight and better ZANU's position. We had not done the political work that was necessary to win an election. If there had been an election, Muzorewa might have won but not us. We worked for Geneva not to succeed. (Mubako 1987, interview with author)

For Joshua Nkomo, the leader of ZAPU, Geneva was a mixed bag. He had lost support within the country after his failure to wrestle a settlement from Smith in March but maintained firm control of ZAPU and its army. Although Nkomo had always preferred a negotiated settlement, pressures from inside and outside his party dictated that he harden his stand. When Nkomo's bid for negotiating majority rule from Smith had failed, he was left with the need to prove his revolutionary credentials. Within his party, important leaders such as Jason Moyo and George Silundika were pressing for a harder line. His military was once again active in Rhodesia in 1976 and younger commanders such as Dumiso Dabengwa favored an intensification of the struggle. Outside of his party, his new alliance with ZANU offered him the chance to rekindle his revolutionary legacy, but precluded moderation.

Throughout this period, Nkomo was the most misunderstood of the nationalist leaders. He desperately wanted to participate in legal politics within his country and preferred a negotiated settlement to a bloody war. Many, including Americans, British, South Africans, and some Rhodesians, misread his desire for constitutional politics and his tremendous penchant for politicking as signs that he could be easily compromised. This ignored, however, the other side of Nkomo: his yearning to be considered a revolutionary leader and a patriot. One side made him seek political solutions at all times and investigate any and all possibilities of alliances to achieve majority rule for his country; his ambition to lead an independent Zimbabwe tempted him to consider many a deal. The other side—the revolutionary side—prevented him from accepting anything less than genuine majority rule in Zimbabwe.

Bishop Muzorewa was perhaps the only leader in the world who thought a settlement could be reached in Geneva. More important, he was one of two black leaders at Geneva without an army. That fact, combined with the tremendous reception he received on his return to Salisbury, prompted him to insist on the demand for a one person–one vote election to decide the members of the interim government. He calculated correctly that he would be relegated to a minor position within the transitional government if it was chosen by the Front Line presidents. Muzorewa had burned his bridges with Nkomo and was close to torching them with the Front Line leaders, whom by that time Muzorewa saw as kingmakers and not disinterested third parties.

Ndabaningi Sithole was there as a last-minute addition. He had not been invited to Geneva until he pleaded with Nyerere, who then asked the British to include him. Having been ousted from ZANU, he was, like Muzorewa, without an army. Having broken away from Muzorewa's leadership of the ANC, he was in reality without a political party. Being a member of the Ndau ethnic group, which constitutes only 4 percent of the Zimbabwean population, he was without a natural power base within the country. That he was at Geneva at all is testimony to his reputation as a national leader, his willingness to fight for power, and his mean ability to bluff. As Ivor Richard described Sithole's situation: "If I had bad cards at Geneva, Sithole had none. Yet by the end of the conference he was a player" (Richard 1987, interview with author). Sithole's goal at Geneva, totally dictated by his circumstances, was the simplest one of all the parties there: to ensure that he was part of any solution that was reached.

The conference began on October 28. The nationalists wasted little time in attempting to portray each other as stooges of Smith, each claiming that he separately held the revolutionary mantle and leadership of the Zimbabwean people. Smith, for his part, repeated his intention to deal only with the Kissinger proposals. The only common ground that Richard could find was that the delegations accepted majority rule in two years. Therefore, he attempted to find a specific date for independence acceptable to all the delegations. The whites held out for twenty-four months, the nationalists insisted on twelve. Muzorewa and Sithole agreed to the British compromise of fifteen months. On November 26, believing that he had the agreement of the Patriotic Front, Richard tabled March 1, 1978, for the day for independence. On November 29, the conference moved on to discussions of the interim government, but not before the Patriotic Front stated that they held firm to a one-year period for independence but would postpone discussion so that the conference could continue.

During the public disputes over the date for independence, Richard had been canvassing the delegations about their ideas on the transitional period. Muzorewa's views had been outlined during his opening speech and were refined on November 17. His plan centered on a one person–one vote election to determine the interim prime minister and a thirty-four–member Executive Council made up of people nominated by candidates for prime minister who received 10 percent of the vote. The Executive Council, in addition to administering the country, would appoint a commission to draft a constitution. Britain would appoint a governor with minimal duties to aid in the transition ("Proposals by the ANC [Muzorewa] on the Structure of the Interim Government and Elections, 17.11.1976," in Baumhogger 1984, 215–216).

Nyerere, on November 10, told reporters that Britain must supply the ministers of defense and foreign affairs in any transitional government. He urged Britain to assume its "full colonial responsibility" during the interim period, but did not spell out what that meant other than control of the defense and foreign affairs portfolios. He further stated that the transitional government should be a "government of national unity, a government of consensus, of Africans and whites who are acceptable to the majority of the people" (Baumhogger 1984, 209).

On the last day of November, Richard put forth "a British-U.S. proposal for a two-tier government consisting of (i) a small legislature responsible for drafting a new constitution, and (ii) a council of ministers in which control of the Army and the Police would remain in white hands." The British did not foresee the possibility of having elections for the interim government or prime minister. Nor did they envisage a British role in the transition.

The Patriotic Front then produced their own proposals for the transition. Their basic idea envisaged a single-tier government—a council of ministers with "full legislative as well as executive powers." The ministers would consist of a "clear majority drawn from the liberation movement"—later defined as four-fifths—"one of whom would be Prime Minister." Decisions would be taken by simple majority, "save on matters where the interim constitution requires a two-thirds or other special majority." Ministers taken from the liberation movement would control all portfolios "directly or indirectly concerned with the completion of the pre-independence process." During the transition there would be "a Resident Commissioner answerable to Britain" with "the functions of a governor in a dependent territory but with certain specific limitations on his powers to meet the exceptional situation of Southern Rhodesia" (Baumhogger 1984, 224). In a "Statement of Guiding Principles," the Patriotic Front made clear Southern Rhodesia's "exceptional situation" and its implications. Since Rhodesia was in rebellion against the Crown, Britain would be responsible for the dismantling of the Smith regime and "the total transfer of power from the colonial power to the national liberation movement." Effective transition would begin "with the Zimbabweans taking over the physical instruments of power which ensures the effective and irreversible transmission of total power" (Baumhogger 1984, 225).

At this time, the Patriotic Front experienced its most difficult marital problems until then. A serious difference of opinion arose between Mugabe and Nkomo on the question of whether there would be elections for the *independence* government. Nkomo insisted that elections should take place, but Mugabe argued that those in power during the transition would form the independence government as had happened with FRELIMO in Mozambique (Legum 1977, A44). Mugabe flew to Maputo to consult with his commanders there. After Mugabe had returned to the conference, Rex Nhongo flew to Geneva with some of his lieutenants. At first the guerrillas hinted that they wanted to be recognized as a separate delegation, but in the end they rejoined ZANU and the Front.

The next four days were spent amidst a barrage of clarifications, additions, and postures. On December 2, Van der Byl rejected the nationalists' proposals as being outside the scope of the Kissinger proposals and described the nationalists' demands as "most weird and wonderful. . . . There is an atmosphere of total unreality about it in that they choose to disregard the fact that the Rhodesian Government is in de facto control of Rhodesia and none of the strange esoteric suggestions they have made can possibly be put into effect without the co-operation and connivance of the Rhodesian Government."

The same day, Foreign Secretary Crosland announced that Britain was "ready to play a direct role in the Transitional Government if it is the general view that this would be helpful." Such a presence was immediately rejected by Van der Byl and Sithole. Muzorewa, however, welcomed such a presence and suggested that a British governor preside, "while holding a deliberative and a casting vote, over a national security council which would form a national army out of the existing guerrilla forces." Such a security council would "comprise the Prime Minister, other leaders of parties and three nominated members."

Sithole also "steadfastly" backed Muzorewa's demand for elections for the interim government, a proposal dismissed by the Patriotic Front. However, it was unclear how such elections would fit into the plan suggested by one of his deputies, who on the next day called for "the establishment of a presidium composed of members of the five delegations present at the conference, as well as of a council of ministers" (Keesing's, 28200).

On December 8, Ian Smith returned to Geneva for four days and met with Richard. Richard then left for London to brief Callaghan and Kissinger. It had become clear that keeping the delegations in Geneva without a baseline for negotiations was doing more harm than good. It was decided that Richard would adjourn the conference, which would give the British time to wade through the bewildering morass of issues and positions on the transition, in the attempt to develop a coherent framework for negotiations. During the adjournment, Richard would set off to Washington and Southern Africa to canvass opinion and support in the hope of finding some fuel for the settlement fire. Less than a week later, the Geneva talks were formally adjourned.

During November, events away from the table had reinforced the deadlock and had taken away any possible leverage from Richard. First, the Rhodesians carried out a series of air attacks on Mozambique, which did not earn a reproach from South Africa. Mozambique, in turn, signed a security pact with Cuba that promised Cuban assistance, if requested by Mozambique, to fight foreign aggression. Although the Front Line presidents met and promised mutual defensive measures, Nyerere made it clear that they would not bring in foreign troops (Cubans or East Germans) and hand to Smith the excuse he wanted to prompt Vorster's help.

South Africa's acquiescence to Rhodesia's Mozambique raids and its public backing for sticking to the Kissinger proposals signaled that Vorster's "realist" policy had come to the end of its reign. Until September 1976, the only single benefit that Vorster could point to from his approach was his meetings with Kissinger. The two leaders had clearly reached an understanding beneficial to South Africa, and the mere fact of their meeting brought a veneer of legitimacy to the South African state and provided Vorster with ammunition against his hard-line domestic critics. Vorster was willing to play along with Kissinger on Rhodesia because it would forestall U.S. pressure on South Africa to take action on apartheid at home or independence for Namibia. If Kissinger could produce a black, moderate, "anti-communist" regime in Rhodesia and a larger regional alliance against the "ideological radicals," Vorster would give him his support.

This all changed in November 1976. The election of Carter and the clear indications that the kind of regime Vorster wanted in Rhodesia would not emerge from Geneva spelled the end of South African efforts to pressure Smith. Vorster and the "soft-liners" were impotent at that point. The adherents of the "forward approach" won in November 1976; their influence is tangible from that point on and intensifies when P. W. Botha replaces Vorster in September 1978.

On December 22, Ivor Richard met with Henry Kissinger and Cyrus Vance in Washington to apprise them of British thinking on the talks. Richard believed that the crux of the settlement was "to convince the blacks that progress towards independence would be irreversible, and convince the whites that it would be peaceful and orderly." On British involvement during the interim period, Richard envisioned a "balancing" presence, with no direct role in day-to-day administration. Nor would there be a commitment of British troops. Arguing that there were plenty of troops within Rhodesia, Richard indicated that the problem was the integration of guerrilla forces and the Rhodesian army. Such an integration, Richard insisted, must be a product of consensus: "It can't be done by imposition from outside. The political leaders on both sides have to agree that the war will stop, that the forces on both sides will at least come together, and that eventually you will get one integrated defence force after independence."

On the sticky issue of control over the portfolios of defense and foreign affairs, Richard listed four choices: "(i) they could be under the direct control of the British representative; (ii) they could be controlled by committees composed equally of Blacks and Whites, with a British chairman; (iii) one ministry could be controlled by a White and the other by a Black; or (iv) both could be run by Rhodesian Whites not connected with the ruling Rhodesian Front" (ARB, 4264).

Richard's message shows, first, the limited role Britain desired and intended to play in any transition and, second, how far Richard and the British had come in two months to having a better understanding of what a settlement might look like. What is noteworthy, however, is that the British had not faced up to the contradictions of what a feasible settlement might entail and what the British were willing to do to bring one about.

As Richard prepared to journey to Africa, the signals from Rhodesia were less than promising. Richard's latest remarks and his suggestions of an integrated army and a British presence drove Smith and Van der Byl to apoplexy. Smith, ever the opportunist, turned to another unilateral alternative. On December 30, the tribal chiefs that Smith had appointed to his cabinet in April resigned and announced that they had formed a new political party (ZUPO—Zimbabwe United People's Organization) under the leadership of Chief Chirau. ZUPO promptly put out feelers for getting an invitation to Geneva, but none was forthcoming. Talk about Smith having to go it alone and reach an internal settlement with responsible blacks was promptly resurrected. Smith let it be known privately that he was once again impressed by Muzorewa's moderation at Geneva and by his public support at home, and that he was also surprised to find Sithole so reasonable. All in all, this was a far cry from the previous year, when Smith arrested Sithole as a terrorist who wrecked his settlement talks and dismissed Muzorewa as a leader without a following.

On December 30, Richard arrived in Lusaka for a thirteen-day consultation trip with all parties concerned, including the Front Line presidents and Vorster. In Lusaka he repeated what he had said in Washington, that British troops would not be sent into Rhodesia. On January 1, he met Smith in what were described as acrimonious meetings. Smith's major fear was that Britain's proposed role in Rhodesia would be one of power without responsibility. Smith told Richard, "What if the transition goes wrong? Where does it leave us if we agree to all this? The only thing you've got is a helicopter on the back lawn, and the British chairman of the interim government as soon as anything starts says bye-bye and gets into the helicopter" (Richard 1987, interview with author).[10] It was reported that Smith told Richard that he trusted neither him nor the British government and would not accept any of his proposals, but would examine them until Richard returned later in his journey.

The British emissary still believed that the only road to Smith ran through Pretoria, and so he left for South Africa where he met Vorster, Hilgard Muller, Brand Fourie, and R. F. Botha. Richard described his meetings as "useful, helpful and constructive," not realizing that the South Africans had washed their hands of the settlement. In Vorster's New Year's Eve address, the South African prime minister blamed the deadlock in Geneva on "some of the delegates' refusal to negotiate a settlement of the plans devised by the British and the Americans, the essentials of which, it was said, the 'frontline' Presidents had concurred." A more ominous message was provided in a government commentary on Radio Johannesburg on January 3 that laid out Pretoria's interest in a settlement: "South Africa's interest is directed at preventing a further expansion of the Soviet sphere of influence in this part of the world either by military means or political means through the capitulation of the West. In the final analysis, further Soviet and Cuban adventures in Southern Africa can only be discouraged if the West, mainly Mr. Ivor Richard himself and the new American administration, are prepared to face up to the fact that majority rule in Rhodesia is no longer the issue. What is at stake is the type of majority rule; a moderate pro-Western, free enterprise government or a militant Marxist regime. . . . If the West however chooses salvation in policies of appeasement, in the exertion of pressures on South Africa. . . . South Africa is prepared to stand alone" (Baumhogger 1984, 240–241). Vorster, Fourie, Botha, and

Muller were sympathetic to Richard's mission, for they personally disliked Ian Smith.[11] But as far as South Africa's Rhodesia policy was concerned, these men had lost.

Richard ventured on to Maputo and had talks with Machel, who Richard found was willing to work on a settlement. The meeting was important because the British realized that Machel was not an "ideologue" but someone who could be dealt with. On substantive issues Machel gave Richard his support for elections before independence, thus siding against Mugabe. After the talks with Machel, Richard met Nyerere, who assured him that the fighting would stop once an interim government was formed, which the British were pleased to hear.

On January 8 and 9, the Front Line presidents met in Lusaka and announced that they would recognize only the Patriotic Front as the legitimate liberation group in Zimbabwe. The move should be seen in the context of Richard's trip; it would make Nyerere's promises credible that the fighting would stop once a new government was established, but, more important, it signaled that a settlement would have to include the Patriotic Front. Any illusions that a compromise was possible without the Patriotic Front were dashed. If the British or anyone else wanted Front Line assistance, they could not exclude the guerrillas.

The move prompted Muzorewa and Sithole to condemn the Front Line presidents for imposing their choice of leaders on the people of Zimbabwe. Van der Byl announced that "the Front Line Presidents' decision leaves my government with no choice but to negotiate a settlement with more moderate Black groups and to hope that the resultant Government will be backed by Western countries." He pledged that "White Rhodesians will fight to the last cartridge rather than hand over the government to the Patriotic Front" (Keesing's, 28202).

Richard met with Mugabe and Nkomo in Lusaka on January 12 and found them noncommittal: they wanted to see solid proposals in written form. Richard then took the time to put his suggestions on paper and traveled to Pretoria to present them to Vorster, who, according to Richard, signaled his approval. Richard then flew to Salisbury and met Muzorewa, who found Richard's proposals acceptable as a basis for negotiations. The bishop also assured Richard that he had no intention of negotiating directly with Smith.

The British proposals called for a British commissioner with "residual responsibility for certain subjects (primarily external affairs, defence, internal security and the implementation of the programme for independence)," whose job was to ensure the transition to independence. There would be a council of ministers with equal numbers from each of the Geneva delegations and a similar number of whites chosen by the commissioner. The leaders of Geneva would form an inner cabinet or advisory council. It was left unclear whether there would be a prime minister or a revolving chairmanship of the council. Voting procedures in the council were left to be decided. Defense and internal security were to be put into the hands of a national security council consisting of the interim commissioner, the leading members of the council of ministers, the two chiefs of staff of the armed forces, and the commissioner of police. The last three individuals would be appointed by the interim commissioner and could be removed by him or her ("Suggestions for Possible Structure of Transitional Government. Note by Chairman of Conference, January 1977," in Baumhogger 1984, 250–251).

Richard had a two-hour meeting with Smith on January 20, which apparently went better then their meeting two weeks previously. Richard presented his written proposals as a basis for negotiation. To make sure there was no ambiguity about that point, Richard assured Smith that amendments were possible and that everything was negotiable. Four days later, the whole episode of mediation finally reached an end: Smith rejected the British proposals outright, and would not even accept them as a framework for future talks. The Rhodesians at that point felt that Richard was asking them to hand over power to the nationalists; in particular, severe objections were raised concerning the security arrangements.

## Kissinger and Geneva: Evaluating the Failure

For most actors in the Rhodesian conflict, the situation in late 1976 was not ripe for resolution. The objective situation in 1976 stands in marked contrast to the attitudes of Ian Smith and the willingness of the Rhodesian government to seek a settlement. Militarily, with South African assistance, the Rhodesians were holding their own. For two years, top military officials were suggesting to Smith that a settlement was needed—that the war was not winnable. Indications after 1976, however, point to at least General Peter Walls having confidence that a strategy of taking the war into the other Front Line States and striking at sanctuaries in Zambia and Mozambique would keep the Rhodesians on top of things. Some within the top leadership hoped that Smith would use the temporary successes from the raids to negotiate from strength (Flower 1987, interview with author).

Toward the end of 1976, Smith had to heed the warnings from his financial advisers and take note of the exodus of skilled whites from the country. The number of whites entering and leaving was the most important indicator to Smith of whether the Rhodesians were winning or losing (Smith 1987, interview with author). He was therefore prepared to reach a settlement as long as it did not relinquish white control of government. At first this meant that Smith slowly proceeded with his policy of including hand-picked blacks in the government and making superficial changes in the race laws to assuage international opinion. But Smith felt that he did not have to rush, because the external raids would buy time for him and the continuing disunity among the blacks would drive one or two of their leaders to him and make any internal settlement more "sellable."

On the nationalist side, a willingness to undertake serious negotiations was also lacking. The problem again stemmed from ripeness being an internal property of the actors. ZANU, the party with nominal control over the guerrillas fighting from Mozambique, was not consolidated behind Mugabe. At that time, there was no leader who could step forward and say, "Stop the fighting." The guerrillas, moreover, had abandoned any desire for a settlement; they wanted the surrender of Smith's regime. Because Sithole and Muzorewa were still hoping to appeal to the guerrillas in September 1976, they could not afford to take a conciliatory line. Along with Nkomo, they had within the past year had their political fortunes adversely affected by seeking a negotiated settlement with Ian Smith, and politically they could not afford the willingness to seek peace.

If we return to our earlier theoretical discussions, it was argued that in civil wars actors will seek to eliminate their opponent and win unilaterally. Negotiations become possible when the possibility of winning for the actors is foreclosed, prompting them to look for alternatives. A third party, if it has the leverage, may seek to interfere with each side's resources for waging war and thus accelerate the search for an alternative. Such intervention must be combined with an acceptable solution that addresses the causes of the conflict and reduces the fear of cooperation on both sides.

The Kissinger approach was based on the crude invention of a ripe moment. As Martin Meredith and others have pointed out, Kissinger's attack was based on an aphorism of Charles Colson that Kissinger often quoted fondly, "If you've got them by the balls, their hearts and minds will follow." There cannot be a more compelling ripe moment for negotiation than facing a guerrilla war without ammunition, oil, or spare parts, with an economy already bled dry. But the moment stands in contrast to one where the individual becomes personally aware that a solution is desirable. Smith's heart and mind did not follow. Within two weeks, the Rhodesian government was privately arranging plans to continue the war and publicly backtracking on the meaning of majority rule. Moreover, Smith did not believe that when push came to shove,

South Africa would see them collapse.

Kissinger, by using Vorster's muscle, produced Ian Smith's "commitment" to majority rule. The fatal flaw of the exercise was that the alternative he offered Smith was unacceptable to the nationalists and those who had leverage over the nationalists. As Meredith argues, "Although he had achieved the 'conceptual breakthrough,' by ignoring the complexities of the conflict he ensured the eventual failure of the mission" (Meredith 1980, 256). Kissinger, by creating an alternative apart from one that would end the conflict, gave Smith a way out.

It is understood, of course, that Kissinger did not want to let Smith off the hook. But what is unfathomable is that the package he gave Smith did not have Front Line approval. One possible explanation is that Kissinger was unprepared for the moment when Smith capitulated: Kissinger had to have something to demand of Smith and all he had was a package that had not been developed. How else can one interpret a remark he made to journalists on the morning of September 19 in Pretoria: "The likelihood is that Smith is on the brink of making some decision. I expected that the SA riots would reduce Vorster's flexibility, but they haven't. My judgement is that we are on the road to significant progress. *But I might have to take hell for a few weeks*" ("Notes from Kissinger's Conversations, Pretoria," in Legum, 1977, A34; emphasis mine).

It has been written that when Kissinger agreed to Smith's demands, he had stepped out of his role of interlocutor. What I am suggesting and have suggested earlier in this chapter is that when Kissinger *began* discussions with Smith, he had already stepped out of his role of interlocutor. He had to give the impression of negotiating for the blacks and the British, and he did so convincingly—by lying that the package he was giving Smith had the approval of the Front Line presidents. When Smith made demands, Kissinger tentatively agreed to them but cautioned Smith that he would have to pass on the Front Line response. The first response Kissinger received was from Kaunda (and Nkomo), who, although they both saw the proposals as flawed, agreed to reserve judgement. Kissinger knew then that his ruse had failed: if Kaunda was hesitant, Nyerere would be opposed. He therefore did not tell Nyerere the details, and Nyerere responded enthusiastically. (Ironically, Kissinger was worried at the time that Nyerere had been too enthusiastic and might prevent Smith from making his announcement. That risk was offset for Kissinger, because it "would preempt Machel, Neto and the black Rhodesian groups" [Legum 1977, 36].) Kissinger then sent a telegram to Smith professing his belief that the Front Line States would accept. In the blunt appraisal of an aide to James Callaghan, Kissinger had relied on "lying to both sides" to save the day (Martin and

Johnson 1981, 253).

Kissinger could only hope that the Front Line presidents would accept the package or, barring that, that the parties would agree to enter into negotiations with the possibility of further compromises emerging. The accepted interpretation is the latter, but the evidence is dubious. Most likely the decision to continue talks under the facade that "everything is negotiable" was a fallback position forced by circumstances on the British. For one, the package that Kissinger put forth was judged and accepted by Vorster as well as Smith. Kissinger could bet on further compromises from Smith only if Vorster was willing to pressure for further compromise. But why would Vorster do so? The package was eminently reasonable from the shared viewpoint of Vorster, Kissinger, and Smith; it produced the solution they wanted to see, had the supposed backing of all concerned, and *was the most that hard-liners in Vorster's government, such as P. W. Botha, would condone.*

Kissinger's only hope was Front Line acceptance. Callaghan, after being briefed by Kissinger, urged the Front Line presidents to accept. When they turned it down on September 26, Kissinger and Callaghan were supposedly shocked. Such shock, however, is difficult to fathom: Nyerere had already voiced his opposition *to a milder agreement* than the one reached with Smith, and Nkomo and Kaunda had already recognized the deal as "seriously flawed." Thus, even those blacks Kissinger considered "pragmatic" were opposed. Moreover, I can only speculate that the presidents' reaction was one of indignation or perhaps astonishment at being asked to ratify an agreement for the blacks of Zimbabwe that was negotiated by Kissinger (and perhaps Callaghan), Vorster, and Smith.

Part of the failure must lie with Kissinger's hubris concerning the easiness of a Rhodesian settlement and, in particular, the procedures necessary for a transition to majority rule. What became evident at Geneva was the depth of difficulties involved in the interim period: What should be done with the armed forces, police, and judiciary? How could one provide assurances that each side would carry out its part of the bargain? What kind of British presence might be necessary? How should the ruling members of the interim government be chosen? When would elections be held and who would supervise them? Any prospective mediator had to have answers to these questions that satisfied the antagonists and reduced the fear of cooperation.

The details of the transition took on an even larger importance in people's minds because the end point of the process was vague: majority rule and independence in two years. Everyone assumed that once that had been accepted and an interim government came into place, all problems would be solved. But like the Victoria Falls talks of the previous year, there was no understanding of what the prize was at the end of the contest. What would the new constitution mandate? Who stood to gain and who stood to lose at the end of two years? These aspects were crucial, for *what dominated the calculations of all parties at Geneva was the search for interim arrangements that provided each individual party with an advantage for gaining power in a transitional Zimbabwe.* And the stakes were enormous, for *the party that controlled the transition controlled the framing of the constitution, and who controlled framing the constitution controlled independent Zimbabwe.*

A British diplomat told Kissinger later, "Henry, where you went wrong was that you had Smith down but you did not nail him into the floor" (quoted in Martin and Johnson 1981, 256). There are two variations to explore on this theme. The first presupposes a Kissinger prepared for Smith's commitment to majority rule and armed with a deal acceptable to the Front Line presidents. Would a settlement then have been possible? Alternatively, barring such a deal, why did Kissinger not force Smith to step down as part of the bargain? Would that have at least increased the viability of a negotiated settlement?

The first variation fails because it assumes that any such deal approved by the Front Line presidents would have been acceptable to Vorster before being presented to Smith. Recalling a point made in the first chapter, that the goals of mediators place limits on possible solutions, such acceptance was out of the question. South Africa wanted a negotiated settlement, but one that provided stability on its doorstep, included a continuing white presence, and prevented the influence of "radicals" and their possible coming to power. Kissinger, before reaching Pretoria, had told journalists that Vorster was still not behind the U.S.-U.K. package. If that is so, it would be hard to imagine Vorster's approval of a package such as that suggested by Nyerere (and, presumably, Machel), which could bring to power the kind of people Vorster was trying to circumvent.

The second variation provokes more compelling counterfactual questions. Why did Kissinger not demand that Smith resign? Why did Kissinger insist on a package deal? Why did he insist that it had the support of the Front Line presidents? Why did he bring in the U.S. election as a factor? Why did he assure Smith that Rhodesia's position would be strengthened if he accepted?

The answers reside in Kissinger's belief that Smith would be useful in a transition. Kissinger assumed that Smith's active participation would be a positive one and would bring the white community firmly in line with a settlement. Given Kissinger's belief that he could work with Smith in order to bring about the kind of regime the United States and South Africa wanted to see in Rhodesia, Kissinger played all his cards on getting Smith to accept the principle of majority rule: an election soon and you won't get a better deal; a package deal; prior agreement of all concerned; benefits to follow. And a common language: the fight against communism; stability in Southern Africa. Each card that Kissinger played, however, encouraged Smith to be intransigent later on.

A related issue concerns Kissinger's timing—in particular, conducting this episode in the midst of a close election battle at home. Kissinger was able to use the proximity of the U.S. election date as pressure against Smith (and Vorster). But it also made the negotiations hostage to that election. It is impossible to ignore Gerald Ford's need for liberal votes and the grandstanding nature of Kissinger's trip. What is striking is the publicness of Kissinger's diplomacy during the trip: the confiding of intimate details to journalists, the attempt to provide proximity to genius for the reading public, a look at how the quick study solves the problems of the dark continent. It all stands in contrast to the tight-lipped nature of Kissinger's talks with Vorster at the end of June. Returning to the point that the goal of the mediator sets limits on a possible settlement, if Kissinger's goal was simply a quick diplomatic coup, then he was willing to get Smith's public declaration for majority rule even at the cost of no settlement coming from it.

But we should step back and ask ourselves whether there was a plan on Kissinger's part if Ford won the election. According to Ivor Richard, "The most important thing as far as Kissinger was concerned was to make sure that it didn't break down before polling day. I don't mean that in any cynical sense, but just that having set it up, it was important from his point of view that the thing was given a proper run" (Richard 1987, interview with author). If Ford had been elected, would Kissinger have come down hard on the guerrillas and Front Line presidents to accept the package? Would he have handed them the fait accompli: accept the package or we go ahead with it anyway with any party welcome to join? Or would he have reentered the negotiations in a forceful way after the election, expecting to extract further concessions from Smith?

We know that Kissinger played it very close to the vest during Smith's insistence that it was a package deal. When Smith went public in October and stated that Kissinger had promised support and recognition, Kissinger and the State Department did not deny or acknowledge such a promise. On October 28, the South African government stated publicly that they backed Smith: it was a package deal and nonnegotiable, a statement indicating that South Africa felt that Smith had conceded enough. Such a sign makes it difficult to imagine Kissinger hoping to further pressure Smith through Vorster, if

Ford was elected.

Ivor Richard later recalled, "I don't think Smith came to Geneva with any intention of settling at all. I don't think he believed that he had to and I don't think that he thought people were going to lean on him sufficiently that he had to; he certainly hadn't accepted the principle of majority rule. . . . He was waiting for the result of the election . . . he had no desire to settle at all" (Richard 1987, interview with author). Indeed, Smith left the Geneva conference the day after the U.S. election, leaving P. K. Van der Byl in charge. Approximately two weeks later, on November 19, came an official announcement from Kissinger denying any promise of U.S. support or aid for Rhodesia if the talks broke down. And although it was in response to a claim by Smith the day before, it was similar to what Smith had been claiming for at least a month. This at least suggests that Kissinger was keeping the option of U.S. support open until after the election.

The irony of Kissinger's professed strategy of isolating the ideological radicals is that he looked for ideologues only on the left. There was a fundamental assumption that the ideological radicals who could not be coopted into the kind of majority rule Kissinger wanted to see were black. The true ideological radical, however, was Ian Smith, whose radicalism was not "geared to specific issues." His objection to majority rule was philosophical and not practical. That Kissinger failed to appreciate this was blindness of the most odious sort. The British, however, held no illusions about Smith. One British representative at Geneva whom I asked what might have made for a different outcome, replied, "Well, I remember thinking if Ian Smith had had a heart attack or slipped under a car or something."

The Geneva conference was destined to fail from the outset. However, British behavior after picking up Kissinger's droppings did little to move the parties toward a settlement. Although much was accomplished as a first round of problem solving, British opinion of Smith clouded their understanding that there were real concerns and hesitations on the part of white Rhodesians. What would be necessary in the future was to isolate Ian Smith from his supporters in the government, not drive them closer together. While this would provide another lesson for the future, such lessons were becoming increasingly costly for the lives of Zimbabweans.

## Notes

1. When the Portuguese pulled out of Angola, a rough truce that had been in place between the three major liberation movements there collapsed into

civil war. Intervention immediately followed as South Africa directly (and the United States indirectly) backed UNITA—the National Union for the Total Independence of Angola. Cuban troops intervened to assist the MPLA— the People's Movement for the Liberation of Angola—fight back against the South Africans. A third movement, the FNLA—the National Front for the Liberation of Angola—also received U.S. assistance. For a full discussion of the Angolan situation, see Bender (1978) and Marcum (1969, 1978). On Kissinger's strategy of gaining "escalation dominance" in Angola, see George (1983b).

2. See Lake (1976) for background on the making of U.S. policy toward Southern Rhodesia before 1975. (Mr. Lake was head of policy planning in the U.S. State Department under President Carter.) NSSM 39, the infamous memorandum behind what came to be known as the "tar-baby" option, is produced in its entirety in El-Khawas and Cohen (1976). Rothchild (1979) places U.S. policy toward Africa in its larger international context.

3. The stumbling block was again Smith's refusal to accept even the principle of majority rule. In a sentiment that appears numerous times in this study, spoken by individuals of varied political persuasions, Nkomo complained after the breakdown in the talks that "after months of evasiveness and prevarication by the regime, it has become clear that we live in different worlds and speak different languages" (Flower 1987, 129).

4. Samora Machel described Kissinger's strategy succinctly:  "In Zimbabwe the war was in the phase of armed struggle. 'That is the secondary school. When it becomes a revolutionary struggle that is the university. Dr. Kissinger is coming to close the university before they can get there'" (Martin and Johnson 1981, 236).

5. I am unable to find a yearly statistical breakdown on the number of black civilians killed as opposed to white noncombatants killed. One author states that at the beginning of 1979 the cumulative figures were 310 white civilians killed and 3,845 black civilians killed (Wilkinson 1980, 114).

6. Nyerere based his calculations on three factors. First, he was skeptical of Smith ever conceding to majority rule. Second, if Kissinger wanted results from Vorster, Nyerere thought Kissinger should put his priority on Namibia, where South Africa was the direct negotiating power, and not Rhodesia, where too many factors were outside of Vorster's control. Third, since Zambia, Mozambique, Botswana, and Tanzania could control armaments entering Rhodesia, Nyerere felt that escalation could be more easily controlled there. In Namibia, however, those states did not have such direct influence on SWAPO's ability to get arms.

7. Vorster, at a press conference, quoted Kissinger, who on September 28 maintained that the proposals he gave to Smith had the approval of the African leaders.  Although the State Department subsequently denied Kissinger's claim, Vorster stated that since Kissinger had told him that was the case, he had no reason to disbelieve him.

8. Note that two weeks after October 25 would have put the talks after election day in the United States.

9. Nkomo and Mugabe, under enormous pressure from the Front Line presidents, agreed in principle to merge their fighting units. Nothing more than an acronym (ZIPA) came out of this merger: neither ZANLA or ZIPRA surrendered their autonomy to this new entity.

10. Richard continued to say, "And in a sense he was absolutely right. There was no force backing up the interim government. All we had agreed to

do was to provide a chairman and if that broke down where were they?"

11. This dislike stemmed primarily from repeated experiences with Smith's obstinacy in the face of South African demands and with Smith's attempts to manipulate the Vorster administration by appealing directly to the white South African public.

# 4

# The Anglo-American
# Initiatives: "Calculated
# To Upset Everybody"

*So foul a sky clears not without a storm.*
—William Shakespeare

The Kissinger initiative and the Geneva conference that resulted from
it, although not successful in settling the Zimbabwean civil war,
marked a turning point in attempts to mediate a settlement there. First,
although the transition to majority rule was not won by the liberation
movements, the fact that Smith had conceded the principle of majority
rule meant that future conferences could concentrate on the hard details
of how to get there. Second, until Geneva, all concerned believed that
if the principle of majority rule was conceded by Smith, everything else
would fall into place. At Geneva it became apparent to all that the
difficult part lay ahead and involved developing specific proposals
concerning the constitution of an independent Zimbabwe and the
arrangements of the transition and cease-fire necessary to get there.
Third, Geneva put to rest the notion that a negotiated end of the war
could be obtained by the parties on their own. Finally, while the
purpose at Geneva was to establish a transitional government in
Rhodesia, the British learned that it was crucial to first reach agreement
about the constitution for the new country before deciding how power
would be transferred.

   The quest for a negotiated settlement continued in 1977 and 1978
with new actors attempting to play a mediating role. Cyrus Vance, the
new U.S. secretary of state, and David Owen, Britain's new foreign
secretary, decided to take upon themselves the trouble of finding an end
to the Zimbabwean war. Their efforts did not produce a settlement
because the antagonists perceived that their alternatives were superior
to any likely political settlement. These perceptions, however, were
affected by the actions of the mediators. At various times, the policies
of Vance and Owen shaped or reinforced the preferences of the actors
in ways that tended to lessen the possibility of settlement.

## The Origins of the New Initiatives

In October 1976, Cyrus Vance prepared a briefing for Jimmy Carter on new directions for U.S. foreign policy should Carter win the presidential election in November. Vance argued that an important priority be placed on human rights and relations between industrialized and nonindustrialized countries. It was important that a new administration not permit its conflict with the Soviet Union to be a dominant lens for viewing global and economic problems. As for the specific problem of Rhodesia, Vance counseled:

> The proposed Kissinger formula is fraught with pitfalls which I will not attempt to sketch. It is clear, however, that the new Administration will probably be faced with a decision on the implementation of the Kissinger plan. Among the available possibilities, I would recommend that the U.S. be prepared to modify the Kissinger proposals to make them more acceptable to the Africans, should that prove to be a stumbling block, and use our leverage on South Africa and Southern Rhodesia to gain acceptance. This should be coupled with letting the British take the lead, as they appear to be willing to do. (Vance 1983, 451)

Vance did not spell out what leverage he had in mind with regard to Rhodesia and South Africa.

Upon taking office, Carter and his advisers on Africa—Andrew Young, Richard Moose, and Anthony Lake—chose Rhodesia as a "test case" for U.S. intentions:

> American participation in resolving the conflicts in Rhodesia and Namibia and in seeking an end to apartheid in South Africa was vital. It was essential to demonstrate to the Third World our understanding of and willingness to take a leading role in dealing with their problems. . . . If the only alternative for the Africans was civil war, our ability to influence events would be greatly reduced and that of the Soviets correspondingly increased.
>
> If the United States did not support social and political justice in Rhodesia, Namibia, and South Africa itself, Africans would correctly dismiss our human rights policy as mere cold war propaganda, employed at the expense of the peoples of Africa. (Vance 1983, 256–257)

In December, Vance had told Ivor Richard that the United States was willing to help bring an end to the war in Rhodesia. Early in 1977, Jimmy Carter wrote to the Front Line presidents to assure them he would work for a negotiated settlement. He took firm action in moving to repeal the Byrd amendment, which permitted the United States to import chrome in violation of the United Nations boycott of Rhodesia. He also contacted the South African government and urged it to warn Smith that the United States would not accept a solution that excluded the Patriotic Front.

Vance's perception of the actors in the conflict differed dramatically from Kissinger's. Mugabe, who to Kissinger was an ideological radical, was to Vance "a professed Marxist," who was "in fact a pragmatist." Vance also had no aversion to bringing Samora Machel into the peace process, and even welcomed the addition of President Neto of Angola, the leader that Kissinger and South Africa had wanted to overthrow. As for Muzorewa, Vance felt that "particularly because he was exploring the idea of an arrangement with Smith, the rest of Africa increasingly regarded him with suspicion."

In sounding out the various players in the Rhodesia game, Vance learned from Pik Botha that although "Pretoria had been upset by Smith's rejection of Ivor Richard's recent proposal," South Africa "would not pressure Smith to join a settlement unacceptable to the Rhodesian whites." In talks with the British in February 1977, Vance learned that the British were apprehensive about the Rhodesian situation, but did not want to get involved in the peace process without U.S. assistance. It was felt that only the United States "could influence the South Africans and the front line states to persuade Smith and the guerrilla groups to resume negotiations."

Vance describes Britain's apprehensions as primarily economic:

> The British feared that if a serious peace process—which they believed could not mount without American political support—did not get underway soon, African efforts to impose a mandatory economic embargo against South Africa, the main loophole through which Rhodesia evaded sanctions, would intensify. Britain could veto UN sanctions, but only at the risk of retaliation against Britain's growing economic interests in black Africa. However, to acquiesce in sanctions would cause damage to the large British economic stake in the Republic of South Africa. . . . For my part, I had doubts about the effectiveness of the sanctions and agreed that the best way to avoid them was to breathe new life into the negotiating process. (Vance 1983, 261–262)

Vance believed, like those before him, "that the path to breaking down Smith's obduracy and deflecting him from an internal settlement was through Pretoria" (Vance 1983, 262). As for the details of the mediation effort, Vance, in conjunction with the new British foreign secretary, David Owen, outlined a plan whereby the United States and Britain would call a conference to work out a new constitution and arrangements for a six-month interim period during which the British would take over the government of Rhodesia and sponsor all-party elections. After sketching the outline, Owen traveled immediately to Southern Africa to canvass the antagonists and their patrons about such a plan.

While Britain and the United States were developing a united front toward Rhodesia, the participants in the conflict began a three-year process of maneuvering to form alliances that could win power. The driving motivation behind this process was the desire of each party to build a minimum winning coalition (Riker 1962). In the Zimbabwean conflict, this meant that on the Rhodesian side, Ian Smith would seek to provide minimum concessions in the attempt to attract just enough black support to make a new government palatable to Britain, the United States, and South Africa. On the nationalist side, this meant that the parties would ally themselves in ways that would increase their chances of coming to power, while also seeking to minimize cooperation in order to gain a bigger share of the overall prize. Potential coalitions would therefore seek the minimum number of allies necessary to gain power. Between the extremes of Smith and Mugabe sat the swing actors: Nkomo, Sithole, and Muzorewa.

At Geneva, Smith had put out preliminary feelers to Muzorewa to ascertain his interest in an agreement between them. If Muzorewa was initially hesitant to such a deal, he had more incentives January when the Front Line presidents publicly recognized the Patriotic Front as the sole legitimate representatives of the Zimbabwean people. This outraged Muzorewa and Sithole, because they deemed such action as tantamount to foreigners picking Zimbabwe's leaders for the Zimbabwean people. Mugabe and Nkomo had little to gain from Muzorewa or Sithole: neither would contribute to the military resources necessary to gain power. It made little sense to invite potential partners who would benefit from victory without contributing to it. Neither Sithole or Muzorewa could see gaining power in conjunction with the triumph of the Patriotic Front. Moreover, without taking any responsibility for equipping or leading the troops, the two stood to benefit from guerrilla success if Smith felt pressured into reaching some kind of accommodation. The real unknown wild card was Nkomo: even during his partnership with Mugabe, he had remained in contact with high officials in Smith's government. But given the Front Line presidents' decision to give sole support to the Patriotic Front, Nkomo temporarily sealed his fate to Mugabe's future.

Smith's inclination was to proceed step by step to see the minimum action necessary for a positive response from the outside world. First, he had attempted to build a black political movement through Chirau and the African chiefs. When this did not win the response he wanted, the pressure of the war drove Smith to look toward Muzorewa. In December 1976 and January 1977, in a series of briefings on the course of the war, Smith and his cabinet began to yield to the advice of their military commanders to begin a real search for some kind of political settlement.

The importance of the Kissinger initiative did not lie only in extracting Smith's public commitment to majority rule. Kissinger's intervention struck at the heart of the Rhodesian military effort, breaking the morale of many whites. In its own way it was as strong a military attack as had been leveled by the guerrillas to that time. White emigration had increased dramatically, and General Peter Walls had warned Smith in December 1976 that military morale was so low that many of his soldiers were planning on leaving Rhodesia when their enlistments expired (Flower 1987, 175–176).

On January 12, Ken Flower presented the cabinet "the bleakest picture they've ever had." Later that day David Smith, the Rhodesian minister of finance, told Flower that he "had had a bigger impact on his Cabinet colleagues than ever before," so Flower "got the impression that they had made the fateful decision to go for a political solution and accept the inevitability of black majority rule, perhaps under Bishop Muzorewa." Immediately after this, Flower met Jack Gaylord, who informed him "that the Ministers had adopted a hard line in 'Informal Cabinet' (Ministers meeting without officials present)." Such mixed messages brought Flower to despair: "The fact of the matter is that we still do not know where we stand. . . . On the one hand, the political scene has been set better (following the Front Line presidents' decision to support only the Patriotic Front) giving us a better opportunity to produce a settlement; on the other hand the P.M. may feel he has no option but to close his party's ranks and fight it out regardless" (Flower's diary, quoted from Flower 1987, 177).

On January 14, the Rhodesian War Council was also informed of the dire situation:

> Council was advised that the OCC assessment of the military situation was that the country was losing so much ground militarily that even with general mobilization, which would have a detrimental effect on the economy and which should be introduced only as a last resort, matters could only be prolonged. . . . it was stressed that action was required very soon, as the Security forces would be unable to hold the position indefinitely. ("Minutes of Meeting of War Council," in Flower 1987, 177)

Yet, with all of the warnings from the security chiefs, Smith and his cabinet moved slowly. Flower complained that he "continued to make the point time and time again in War Council that the war could not be won militarily," but was stymied by "a group of politicians in that forum who could not have been more retrogressive" (Flower 1987, 178).

By late January, Smith publicly stated his intention of looking toward an internal settlement, a move that brought the support of John Vorster. Smith's announcement came immediately before the region was again the focus of international attention. From February to the end of March, Southern Africa was visited by no less than Andrew Young, Fidel Castro, and Soviet president Nikolai Podgorny.

## Developments, April to September 1977

In April 1977, David Owen embarked on his own trip to Southern Africa to consult with the nationalist parties, Ian Smith, the Front Line presidents, and John Vorster. He brought only the skeleton of a settlement plan, a fact that angered the Patriotic Front and pleased Ian Smith. Both Kaunda and Nyerere expressed doubts about a new round of initiatives. Nyerere, especially, felt that the conflict should be allowed to mature, that Smith understood only force and would never relinquish power. The Tanzanian president also expressed his view that Vorster could not be expected to pressure Smith. The best that could be hoped for, urged Nyerere, is that South Africa not prevent majority rule from coming to Rhodesia.

Even with the Front Line presidents' skepticism, Owen received their backing on two fundamental points: a large U.S. role in any conference and the inclusion of all the nationalist parties in any talks that were held. These points, however, were contested by Mugabe and Nkomo, who set out three conditions for their participation: (1) the Patriotic Front and Britain would be the only actors at any conference; (2) U.S. involvement would be prohibited, for it threatened to further internationalize the conflict; and (3) the British had to give assurances that they would back up the conference with explicit action to strip Ian Smith of power.

Owen traveled to Cape Town, where he met Vorster and Smith, both of whom listened to Owen but remained noncommittal to his framework. Owen then proceeded to Rhodesia, where he spent two days. In a televised interview in Rhodesia, Owen was forthright and candid. He responded once by saying that he believed that the guerrillas would win if a settlement was not reached; he emphasized that trust was the necessary ingredient for a settlement to work; and he also admitted that it was a gamble for the whites to hand over power but that his role was to "reduce the amount of the gamble." Upon his return to London, Owen's candor slipped into tactlessness. In a line that would come back to haunt him, he finished a public briefing with Parliament by saying, "I must tell the House that if anyone believes that guarantees can be built into constitutions, or into statements, he is living in a fool's paradise" ("Extracts from Debate in British House of Commons, 4.19.77," in Baumhogger 1984, 315). Such statements did little to increase Rhodesian confidence in the negotiation process.

Smith emerged from Owen's journey in good position. By listening to Owen and not demanding preconditions for talks, he looked more reasonable than the Patriotic Front. More important, relations between Smith and Vorster seemed to have mended substantially. The *Times* (London) reported that officials in Rhodesia and South Africa considered their ties to be at the "highest point for years. The Rhodesians now regard the South Africans as an ally rather than a neutral referee." Such closeness was backed up by South African increases in weapons to offset new weapons that ZIPRA was receiving from the Soviet Union (*Guardian*, April 28, 1977).

In the aftermath of Owen's trip, the British and Americans decided to form a joint consultative team composed of Under Foreign Secretary John Graham and U.S. Ambassador Stephen Low, who were given the tasks of hammering out specific proposals on a constitution, interim government, and cease-fire. They were to do this in a series of shuttle trips between the various capitals of Southern Africa, where they would discuss proposals with all of the participants.

On the U.S. side, the Carter administration had decided to hold direct talks with the South African government. Walter Mondale met John Vorster in Vienna on May 19 and 20. Unlike Kissinger's meeting with Vorster the previous year, Carter felt that, although the United States desired Vorster's practical help on Rhodesia, it should be made clear to Vorster that the United States wanted change within South Africa. Carter and Mondale did not want the meeting to be used to legitimize South Africa's domestic politics. The most incisive evaluation of the Mondale-Vorster talks came from Vorster himself, who claimed that they "might well have been talking different languages."

The meeting was indicative of what happens when words cease to have similar meanings. When Henry Kissinger approached Vorster, the two leaders shared an understanding about the need to fight communist aggression and their mutual interest in "moderate" black regimes and South Africa's stabilizing role in the region. South Africa, by working for change in Rhodesia, would buy themselves time in Namibia and at home, while also assisting the United States to hold the line against Soviet intercession in Southern Africa. When Mondale met Vorster, the U.S. vice-president argued that South Africa's racial policies were contributing to communist aggression by providing the injustice that others could manipulate. Mondale was said to be careful not to use the term "majority rule," preferring instead to talk of "full participation." Vorster chose to see the two as the same thing and came away berating Mondale.

At the time, Mondale took criticism for his performance, and it was inferred that this meeting marked a turning point in South Africa's views toward its role in the region. I have argued otherwise: that by the end of 1976, Vorster could no longer actively follow a policy of limited change in Southern Africa. Although the proponents of the "total onslaught" perception had not triumphed, they had been able to block their domestic opponents from carrying out an alternative policy. In the interregnum, South Africa refused to pressure Smith, and hard-liners such as P. W. Botha could push for increased military aid for the Rhodesians. The only effect of Mondale's behavior was to bolster the position of those in the South African government who had argued that the soft line in Southern Africa would never be enough to satisfy international opinion.

In the aftermath of the Mondale-Vorster talks, there were signs of renewed intransigence by Ian Smith. Smith informed the Graham and Low team that he would accept only conditional suffrage accompanied by educational qualifications for voting. At the end of May, the Rhodesian army struck sixty miles over land into Mozambique on a five-day attack against refugee camps and guerrilla bases. The attack came amidst increasing reports of diminishing morale within the Rhodesian army and increasing penetration by guerrillas into the country.

Against this backdrop, Vance and Owen met in Paris in June to evaluate the results of Graham and Low's shuttle diplomacy. As to the peace process itself, the Patriotic Front had refused to meet Low but had discussions with Graham (British Diplomat B. 1987, interview with author). On substantive issues the Patriotic Front was adamantly opposed to Smith's demand for arrangements that would afford special protections to the white minority or provide anything less than one person–one vote. The transitional arrangements were equally deadlocked. A final difficulty concerned what to do with the armed forces of each side. Should the guerrillas be immediately merged into the Rhodesian army? Should one or the other force form the backbone of a new Zimbabwean army? Should the merger take place before elections or afterward?

Owen believed that the parties would need the armed presence of outside troops to increase the success of a cease-fire. Owen's first idea—the use of British troops—was vehemently opposed in Parliament, with some members going so far as to predict that a "British Vietnam" would result. An obvious alternative was a United Nations force, but Owen felt that the Rhodesians would view such a force as partial to the Front and therefore veto that option. Vance and Owen chose to present to the parties the possibility of a force composed of Commonwealth troops, who would supervise the elections and cease-fire and remain in Rhodesia for only a brief time.

With new questions and ideas in hand, the consultative team set off for another round of visits in July. In Vance's words, Low and Graham returned to Africa "only to encounter intransigence on all sides":

Nkomo demanded that negotiations be solely among the Patriotic Front, Smith and the British, thus excluding Muzorewa, Sithole and other black nationalists. Nkomo, presumably speaking for Mugabe, seemed willing to accept a Commonwealth peacekeeping force during the transition and acknowledged the necessity for elections. Smith was adamant that he would not accept any solution that turned over power to Nkomo and Mugabe after a short transition period. We felt that he was trying to develop a parallel negotiating track with Muzorewa and Sithole as a way of splitting the Patriotic Front by attracting Nkomo into a black majority government, leaving Mugabe isolated. (Vance 1983, 267)

In July and August, the British government worked out specific proposals to be handed to the antagonists. The United States was willing to stand by such proposals and back Owen's idea that no party should be allowed to veto a settlement. In theory, if either Smith or the Patriotic Front accepted the conditions and the other did not, Britain would be willing to bring that party to legality. To ensure that all of the patrons were "on-side," Owen thought it best that the specific proposals be presented to Julius Nyerere during his scheduled visit to Washington in August and to Pik Botha in London at about the same time.

The proposals called for an independence constitution that would provide universal suffrage; 20 percent white representation in a national legislature; a presidential system of government; an eight-year guarantee of protected representation for whites, after which disproportionate white representation could be voted out by simple majority; and an extensive bill of rights that called for compensation for any property that was appropriated for redistribution and that ensured the honoring of civil servant pensions from the preindependence regime. The plan envisioned a six-month period during which a British resident commissioner would take over the reins of government and conduct elections. During that period, the country would abide by a transitional constitution. Police functions would remain in the hands of the existing Rhodesian police, but a merged Zimbabwean National Army would be formed during the transition. The British presence would be supplemented by a United Nations force. Finally, the plan foresaw the establishment of a billion-dollar international development fund to be made available to Zimbabwe on its independence (United Kingdom 1977).

President Carter presented the proposals to Julius Nyerere during a state visit in early August. Nyerere gave qualified approval but felt that as the proposals stood, it would be difficult to obtain Patriotic Front approval. Nyerere suggested that during the transition period the guerrillas should constitute the national army. Carter, acting unilaterally, accepted this provision and Nyerere promised to push the Front toward settlement.

When Owen heard that Carter had promised this to Nyerere, the British foreign secretary turned irate. The British Foreign and Commonwealth Office knew that the Rhodesians would never accept Nyerere's condition and that the proposals would therefore be a nonstarter. Vance met Nyerere in London on August 13 to attempt to retract Carter's commitment. Nyerere, however, came away from the meeting convinced that Vance endorsed his stipulation. In contrast to Vorster's description of his meeting with Mondale in May, Nyerere described his talk with Vance in glowing terms: "We found that we are talking the same language. It is very encouraging to find out that the secretary of state of the United States can be talking the same language with somebody who is trying to achieve independence for Zimbabwe" (Baumhogger 1984, 401).

The day before the Vance-Nyerere discussion, Owen met R. F. Botha to sound out his opinion on the proposals. Behind the scenes in South Africa, Vorster was encouraging Smith to proceed with his own settlement. South Africa's commitment to an internal settlement could have been read from a speech that Botha gave in New York in June. At that time Botha hinted that

> the British/American initiative on Rhodesia may, however, be faced with a dilemma whether or not to proceed with a constitution, and with subsequent election based thereon, which has enjoyed the endorsement of the supporters of the major black and white parties who support a peaceful negotiating process towards independence, as against the implacable opposition of the Patriotic Front which believes that power stems from the barrel of the gun.
>
> The decisions to be made in this context will prove as good a test case as any of the genuineness of the commitments of the United States and British Governments to the list of principles—which particularly the United States Government—has propounded with such forthrightness, indeed with such dogmatism, in the last few weeks. (Baumhogger 1984, 365)

Botha had visited Rhodesia three times in the two months preceding his visit with Owen, and his most recent trip there, on August 6, had prompted Ian Smith to claim publicly to have "full backing" from South Africa for his internal plans (Baumhogger 1984, 393). This meeting prompted Flower to write to Peter Walls that "if we are reading the signs correctly, John Vorster and those who count in South Africa have come to the conclusion that 'enough is enough' and that they are neither going to apply more pressure of any sort on Ian Smith nor give way to further pressures on themselves" (Flower 1987, 183). Not surprisingly, Botha refused to support the proposals when they were presented by Owen.

When Nyerere returned to Dar es Salaam on August 15, he gave a press conference at which he heaped praise on Carter and Vance, but confessed to some confusion because he had not found the same urgency and commitment in London as he had found in Washington. Five days later he provided the press with the source of his confusion:

> That army (the Patriotic Front's forces) will either by itself alone without any assistance from the international community get rid of Smith and become the army of independent Zimbabwe; or with the assistance of the international community might end the war much more quickly and get rid of Smith and become the army of independent Zimbabwe. Now that is the issue.
> I thought that in Washington I had made this position clear.... My purpose in going to the United States was to try and find out, since the Americans and the British were co-operating in evolving a solution of the Rhodesian problem, whether the Americans also understood this essential point, that Smith and his army must go. Having explained this in the United States, I found that President Carter and colleagues understood it and accepted it.
> ... it is in London where I got the confusion I told you. I was seeking for a little clarification.... I have received information both from Washington and London. Both the British High Commissioner and the American Ambassador saw me to clarify this point. On the basis of this clarification, I believe we are agreed.... The essential point is Smith's army has to be removed and the future army of independent Zimbabwe has to be based on the present army of the Patriotic Front. (Baumhogger 1984, 404)

The presentation of the formal proposals was then botched in almost every conceivable way. Nyerere's announcement coincided with a leak from Andrew Young or his staff of the details of the proposals on August 25, a full week before the planned formal presentation. Although Smith issued no formal response to the leaked proposals, he made it known informally that the new proposals were "totally unacceptable."

Owen and Young traveled to Lusaka on August 27 and 28, where they were told by the Patriotic Front and the Front Line presidents that, although they did not reject the proposals, their acceptance hinged on the disbanding of the Salisbury forces. In private, the presidents were dismayed at Owen's take-it-or-leave-it attitude and inferred that they would view the proposals solely as a basis for further negotiation (Martin and Johnson 1981, 269). Owen and Young then flew to Pretoria, where they failed to gain encouragement from John Vorster. Vorster raised Nyerere's comments and stated that they were unacceptable. The South African newspaper, the *Citizen*, claimed that Vorster told the mediators that their terms were "a non-plan, completely unworkable" (ARB, 4539).

The trip by Owen and Young coincided with a general election in Rhodesia. On August 31, the Rhodesian white electorate once again returned Ian Smith to office in a landslide victory, which all in Rhodesia acknowledged as a referendum concerning Smith's pursuit of a settlement with Muzorewa. On September 1, the Anglo-American proposals were made public. They contained no specific decree that the Patriotic Front forces would make up the army or police. Indeed, police duties were to be handled by the existing Rhodesian police, who would be under the supervision of the British resident commissioner. While Carter's pledge to Nyerere about the composition of the army was not in the specific proposals, Owen specifically announced that the liberation army would form the core of the armed forces (Baumhogger 1984, 423). The first proposal, in either an attempt to slough off the plan as meeting Nyerere's demand or through an unthinking choice of words, called for "the surrender of power by the illegal regime and a return to legality" (United Kingdom 1977, 3) and repeated three pages later that it was "a basic premise of the British and United States Governments that the present illegal regime will surrender power" (United Kingdom 1977, 6).

On the Rhodesian side, the phrase alienated the one group in power who could have pushed hard for a settlement: the military commanders and top intelligence officers. Not only was their pride wounded by the connotation of surrender, it was a practical matter as well. If a settlement was to be reached, any mediator would need the Rhodesian commanders in position during the cease-fire and transition to ensure that no troops would rebel against the arrangements.

Owen and Young, however, tried to bluff that they had the leverage to coerce the parties into settlement. During their stay in Salisbury, the two met Sithole and assured him that the consequences for any party that refused the plan would be prohibitive. The minutes of the meeting reveal the mediators' confidence in their powers of persuasion:

> The question was asked . . . "What if Smith throws this plan out of doors . . . What then?"
> Dr. Owen stated categorically that both the American and British Governments would go ahead with the plan.
> Ambassador Young interjected that Smith has never had to face a "United" United States Government before this. . . . President Carter was committed to see this [plan] through to the end. . . . Pressure, Ambassador Young said, would be applied where necessary.
> Dr. Owen said that there were many options open to the American and the British Governments in terms of pressures to be applied to any dissident governments. . . . There could be a ratification of the White Paper by the United Nations with penalties to be imposed on any Nation attempting to undermine the settlement. . . . It was . . . intimayed [sic] . . . that South Africa could be a leading candidate for such pressures should they not abide by the terms of the White Paper. . . .
> . . . Discussing the possibility of some party using the veto against

the proposals, Ambassador Young said that any such party would have to mount more power than the United States, the Western World and Great Britain put together to defeat the plan. (Minutes 1977)

Neither the Patriotic Front nor Salisbury officially rejected the proposals, but neither party endorsed them. The Front wanted the transition period used to disarm the white regime so that progress toward independence would be irrevocable. Smith refused to countenance guerrilla control of the army and reacted angrily to the notion that what was demanded of him was surrender instead of a negotiated, peaceful transfer of power. He went so far as to say that Owen was revenging some long-held personal grievance toward the Rhodesian people. Stuck in the middle were Muzorewa and Sithole. The *Times* summed up their dilemma:

> Bishop Muzorewa and Mr. Sithole have no interest in the Nkomo-Mugabe demand, which they would see as a licence for civil war. They urgently want peaceful elections on adult franchise to produce a black government with one or other of them as prime minister. They cannot want the guerrillas in charge of those elections.

It was as if, as one reporter described it, the proposals "were calculated to upset everybody" (quoted in Martin and Johnson 1981, 273).

## *September 1977 to March 1978: The Politics of Partnerships*

The next six months would be full of uncertainty as the individual parties weighed the prospective gains and risks of potential partnerships against the backdrop of an intensifying war that Rhodesia was losing. In the immediate aftermath of the announcement of the Anglo-American proposals, Smith looked inward for allies to Muzorewa and Sithole and outward to Nkomo. His first choice for partnership was Nkomo, and in mid-September Smith arranged to meet with Kaunda on September 25 to discuss possible solutions to the conflict. Although no agreement was reached, Smith and Kaunda felt it worthwhile to hold more talks. When a week later word leaked about the meeting, the two leaders were rebuked from all sides. Muzorewa and Sithole argued that the parties were stepping outside the bounds of the Anglo-American proposals; Nyerere sharply criticized Kaunda for such a potentially divisive move; and Mugabe, who did not accept Kaunda's assurances that Nkomo was not present at the meeting, postponed discussions on the further merger of the two guerrilla forces. Although this dissension did not force a public split between ZANU and ZAPU, "months of careful preparation aimed at strengthening the fractious alliance were wrecked overnight" (Meredith 1980, 318).

Just as Nkomo was the lesser committed partner of the Front, Kaunda was the weakest link in collective action by the Front Line presidents. Kaunda's own political survival began to hang in the balance because of the Rhodesian conflict. As Ronald Libby explains,

> The leadership of the ruling United National Independence party adopted a doctrinaire foreign policy of complying with United Nations Security council Resolution 232 against Rhodesia for declaring Unilateral Declaration of Independence despite Zambia's exemption. Zambia complied with the sanctions from 1973 to 1978 by discontinuing its trade with Rhodesia. This action involved great economic costs to Zambia since Rhodesia was the country's major lowest-cost supplier.
>
> When Zambia's means of paying for its imports—the sale of copper on world markets—declined seriously beginning in 1975, the government was forced to drastically curtail its imports. The reduction significantly affected the availability of consumer goods for the large urban wage-earning population, resulting in severe shortages of consumer goods, high unemployment, inflation and industrial strikes. (Libby 1987, 230)

By 1977, 25 percent of the urban work force in Zambia was unemployed, and a devaluation of currency by 20 percent in 1976 had dramatically raised the cost of living, especially for the poorest urban dwellers (Libby 1987, 241). By 1977, the "pressure on the government from urban wage earners reached the point where the Minister of Finance John Mwanakatwe was forced to acknowledge that the shortages of essential commodities were the most sensitive political issue in the country" (Libby 1987, 241). Such pressures forced Kaunda to look for possible routes to end the Rhodesian conflict, even if it meant he traveled alone.

In November 1977, the British decided to push the parties to settlement. They dispatched Lord Carver as the designated British resident commissioner for Rhodesia, and General Prem Chand of the United Nations as his assistant, to Southern Africa to attempt to work out details for a cease-fire. The first meeting of Carver and Chand with the Patriotic Front was held in Lusaka. When the two generals arrived in the Zambian capital, they found that Mugabe—still angry with Kaunda—had refused to travel to Zambia. Carver and Chand proceeded to Dar es Salaam to meet the Front in what were to be two days of meetings. The meeting instead lasted one hour; a spokesman for the Front claimed that the meeting would have been briefer, but Carver spoke much more slowly than expected. When the two emissaries traveled to Rhodesia, they were met with basic hostility by the Salisbury government. On November 19, Ian Smith dismissed the visitors as "a travelling circus" (quoted in Flower 1987, 185).

Both sides of the struggle were equally critical of the mediators' focus on a cease-fire without having attained agreement on the end stage—the constitution. Owen and Vance had originally believed that the constitution was the key to a settlement, but they chose to work simultaneously on the three aspects of the package—constitution, transition, and cease-fire—rather than addressing each aspect in progression. The end result was a lack of clarity as to what would come first: a settlement or a cease-fire.

Coinciding with the confusion engendered by Carver's visit, trouble was again brewing for the ZANU-ZAPU alliance. On November 18, Zambia's foreign secretary announced that independence should be granted to a new Zimbabwe before elections took place, a demand that was reiterated by Kaunda two days later. The Zambians suggested as an alternative a plan for all parties to form a Government of National Unity that would govern for four or five years and then call elections. This was a proposal way out of line with the Owen and Vance ideas and threatened to bring their mediation to a halt. Mugabe immediately denied that the Patriotic Front supported such a demand. Nyerere chastised Kaunda for proposing the idea and hinted that Kaunda could only be reasoning that his choice for president of Zimbabwe, Nkomo, could not win an election. Nyerere added that the price for such a demand would be a fundamental loss of legitimacy by the rebels, who claimed to be the genuine representatives of the Zimbabwean peoples. The split spilled over to the Patriotic Front when George Silundika, ZAPU's vice-secretary for publicity and information, referred to the demand for preindependence elections as an "influenza which is likely to sicken the body-politic of Zimbabwe" (*Zambia Daily Mail*, November 25, 1977, in Baumhogger 1984, 471).

While the Front Line presidents were wrangling over Kaunda's demand, Ian Smith announced on November 24 that he had entered into talks with Muzorewa, Sithole, and Chirau to reach a settlement that would include majority rule. At the same time, the Rhodesian military struck into Mozambique and massacred more than a thousand guerrillas and refugees at one of ZANLA's main bases. Owen, showing his exasperation at the foiling of his initiatives, tactlessly remarked that maybe such an attack would convince the Patriotic Front that the Rhodesian military "was not yet on its back." The Front pointed out to Owen that the ability of an army to kill and maim unarmed civilians could hardly be read as a sign of strength, and that, moreover, such a statement implied tacit approval of the raid as a bargaining move. The direct effect of Owen's statement was for the Front to decline an invitation to meet with him in London in mid-December.

By then the situation was in extreme flux for every party in the conflict. The Smith-nationalists talks faltered through fits and starts, and by late December the halting nature of the internal negotiations "put everyone in a quandary: whether to support the Anglo-American initiative, Smith's initiative, or indeed any initiative at all" (Flower 1987, 193). The Front Line presidents and Patriotic Front had a heated meeting in Beira, Mozambique, on December 19 to bring back a semblance of unity to the alliance. Nyerere, in particular, wanted Nkomo to merge his army with Mugabe's, a demand that Nkomo dismissed. Such a move by Nkomo would reduce his flexibility if he decided to seek his own settlement with any of the internal parties. At one of the breaks, Nyerere, Kaunda, and Nkomo could be heard outside the conference room in an argument that concluded when Nkomo replied in Ndebele, "I am not a kid. If I have refused, I have refused" (*Zambia Daily Mail*, December 20, 1977, in Baumhogger 1984, 494).

As 1978 began, the security situation in Rhodesia was significantly worse. In April 1977, Peter Walls had estimated that there were 2,350 armed guerrillas inside the country; in January 1978, the estimate had climbed to 8,000 inside Zimbabwe with ZIPRA force levels in Zambia over 8,000. The GDP for the year was –7 percent; defense expenditures exceeded a million dollars a day; the inability of the Rhodesian regime to provide basic services to its farmers led to the decimation of livestock; and white emigration totaled almost 11,000 for the year. Casualties for guerrillas, Rhodesian soldiers, and civilians in 1977 surpassed the totals in each category for those from 1972 to 1976 combined. In anticipation of future success, the Patriotic Front had christened 1978 the Year of the People, which, they assured everyone, would be the forerunner of the Year of the People's Storm, when the Front would sweep the whites out of power (figures from Wilkinson 1980; Cilliers 1985; Martin and Johnson 1981).

The Smith regime could not plead ignorance of the situation. On January 17, 1978, Flower briefed the Rhodesian cabinet on the war:

> The overall picture is sombre. Our Half-Yearly Threat assessment, just completed, confirms the steadily deteriorating internal security situation, as forecast, and holds out little prospect of improvement other than through the achievement of a political settlement. Time is no longer on our side. Like never before, it is vital to our interests to secure African allies against the Patriotic Front before they become disinterested or are swamped by numbers and the overall spread of terrorism throughout the country. ("Briefing," in Flower 1987, 193)

Vance and Owen decided to breathe some new life into the peace process by inviting the Patriotic Front to Malta at the end of January to once again discuss security arrangements for the transition. Small progress was made there as the Front softened their stand against an outside military presence.  Mugabe, Nkomo, and Owen agreed on a lessened role for the British commissioner, who would now answer to a governing council made up of leaders from all of the different parties. There remained, however, a great distance between the two sides on the composition of the army.  Finally, Mugabe and Nkomo were angered at Owen putting Sithole and Muzorewa on a par with them.  The parties concluded by agreeing to meet again in March for a second round.

Mugabe returned to Mozambique to find that a remnant of soldiers who had opposed his leadership at Geneva had attempted a coup in his absence.  Mugabe, with the aid of Tongogara and Samora Machel, put down the uprising and eliminated the last threat to his leadership in ZANU (Cabezas 1978, 60).  The cost to Mugabe, however, was that his power rested on the shoulders of Machel and Tongogara.

The first major move in the coalitional game occurred on February 15, when Smith, Muzorewa, Sithole, and Chirau announced that they had reached an agreement in principle on a settlement that would provide one person–one vote.   The announcement brought widely different replies from the would-be mediators. Andrew Young dismissed the agreement as "a recipe for civil war."  Owen, on the other hand, embraced the tentative agreement, telling Parliament on February 16 that "this is a significant move towards majority rule and it should be welcomed" (ARB, 4757).

Vance detected a willingness on Owen's part to accept the internal settlement:

> David Owen's faith in the Anglo-American proposal was waning, and he was increasingly drawn toward the idea of building upon the internal settlement. He saw in it both an opportunity and a danger.  If a way could be found to broaden participation in the Salisbury agreement—by which Owen meant including Nkomo—and to modify it sufficiently to make it acceptable to African opinion, it might provide the basis for an early settlement. On the other hand, even if the Salisbury agreement failed to gain international support, once elections were held there would be heavy pressure from Parliament to recognize the new black government and finally have done with the Rhodesian millstone around Britain's neck. Owen was acutely sensitive to the harm this outcome would do to British and Western interests in Africa and the strains it would place on U.S.-U.K. relations.
>
> Against this background, Owen concluded that he must intensify his efforts to bring Nkomo and Smith together. (Vance 1983, 287)

Owen met Sithole in a series of meetings between February 20 and 23.  Sithole's minutes from the meeting show that Owen was at a loss as to how best to keep the mediation effort alive.  After Owen briefed Sithole on the Malta conference, Sithole informed Owen of the specific contents of the internal settlement.  Owen pointed out potential problems that would impede international recognition: white control of the military and law and order; 50 percent white representation within the cabinet, and Smith's presence in any government. Owen made it clear that he wanted a way to marry the internal settlement to the Anglo-American process.

Owen was often contradictory in the meetings. At one point he asserted that he stood by his pledge that no single group be afforded a veto, yet he insisted that Nkomo and Mugabe be involved in talks. Toward the end of the first meeting, most of Owen's comments concerned splitting Nkomo from Mugabe:

> In Mugabe's organization there is more friction and fragmentation than in ZAPU. The Mugabe people have an element that would never accept a compromise . . . how you handle Nkomo and his people seems to me to be crucial. . . . If you can include one of the External Nationalists, then that would help in gaining recognition at the earliest time . . . the real question is how do we bring Joshua in . . . the further you go down the road without Joshua, the harder it would be for him to come . . . Joshua has been realistic to me. He now wants direct negotiation with Smith on the Anglo-American proposals . . . His problem is that he cannot be seen to be breaking from Robert Mugabe before he gets a concrete offer. . . . Before he breaks with Robert, he must be assured of success. (Minutes 1978)

Sithole suggested that a direct confrontation with Nkomo might be the best option. This horrified Owen: "You should be very careful on that. We have stopped invasions into Zambia. This could create an international problem of immense dimensions. Kaunda has been under enormous pressure to involve the Cubans and Russians. Given enough pressure he could go"[1] (Minutes 1978).

The settlement between Smith, Muzorewa, Sithole, and Chirau was finalized on March 3, 1978. The agreement reserved twenty-eight out of 100 seats for whites, a clause that would be reviewed in ten years for possible renewal. The twenty-eight white seats would be prevented from entering into a coalition government. The agreement contained clauses for a bill of rights, dual citizenship, and police and security forces "free from political interference." Any vote on altering provisions of the constitution would need seventy-eight votes to pass, thereby providing the whites with a blocking mechanism. A transitional government consisting of an executive council composed of the four leaders and a ministerial council composed of "equal numbers of black and white ministers" would be responsible for the future composition of the military services and the bringing about of a cease-fire ("Internal Settlement Agreement," in Baumhogger 1984, 531).

The agreement put incredible strains on the Anglo-American partnership. Vance expressed to Owen that the United States would not be a party to splitting the Patriotic Front. Within a matter of weeks, two diplomatic tiffs were rumored: the first between Owen and the U.S. undersecretary for African affairs, Richard Moose, who criticized Owen for welcoming the settlement, and the second between Owen and Andrew Young, who accused the British of wanting to "wash their hands" of the Rhodesian problem. The British-American split mirrored a split that was occurring within the U.S. administration, as Jimmy Carter expressed interest in the internal settlement, much to the consternation of Young and others. Carter went so far as to order Andrew Young to refrain from comments on the agreement. As a compromise among all parties, Carter labeled the internal settlement inadequate and announced the intention of the United States and Britain to hold an all-parties conference on Rhodesia to find some common ground between the Anglo-American proposals and the internal agreement. The conference, however, never got off the ground. The Salisbury coalition demanded that any conference should simply recognize the change they had ushered in, and the Front refused to attend any talks that would venture outside the scope of the Anglo-American talks.

In an attempt to salvage their position, Owen, Young, and Vance traveled first to Dar es Salaam, on April 14 and 15, to meet Mugabe and Nkomo in order to continue the Malta discussions on security arrangements. The postmeeting statements of the parties reveal widely different interpretations of what happened. Owen implied that the meeting had been a setback to the Anglo-American proposals, but the Front felt that they had made substantive concessions, including agreeing to further talks. Mugabe and Nkomo stated that since the last meeting in Malta, they had accepted that the British resident commissioner be given the wide-ranging powers the British demanded and that the police and military could be under his control, as long as the Front's forces were included in the transition police and army. When, in the aftermath of the talks, Owen downplayed the Front's concessions and accused the Front of intransigence, the Patriotic Front assumed that the British were setting them up in order to recognize the internal settlement.

Vance's memoirs support Owen's version of the meeting but suggest that the parties brought very different mindsets into the negotiations. Vance prefaces his description of the meeting by noting that "despite everything that had occurred since Malta, Nkomo and Mugabe still insisted on ignoring the changes in Salisbury" (Vance 1983, 288). This introductory line is central to understanding how each group approached Malta II, as it was called. Clearly, Vance and Owen had not ignored the changes in Salisbury and had reformulated what kind of settlement they were willing to live with. They viewed the internal agreement as a fundamental change that should have prompted the Front to radically reconsider their position. Before, Vance and Owen had viewed the

Anglo-American accords as a compromise lying between the extremes of the Front and Smith, but now the mediators were seeking a compromise between the extremes of the Anglo-American accords and the internal settlement. The Front, thinking that the mediators meant what they previously said about no party having a veto on their proposals, did not realize the range of settlements had changed. They came to Dar es Salaam believing that the Anglo-American settlement was a midpoint, and to show good faith, Mugabe and Nkomo tried to move toward it. The mediators, perhaps feeling the strain and pressures of having been presented with a fait accompli by Smith, entered the talks expecting that at a minimum the Front would heel to the Owen-Vance terms.

Upon visiting South Africa on April 16, the mediators interpreted Vorster's position as support for their efforts but an unwillingness to pressure Salisbury. In Rhodesia the next day, the mediators found no party willing to budge from the terms of the interim settlement. For one, the signals from Owen, in particular, gave Smith, Sithole, and Muzorewa reason to believe that if they held out, the British would eventually recognize them. Moreover, the positions of the Salisbury leaders precluded joining any talks that would call into question the terms of their agreement. To win domestic approval of blacks and whites within Rhodesia, the Salisbury leaders could not afford to have people doubt the viability of their plan. If immediately upon reaching an agreement the leaders were to enter into talks to alter that agreement, doubts would be raised about the efficacy of the internal settlement.

The Owen and Vance visit posed a real dilemma to the new regime. On March 13, ten days after the signing of the settlement, the new government established two official working parties whose purpose was "to put over an agreed and consistent explanation of the facts contained in the Constitutional agreement signed in Salisbury on 3 March, 1978" (Findley, March 13, 1978, in Rhodesia, Internal Working Party). The charge of the group was to "sell" the agreement, not only to those Western countries whose support was necessary if Rhodesia was to survive, *but also to the people inside Rhodesia.*

An immediate concern of the Internal Working Party was that the visits of Owen and Vance made it very difficult to sell the agreement within the country. Thus, not only were the internal settlement leaders not interested in the Anglo-American initiatives, they deemed them harmful to the implementation of their own settlement. The minutes of April 19, just two days after the Owen and Vance visit, stated:

> The vital need for unity in selling the Agreement was discussed again. . . . Mr. Mukone (UANC) then stated that as long as the Executive Council left room for the U.K. and the U.S. to change the agreement there will be doubt in the public's mind. He believed the Executive Council had to be forthright in statements as to whether the

Internal Agreement was final or not. Certain people were hesitating, "How can you sell an incomplete jacket? People don't know what it will look like."

For the good of the settlement there should be as few Owen/Vance type meetings as possible. They leave doubt in people's minds. In the final analysis the Agreement will be judged by the behavior of the Top Four (the executive council). People's doubts will be given substance if the Transitional Government gives the impression of entertaining the possibility of change. (Rhodesia, Internal Working Party, April 19, 1978)

The strategic dilemma for the leaders stemmed from the need to make a good impression on Vance and Owen (to sway them to recognition) and, at the same time, avoid any misunderstanding by the Rhodesian public about the leaders' commitment to the internal agreement. Vance and Owen's presence and their demands for inclusion of Nkomo and Mugabe did create confusion in Rhodesia as to whether the internal settlement was genuine and permanent. Attendance at an all-parties conference would have the same effect, so the internal leaders refused to accept the British and U.S. invitations to such an affair.

## May to August 1978: A Waiting Game

The viability of the new Salisbury government rested on four assumptions: first, that Muzorewa and Sithole could attract the guerrillas through an amnesty program; second, that active measures would be taken by the government to erase discriminatory laws; third, that an election for prime minister would take place and would act as a symbolic referendum of African acceptance of the internal agreement; and fourth, that the international community would recognize the government and lift sanctions. For the next year, contradictions and tensions would render the government ineffective against the guerrilla war. During that time, the Salisbury government waited for domestic pressure in the United States and Britain to alter those governments' policies on Rhodesia, while the mediators waited for the settlement to fail and drive Smith, Muzorewa, and Sithole back to the negotiating table.

In the wake of the refusal of the internal leaders to attend a conference, the Anglo-American process was at a loss. The best that could be done under the circumstances was to continue the Low and Graham team as interlocutors with the principal actors, and keep the proposals and conference on the table as an alternative. While the Patriotic Front was willing to accept such a conference, Sithole and Muzorewa absolutely refused. Vance recalls that as time went by, Muzorewa was becoming even more determined than Smith not to negotiate with the Patriotic Front. He expected to be leader of Zimbabwe by 1979 and was confident that once he acceded to power many of the rank-and-file guerrillas would choose peace rather than fight a black government. . . . I doubted Muzorewa would be receptive to negotiations with the Patriotic Front until he recognized that the Salisbury agreement would not produce international recognition. (Vance 1983, 290)

Owen persisted in trying to bring Smith and Nkomo together, a policy that worried Vance. On Smith's part, there were signs of growing support of the internal settlement in the United States, as some conservative members of Congress began to snipe at Carter's nonrecognition policy.

On June 7, 1978, Kenneth Towsey, the director of the Rhodesian Information Office in Washington (and unofficial Rhodesian ambassador), returned to Rhodesia to counsel on "what must be achieved internally before the agreement could be sold in America" (Rhodesia, Internal Working Party, May 30, 1978). In his briefing to the Internal Working Party, Towsey stressed that public opinion and 90 percent of the U.S. media were behind the settlement, but that the administration still had concerns about it. He mentioned three sources of the Carter administration's hesitancy about the new regime:

1. Certain reservations about the honesty of the Agreement. . . . These misgivings exist in the official mind and are constantly being paraded in columns of the NY Times, which pretends that the Agreement is a contrivance. It is important for you to remove these suspicions.

2. [Concern] that if the PF is not included . . . there will be an escalation of conflict here . . . greater and more Soviet aid . . . creating an extremely dangerous international situation . . . the possibility that South Africa might be drawn into the conflict if the Cubans and Soviets got into direct front line confrontation with Rhodesia. Concern would then be felt in American circles about their being seen to be fighting a war on the same side as the South Africans.

In my public statements I am offering a different point of view. I am suggesting that with the Cubans already very heavily involved in Africa, they would, if they got involved militarily in Rhodesia, be facing a far more formidable opposition than they had encountered anywhere else. This might give them pause.

Now the Cuban soldiers are looking like heroes in Cuba. They might not look so heroic if they were taking some casualties. Conceivably, if this happened the African adventure would not look very good in Cuba itself. If the undertakings given by Dr. Kissinger were to be fulfilled now—that is to say the removal of sanctions on the formation of the transitional government—there would be a most energizing boost to the Rhodesian economy. It would give us overt access to the weaponry we have to get under the table now, thus transforming the terms of battle in our favour. In view of these considerations, support for the Agreement would tend to diminish the conflict rather than escalate it.

3. A desperate desire . . . to look good in Africa: within the OAU, the FLS and particularly with Nigeria. . . . It is most important to break up the monolith of the OAU's support for the PF.

The success in turning the tide in the United States relied on successful elections and a reduction in the fighting:

If it could be adequately demonstrated that the elections were open, honest, and that a substantial electorate went to the polls, there would be powerful reason to suppose that the U.S. would accept the result of that election. I have to make one reservation. If there continued to be a heavy level of conflict it would seriously affect the decision of the U.S. government. Reducing the level of conflict is a terribly important factor in this situation.

Towsey concluded by summarizing the differences between the British and the Americans on the internal settlement:

There has been some movement. Broadly speaking, before the last Vance/Owen visit, the U.S. Government was more hostile to the Agreement than the British Government. I think that the British Government had moved to a position of greater sympathy towards the Agreement . . . because the Conservative Party was giving him [Owen] a very rough time. I think that the Vance/Owen visit was very useful. I think that Secretary Vance, during the short time he was here, became aware that there was much more to the situation than he had been given to understand by his policy advisers at lower levels. I think the visit opened up a gap between Mr. Vance's perceptions of the position and those of Mr. Young. I think that Mr. Vance is now somewhat mistrustful of Mr. Young's judgement in the Rhodesian situation. This will not lead to any immediate change in American attitudes. (Rhodesia, Internal Working Party, June 7, 1978)

Immediately after Towsey's visits, cracks began to show in the regime: Smith, in a televised interview on June 15, confessed that the regime had been unsuccessful at winning a cease-fire. On June 20, in the Rhodesian Parliament, members of the Rhodesian Front accused the Executive Council of "sitting on their collective posterior," failing to win a cease-fire, and blatantly misleading the government about the size of their support and contacts with the guerrillas. Black members of the Parliament castigated the government for failing to take a single action in repealing racist legislation. Some went so far as to demand talks with Nkomo and Mugabe.

The Salisbury regime had entered into a waiting game to see if their move would win recognition. In July, the black parties sent delegations to Europe and Africa to canvass opinion on recognition. In Britain, a delegation of ZUPO leaders met with a British diplomat at the Foreign and Commonwealth Office who informed them that "if the Transitional Government would agree to go to an all-party conference, the British Government would be forced to take cognizance of the Internal Settlement as it would be expected that Nkomo and Mugabe would walk out. The British Government would be more sympathetic to the Agreement if it was seen that the Land Tenure Act was repealed, all forms of discrimination removed and the protected villages dismantled" (Rhodesia, External Working Party, July 18, 1978).

A member of Muzorewa's newly formed party, the United African National Council (UANC), who had just returned from a trip throughout Africa reported that Kaunda was being squeezed and would crumble in a matter of time:

> Kaunda has a problem. He is seeking aid from Britain and the United States. Those countries have made a condition that their loans be repaid in time. It will therefore be necessary for Zambia to use cheaper export routes for its commodities. This affects Zambia's position regarding Rhodesia if he wants to get the finance. There are two pressures—pressure to de-escalate the war and pressure to re-open the border. He therefore is attempting to pressure Mr. Nkomo into accepting an all party conference. This is a way out. President Kaunda is taking a much softer line. He is no longer attacking the leaders here as he used to." (Rhodesia, External Working Party, July 18, 1978)

On July 26, the U.S. Senate was set to vote on a motion by Jesse Helms to remove U.S. sanctions on Rhodesia. This was a crucial battle for the Carter administration if they were to keep an all-parties solution alive. In Rhodesia, Ian Smith anxiously anticipated the results, calling the vote "the most exciting thing to happen for a long while because, the removal of sanctions, I think would have a far greater effect if it came from America than Britain or anybody else." At the last moment, a compromise bill was introduced by Senators Javits and Case that called for the continuation of sanctions and their removal if the Salisbury regime entered into negotiations with the Patriotic Front and held elections. The alternative bill passed on a 59-36 vote.

### Smith and Nkomo, Round Three

The Senate vote on sanctions proved a hard blow to the internal settlement. The time for waiting had passed. On August 3, Ken Flower, head of intelligence, addressed a joint meeting of the four top leaders and their ministers:

The scene is more than sombre. It's pretty desperate and needs desperate remedies. . . . So far we have failed—and none of us should be surprised if the rest of the world looks at it as failure . . . there are fewer ministers, White and Black, dedicated to your survival as a Government than there are undermining it by default. . . . Our professional assessment is that, individually and collectively, all four members of EXCO have lost support, and will continue to lose support unless the trend is reversed; whereas the Patriotic Front, and particularly the Mugabe faction, has gained and is gaining support. . . . There is hardly anything on record indicating that any faction represented in the Executive Council has achieved anything effective against the Patriotic Front. . . . You have proved more effective in fighting among yourselves than in any way getting to grips with the common enemy— exactly what Nkomo forecast. . . . The security situation has never been so desperate. . . . Over 6,000 terrorists within Rhodesia with plus or minus 30,000 lined up against us, and their numbers probably growing to about 40,000 before the end of the year—with more support and sympathy internally and externally than they have ever had. Meantime, our White Security Forces diminish in numbers and effectiveness. ("Brief by DG CIO to joint EXCO, MINCO, and NATJOC August 3, 1978," in Flower 1987, 207–208)

Flower had concluded that the only alternative was to bring Nkomo into the government, even if that meant conceding the top position to him. Through back channels (the British Government; "Tiny" Rowlands, chief executive officer of the huge conglomerate Lohnro; Joseph Garba, former Nigerian foreign minister; and Kaunda), Flower arranged another meeting between Smith and Nkomo. Flower believed that if Smith could act firmly, there was a real possibility of splitting Nkomo from Mugabe. Kaunda's position was weakening by the day, and his apprehension toward the expansion of ZIPRA in Zambia was growing rapidly. Once again he acceded to a secret meeting of Smith and Nkomo.

Flower succinctly describes Nkomo's quandary going into the talks:

He could see by now that only he or Mugabe could stop the war; he paid no heed to Muzorewa's contention that because the Internal Settlement included a genuine prospect for majority rule there was no point in continuing the war. Being more interested in power than in majority rule, the decision he had to make was based on whether he could more easily obtain power for himself in partnership with Mugabe, or in coalition with Smith, or through the barrels of his guns. (Flower 1987, 209)

According to Flower, in mid-August an agreement was reached between Smith and Nkomo that would install Nkomo as head of the transitional government. Nkomo stressed that he could not enter an agreement without Mugabe, but he believed that he could convince

Mugabe to join. Smith and Nkomo both left to inform their coalition partners of the deal. Nkomo then arranged for Garba, a third party with unquestionable progressive qualifications, to inform Nyerere and Mugabe that Smith was willing to "hand over power to the Patriotic Front." Upon hearing the news, Nyerere immediately vetoed the plan and demanded a meeting of all concerned in Lusaka.

A long, heated, six-hour meeting began with Nkomo presenting his version of the story. With the Front Line presidents and Garba present, Nkomo made it clear that the British, Soviets, and Nigerians knew what he was doing—and he did not intend for a second to keep anything from Mugabe. He said that Smith had called for the meeting and that any possibility for peace was worth pursuing. Nkomo, who found Smith to be "a sick man, a broken man," indicated that Smith offered what in effect was his surrender. Nkomo told the meeting that he had made it clear to Smith that he could not accept the offer unless Mugabe joined him.

Nyerere then led an analysis of Smith's motives. Smith would never surrender power, Nyerere asserted. His sole purpose must have been to split Nkomo from Mugabe and divide the Front Line presidents. Nyerere claimed that Smith, during the meeting with Nkomo, never mentioned Mugabe, which served as evidence of Smith's goal. Nyerere argued that Nkomo, by going along with Smith's charade, had put all the alliances against Smith in jeopardy. He further warned that if the Patriotic Front split, the result would be civil war. The presidents accepted Nyerere's version and pledged that no more secret diplomacy would be tolerated. Nkomo is said to have called Nyerere "a saboteur," and two days later Nkomo made the rift public, stating that he refused to rule out more talks with Smith and that Nyerere could not tell him what to do.

When the tale became public, some white Rhodesians applauded the efforts and hoped that the agreement would come off; others, including the *Rhodesia Herald*, blasted Smith for creating disarray in the transitional government and lying to the public. The secret moves by Smith split the three black leaders of the interim regime: Muzorewa and Sithole bitterly denounced the meeting, while Chirau praised it and publicly called for talks between the Patriotic Front and the Salisbury government.

This tension filtered from the top down in the three black political parties. For example, black members of the working parties became caught between their commitment to the March 3 agreement and to a transitional government that was not implementing any changes. As the transitional government refused to carry out reforms, the black leaders lost more credibility. As the black leaders lost credibility, whatever chance they had of attracting guerrillas in from the war vanished. By September, individuals within the working parties were bickering over the course of the agreement and whether including Nkomo would end the violence. Moreover, the black groups, although nominally allied to fight the Patriotic Front, were engaged in active competition with each other for the right to rule "Zimbabwe-Rhodesia." The weakest link in the group was Chirau and ZUPO: he had the least to gain from the internal settlement because it was unlikely he would be elected prime minister. He could also see that Sithole and Muzorewa could not end the war. Chirau went so far as to campaign in Matabeleland on promises to bring back Nkomo, who would then lead the country. This infuriated supporters of Sithole and Muzorewa,[2] who felt such promises were undermining acceptance of the March agreement and who also knew they would lose out if Nkomo returned. A heated argument erupted in the Internal Working Party on September 6:

> *Mukone* [aide to Muzorewa]: If members of the Ministerial and Executive Councils want to bring Nkomo back, it is important that a policy should be defined so that the authority of the Transitional Government is not undermined. The discussions in the Chiefs' Assemblies in Matabeleland and Mashonaland have not helped the Transitional Government in identifying the common enemy. They should formulate a policy which will not undermine the Transitional Government.

> *Rutsito* [aide to Chirau]: If it is a question of saving lives, why is it not possible to go to an all party conference? Then the world would know that the country wants peace.

> *Masangomai* [aide to Sithole]: It is wrong to believe that if Nkomo returns the fighting will end.

> *Rutsito*: There should be an all party conference. Why is the Transitional Government afraid to go to one? If it failed, the Internal Settlement would be upheld and the British and Americans would have to take note of it instead of trying to foist a leader on an unwilling people. If it succeeds and a leader emerges who can bring peace, which is what the people want, it would be justified.

> *Masangomai*: If Nkomo returns, the fighting will not stop. He has no control. It is the Russians and the Cubans who trained his men in Angola and Zambia who are just waiting to come in. Nkomo is a tool and does not lead the men who profess loyalty to him. (Rhodesia, Internal Working Party, September 6, 1978)

Although there was still a possibility after the Front Line summit in Lusaka for Nkomo and Smith to carry out their deal, a military event put it to rest. ZAPU destroyed an Air Rhodesia Viscount passenger plane carrying fifty-six people. A particularly grisly aspect of the attack is that when the plane was downed, ZIPRA soldiers in the area then shot ten passengers who had survived the crash. It was not known whether the attack had been specifically sanctioned by Nkomo as a way of reestablishing his revolutionary credentials or was carried out by soldiers on their own with or without the purpose of destroying the possible agreement with Smith. This, however, was the effect of the attack: those whites who had hoped for Nkomo to defect from the Patriotic Front were horrified and demanded an end to all talks with him. In the cabinet, Smith and another Rhodesian Front member, Hilary Squires, demanded martial law and an intensification of the war into Zambia. Peter Walls quieted them down with the threat of a military coup (Flower 1987, 211).

As for ZANU's relations with ZAPU, Robert Mugabe seemed to be angrier with David Owen than with Nkomo. Mugabe finally had an explanation why the British and Americans had been so loath to carry out their plans for a conference, even though the Patriotic Front had insisted since April that they would attend. The British goal, Mugabe insisted, was to wait for the internal settlement to collapse and then salvage it by splitting Nkomo from the Front: "This was a complete departure from their Anglo-American proposals. This is the duplicity, utter dishonesty of which I have time and again accused Owen" (quoted in Baumhogger 1984, 681).

While Mugabe seemed to have taken it pretty easy on Nkomo, others within ZANU did not. On September 11, Nkomo, again attempting to reclaim the revolutionary mantle, ruled out any participation in an all-parties conference and claimed that the time had come for "total war." The next day, Edgar Tekere, one of the most radical of Mugabe's lieutenants, said flatly that ZANU had not ruled out a conference and criticized ZAPU for holding back its army against Smith (Baumhogger 1984, 665–666).

Kaunda, who because of the failure of the Nkomo-Smith talks had not received any relief, still faced a deteriorating domestic position. Elections were scheduled for December 12, and the leaders of the opposition were trumping Zambia's burden of supporting the revolutionaries as their main issue in the election. In particular, they opposed Zambia's closed border with Rhodesia, which had cost Zambia 744 million U.S. dollars since 1973 (Libby 1987, 243). The closing of the border had eliminated one of Zambia's main transport routes and had been undertaken even though the United Nations had given Zambia dispensation from complying with sanctions against Rhodesia.

On October 6, Kaunda buckled under to domestic political pressure and reopened the border with Rhodesia. To support the decision, the Zambians cited supply bottlenecks in Tanzania and Mozambique for needed fertilizer. This was immediately disputed by transport officials in Maputo and Dar es Salaam. Nyerere immediately promised to expedite any supplies that Zambia needed, but Kaunda refused. Once again an emergency Front Line meeting was held in Lusaka, where

Kaunda explained his position. Publicly, the other presidents supported Kaunda; privately, they were angered by Kaunda's decision.

The focus of diplomatic activity shifted to the United States as Smith, Muzorewa, Chirau, and Sithole visited the States as guests of a group of twenty-seven conservative senators, led by Jesse Helms. The State Department had originally refused a visa to Ian Smith, but intense pressure from Helms led them to rescind their refusal. The trip was undertaken to win sympathy for the internal settlement and to impress upon the United States the need to revoke sanctions against Rhodesia. A minor flip-flop occurred when, in the course of the trip, the Rhodesian leaders publicly proclaimed their willingness to go to a conference sponsored by the United States. Although this was trumped as a major change in the leaders' position, a closer look reveals the concession as a highly contingent tactical necessity.

When Smith arrived in the United States, the Carter administration and the State Department refused to meet him, citing among other things that the unwillingness of the internal parties to attend a conference had proved to be a major stumbling block to peace in Southern Africa. While Smith was in the United States, his conservative friends pointed out that because of the terms of the Case-Javits amendment, Carter could not rescind sanctions until the regime negotiated with the Patriotic Front and had elections. In front of the Senate Foreign Relations Committee, Smith displayed a willingness to commit to a conference on Rhodesia, prompting the State Department to arrange a meeting with him.

On October 15, Smith told a press conference that all of his colleagues would accede to a conference. Smith had something in mind along the lines of the Camp David meetings between Sadat and Begin: "Two points of significance struck me about the Camp David meeting. Firstly, the terrorist organizations were not invited to participate. Secondly, the decisions at Camp David were taken despite the opposition of a number of Arab states not directly involved in the dispute between Egypt and Israel" (Baumhogger 1984, 708). What Smith was implying was that he would agree to a meeting that would not include the Patriotic Front (a terrorist organization in Smith's mind) or need the approval of the Front Line presidents—a conference that repudiated Owen and Vance's publicly stated criteria for such a meeting.

When asked about their willingness to attend an all-parties conference, Smith's black colleagues expressed bewilderment and denied they had changed their minds on the subject. Muzorewa replied that such a conference was not "in the best interests of my country" and that he didn't "know on whose behalf he [Smith] was talking." A spokesman for Sithole went further: "The varying viewpoints of the different groups involved in the dispute make the idea a non-starter and a futile exercise which will not achieve anything" (Baumhogger 1984,

709).

On October 19, Rhodesia attacked by air five refugee camps and guerrilla bases near Lusaka, killing more than 200 people and wounding upwards of 2,500, including thirty-one Zambian soldiers. The attack, the first of its kind against Zambia, prompted a cautious reaction from Kaunda. He announced that it was in his power to counterattack by bombing Bulawayo or Salisbury, but that such a response would only escalate the conflict, which is what Salisbury wanted. He demanded and received defensive antiaircraft weapons from Britain.

The day after the bombing of Zambia, the four Rhodesian leaders stood side by side and agreed to an all-parties conference to be sponsored by the British and Americans. Nkomo, reeling from the attack the previous day, said such a meeting was out of the question. ZANU believed that Smith's purpose was to try to demoralize their guerrillas by talking peace immediately before Zimbabwe's summer months, which were the guerrillas' most active time.

On October 23, the British and Americans issued revised proposals on the nature of the transitional government. Three options were put to the contestants. Two of the options were variations on the idea of a governing council. The third option marked a significant change in the Anglo-American plans: after three months of a coalition transitional government, a referendum would be held. If the referendum passed, Rhodesia would be brought to independence and elections would be held three months later. All of the parties recognized the intent of the new suggestion: the only player who could benefit from elections coming after independence was Nkomo. The sponsor who would benefit from Nkomo's acquiescence was Kaunda.

November was marked by another Rhodesian raid on Zambia and by the first guerrilla firefight in the vicinity of Salisbury. Toward the end of that month, James Callaghan announced that he was sending a special envoy, Cladwyn Hughes, to Southern Africa to investigate the favorability of Britain calling a new conference on the Rhodesian problem. The results of Hughes's visit were announced on December 20, 1978. He concluded that such a conference could only fail, for "each side in the war is convinced it can reach its goal, or at least not to lose, by continuing to follow its own policies" (Hughes, quoted in Gregory 1980). Hughes's report brought to a close the efforts of Cyrus Vance and David Owen to mediate an end to the civil war in Zimbabwe.

## Analyzing the Failure of the Anglo-American Initiatives

The entrance of Owen and Vance into the Rhodesian melee brought two new actors with goals different from those of previous mediators. On the U.S. side, the most marked change involved a turn from Kissinger's superpower angle to the conflict in Southern Africa to Jimmy Carter's emphasis on human rights there. Such a change coincided with a growing importance of black Africa for the economic interests of the United States and Great Britain. Both of the mediating powers had a bigger stake in Africa than the solution to the conflict in Rhodesia. The change from Kissinger to Vance was important, but one continuity remained: Rhodesia was still a subarena for another game. In the case of Carter, actions taken in pursuit of peace in Rhodesia were aimed at winning friends in the rest of Africa, especially Nigeria and Tanzania. On the surface, such actions would seem compatible, but in fact they were not. At a crucial point in the negotiations, Carter's desire to make friends in Africa interfered with the settlement of the conflict. His ill-thought-out, unilateral acceptance of Nyerere's demand on the composition of the armed forces of Zimbabwe threatened to sink the Anglo-American peace process.

In terms of a strategy for reaching a settlement, there again existed change and continuity. On the one hand, some learning had taken place. The work of Ivor Richard set in motion the search for detailed solutions to the problem. The would-be peacemakers recognized the enormous complexity of the issues at stake, and they decided on the basis of the Geneva experience that a settlement would involve both sides making large concessions and that the parties in conflict were unlikely to reach agreement by themselves. There was thus a shift to an arbitration mode. David Owen believed that since leverage would be necessary to impose a verdict, the United States would be crucial to the success of such an enterprise. Both Owen and Vance were willing to work closely with the Front Line presidents and South Africa as their routes to the respective gladiators. In the latter case, however, Owen and Vance did not recognize the shift in South Africa's willingness to play the role they assigned to it. Machel and South Africa were mutually exclusive leverages: the preferences of these actors prevented a strategy of using both. Finally, David Owen signaled a willingness on the part of the British to play a much more active role than they had previously displayed. Although Owen was out in front of his government on this issue, he at least confronted head-on the contradiction that had stymied Ivor Richard at Geneva: a settlement would depend on an active Britain, but Britain had no intention of getting seriously involved.

Was the conflict ripe for resolution? There were two actors in the conflict who feared the consequences of no agreement and who could see a point in time when the conflict would be worse if no settlement was reached. On the Salisbury side, the military and intelligence commanders made clear to Smith and his cabinet that their situation was tenuous. On the nationalist side, it cannot be said that any of the major parties truly feared a lack of agreement; indeed in the case of Mugabe, he believed that only by making the situation worse for white Rhodesia would Smith ever capitulate. Among the sponsors of the antagonists, however, Kenneth Kaunda desired an end to the war, because his country's deteriorating condition imperiled his own political future. If Kaunda's position led to pressure on Nkomo to break away from Mugabe, it would prompt Julius Nyerere's worst nightmare: a bloody civil war between ZANU and ZAPU.

No significant change of positions occurred between the guerrillas and the Salisbury regime. The Patriotic Front still had the upper hand in the conflict, while Salisbury's military situation worsened by the day. As for the internal properties of the players, new splits were emerging in the Rhodesian camp as the military pressured Smith for a settlement. On the other side, Robert Mugabe had overcome another challenge to his leadership in ZANU.

In contrast to the previous mediation efforts, the Anglo-American initiatives failed to bring the parties to the negotiating table. The trite answer to this puzzle argues that the players' alternatives away from the bargaining table were superior to a possible settlement. What remains to be explained, however, is how the mediation effort influenced the perceptions and preferences of the players. Was there anything that the mediators could have done differently to move the parties toward settlement? Was the objective situation such that no mediation strategy could work? To answer these questions, it is useful to break the peace process into two parts: April 1977 to March 1978 (the pre-interim settlement period) and March 1978 to December 1978 (the post-interim settlement period).

It was obvious to the mediators when they began the peace process that the parties were very far apart on many important issues. Owen decided, with Vance's backing, to adopt an arbitration strategy. The mediators would canvass the different constituencies and put together a package deal that, while not meeting the unilateral demands of any of the participants, would try to meet everyone's minimal needs. Since the nationalists and the Rhodesians would both find some of the terms odious, the mediators would insist on approval of the whole package. As Owen inferred once, if the package were allowed to be picked apart, there would be no hope for agreement. Since the parties were to be handed the proposals on a take-it-or-leave-it basis, it was necessary for the mediators to back up an implied threat against any party that vetoed the proposals.

The Owen and Vance strategy approximated arbitration, where a third party lays down the law after hearing the positions of both sides. Usually, however, arbitration involves parties who have committed themselves to the judgment of the third party, who more often than not has an edifice of law and sanction of police to enforce a settlement. Rarely do we speak of arbitration in international politics. For a third party to pursue such a strategy when the settlement will be self-enforcing by the parties requires leverage, firm control by the mediators, a knowledge of the minimal needs of the antagonists, and some kind of legitimation.

When the mediation effort began in early 1977, the task of the third party was to create a settlement that was preferable for all actors to other alternatives they had away from the table. In the case of the Patriotic Front, ZANU was convinced that Smith would never negotiate in good faith; many were convinced that new negotiations would hinder the intensification of the war, which would be necessary to achieve their goals. Nkomo, although willing to consider negotiation as an option, was in a quandary. His political support within Rhodesia was limited by region and ethnicity to about 15 percent of the population. For him to come to power, he needed an alliance with a nationalist who appealed to the large Shona constituency: Mugabe or Muzorewa. Nkomo also realized that any settlement without Mugabe would not end the war.

The mediators knew that the other parties—Smith, Muzorewa, and Sithole—were contemplating a settlement on their own that would, in a sense, compete with the mediators' proposals. The mediators, therefore, had to raise the costs or lower the attractiveness of the competing settlement. To do this they had to either spell out a punish-ment that would ensue if the Anglo-American proposals were rejected or convince the participants that in terms of efficacy the Anglo-American proposals were a superior settlement to any internal agreement. At a different level of analysis, the mediators would have to strengthen those actors within the various parties who might favor an all-parties agreement. The two methods available to the mediator to forge an agreement were direct leverage against the parties and the crafting of an agreement that would split other alternative coalitions.

As for leverage, the mediators were to rely on resources that had previously been used: South Africa against the Rhodesians and the Front Line States against the Patriotic Front. The mediators also sought leverage through their promise to carry through the plan, if one side vetoed it. Other than this bluff, Vance and Owen never really considered what incentives or punishments they could utilize with Muzorewa or Sithole.

If we go through various scenarios, it is easy to see that the British and Americans in 1977 and 1978 had neither the carrots nor the sticks to dictate a solution. First, if we imagine that in September 1977 the nationalists were to accept the Anglo-American proposals, while the Salisbury regime rejected them, would it have been credible for the

British and Americans to proceed and in some sense bring the nationalists to legality? The short answer is no: neither Britain nor the United States was going to intervene in Rhodesia to help install the nationalists in power. It was common knowledge to all that the British Parliament in June 1977 had shot down the possibility of using British troops in Rhodesia *after* an agreement had been reached. It would therefore be highly improbable that the British or Americans would intervene militarily *before* an agreement had been reached.

The mediators believed that a second option would be to request South Africa's muscle to push Rhodesia to accept. As we know now, that was not a possibility after 1976, but there was a vague implicit threat by Vance, Young, and Owen that if South Africa did not cooperate, it would be punished. Was this threat credible? Both Owen and Vance represented relatively progressive regimes that had made their relations with black Africa a high priority. The South Africans may have been swayed by this to think that these administrations would push for sanctions against them. We also know that one of the specific motivations behind Vance and Owen's initiatives was to avoid sanctions, because they would be devastating to British investment in South Africa and neither Vance nor Owen believed them to be effective. Thus, it may have been possible to bluff Pretoria into action, but the costs of the bluff being called were prohibitive.

If we turn the scenario around and imagine the Rhodesian regime accepting the September proposals, would the mediators have had leverage on the nationalists? The first option—recognizing Salisbury— was unlikely, given the larger goal of Britain and the United States to strengthen relations with black Africa. The second option—indirect leverage through the Front Line presidents—depended in large part on what the presidents believed to be reasonable. By choosing Nyerere as the barometer of Front Line opinion, the United States locked itself into the most strident of the presidents. In part, just as South Africa gradually turned away from pressing Rhodesia, Nyerere himself had grown more radical through the war, so that he believed that Smith would never negotiate away power. To get Nyerere's approval, the Carter administration acceded to a demand that Smith, Muzorewa, Sithole, and the Rhodesian military would all reject: the surrender of the armed forces to be replaced by the liberation armies during the transition period.

This last point relates to the ability of mediators to frame alternatives to break existing coalitions and create new ones. To prevent Ian Smith from joining with Muzorewa and Sithole, the Anglo-American proposals needed the support of the internal nationalists and the support of the Rhodesian military, which would have been powerful leverage to push Smith toward the Owen-Vance settlement. Two important questions arise: Did the mediators know or suspect that Smith's military commanders favored some kind of settlement? Was there anything that the mediators could have done to keep the internal nationalists away from Smith?

The answer to the former question is probably. The Low and Graham team felt that Peter Walls was very helpful and indeed that Walls looked forward to working with some of the guerrilla troops and bringing them into the army (British Diplomat B. 1987, interview with author). The British must have had some hints from Ken Flower that important personnel favored a settlement. This perhaps explains Owen's exasperation when Carter, acting unilaterally, promised Nyerere that Smith's army would be disbanded during the transition.

As for Sithole and Muzorewa, the only approach that might have kept them from Smith would have involved a constant "stroking" of their egos and an insistence that they be treated as equals to Nkomo and Mugabe. This would have meant that the mediators would have had to fight against the decision of the Front Line presidents to acknowledge the guerrillas as the sole voice of the Zimbabwean peoples. It also would have meant a public effort of incorporating Muzorewa and Sithole into talks with the Patriotic Front, however much that may have been distasteful to the guerrillas. One example that comes to mind in this respect was the meeting at Malta in January 1978, when Owen and Young met the Patriotic Front to discuss security arrangements. In Ken Flower's memoirs, he points to the failure of the mediators to invite Muzorewa to the conference as one of the reasons that drove him further to Smith. Sithole, in a private letter to Owen, also expressed his bitterness at being excluded (N. Sithole 1978).

Although Muzorewa was clearly leaning toward an internal settlement with Smith, the Owen/Vance efforts pushed him into Smith's camp. Because the mediators put so much emphasis on appeasing the Patriotic Front, Muzorewa began to see his political future as dependent on cutting his own deal. He had little choice: he did not command an army, but he did have political support at home. Smith offered him the chance to use his resources at home and gave him the possibility of taking power. The initiatives of Vance and Owen, were they to have been successful, would have had to drive a wedge between Muzorewa and Smith. Instead, they pushed them closer together, a point readily admitted in Vance's memoirs (Vance 1983, 286).

The second period when the actions of the mediators came into play was after the announcement of the internal settlement in February. The move clearly caught David Owen unprepared; in his first meeting with Sithole after the announcement, Owen found himself vacillating between resolve for the Anglo-American proposals and encouragement for the new settlement. Owen, because of his desire to rid himself of the

Rhodesian problem, and his fear of his country recognizing the settlement, decided on a strategy of grafting Nkomo to the internal coalition.  Smith, Muzorewa, and Sithole therefore received positive reinforcement from Owen, even though Owen's public proclamations attempted to chide those leaders into returning to the Anglo-American framework.

Owen's secret machinations to split Nkomo and Mugabe proved to be the final breaking point in the mediation episode.  In the aftermath of the secret meeting between Smith and Nkomo in August 1978, Owen's credibility had vanished. The rules of the game that the mediators had established called for any unilateral vetoes to be punished. Instead, when Smith announced the internal settlement as a fait accompli, Owen did not carry through with the mediator's promise. This was his first loss of credibility. After his attempts to marry Nkomo and Smith became public, Owen lost whatever trust from Mugabe that may still have existed.

In terms of problem solving, the mediators accomplished much in trying to create a settlement that all could live with.  Given that Kissinger's proposals were so tilted in favor of the Salisbury regime, it was perhaps normal to expect the next effort to rebound too far in the Front's favor.  However, two disadvantages resulted from the thoroughness and openness of the problem-solving exercise.  First, even though Owen believed it was crucial to solve the problem of the constitution before moving on to other matters, by publishing proposals on all three aspects of a settlement (constitution, transition, and cease-fire), it appeared that the mediators were working simultaneously on the problems, therefore causing doubts as to what would come first: an end to hostilities or a new constitution. Second, by publishing all of the proposals at once, the antagonists had that much more opportunity to find pieces that were objectionable.  If presentation of proposals had been sequential, there may have been a slightly greater chance for success.

As 1978 drew to a close, nearly 85 percent of Rhodesia was under martial law.  Within two weeks into 1979, the draft would be extended to calling up men between the ages of 50 and 59.  In December, the guerrillas, in an audacious act, blew up Salisbury's fuel depot that stored the nation's oil.  The fire lasted six days, and the smoke was visible to all in the capital city.  On December 20, 1978, the war within Rhodesia turned thirteen years old. The last year had been its deadliest to date: 2,450 guerrillas, 282 Rhodesian troops, 2,406 black civilians, and 173 white noncombatants killed.  The country lost over 13,000 whites to emigration.  The Rhodesian military estimated that between 10,000 and 12,000 guerrillas were inside the country.

On January 1, Robert Mugabe sent his New Year's Day message to the people of Zimbabwe:

Let the People's fury break into a revolutionary storm that will engulf and sweep the enemy completely from our land. Let every settler city, town or village, let every enemy farm or homestead, let every enemy post, nook or hiding place be hit by the fury of the People's Storm. The People's Storm must come with thunder, heavy rain and irresistible blasting gusts that will ransack the enemy. strongholds. Let us call this year therefore the Year of the People's Storm—*Gore re Gukurohundi*. Let us proceed from the Year of the People to the Year of the People's Storm and storm right through to victory and the creation of a nation based on People's power. The People are a power, the People are a revolutionary storm. ("R. Mugabe's New Year Message to the People of Zimbabwe, 1/1/79," in Baumhogger 1984, 775–777).

# *Notes*

1. It is not clear whether Owen was bluffing on this score or whether he truly believed that Kaunda's desperate straits could drive him to seek Soviet bloc intervention. From the accounts and documents that I have seen, it was not until the autumn of 1978 that Kaunda considered Soviet help. As I point out in the next chapter, eventually Kaunda's deteriorating position and his lack of faith in the negotiation process did lead him in June 1979 to support a Cuban plan for escalating the conflict. As for Owen's claim to have stopped invasions into Zambia, I have found no reference to this in any of the military accounts of the period. Flower, who would have been privy to such information, does not mention any specific instances of British action that stopped a Rhodesian cross-border raid.

2. This competition grew violent as election day (originally scheduled for the end of 1978 but postponed until April 1979) grew closer. At times, the meetings of the Internal Working Party resembled a sordid comedy. In February 1979, two months before the election, the issue of intimidation of African voters was raised. At a meeting on February 1, a representative of ZUPO complained about the UANC (Muzorewa) threatening Africans to vote in the upcoming election. The representatives of the UANC bristled at the accusation, since "It will play into the hands of Dr. Owen and the Patriotic Front if there were to be say an 85% turnout of whites and few, if any, black voters. Therefore the fact of the election and the need to vote have to be constantly put before the black electorate." Another UANC official appealed "to representatives of any party who might consider that people of another party are acting illegally not go to the press." Ferris, the white Rhodesian chairman, missing the context of the discussion, assumed that since the Africans were arguing about intimidation, then it had to mean intimidation by the Patriotic Front. The chairman asked, "Do you think intimidation during the election campaign will be overcome or is it a serious factor which will keep people from voting?" The response from a member named Rumano, an officer of Sithole, made clear that the parties believed that intimidation was needed *to get the vote out*: "In the business of politics in Africa it is not called 'intimidation,' it is called 'reminding.' The truth of the matter is that it is an almost inseparable problem trying to politicize what are strictly unpoliticized

people. One tries words; the people do not see why. One tries to talk politics and they are not interested, but it is vital that these people exercise their vote. It is necessary constantly to remind the people of their political rights. What does one do? . . . Most of our people are not interested in political rights. All they want is a span of oxen and land to cultivate. To win an election, percentages are needed. How does one get them? They have to vote. So they need to be reminded" (Rhodesia, Internal Working Party, February 1, 1979).

# 5

# Lancaster House and
# Harnessing the Storm

*If I go, who stays? If I stay, who goes?* —Dante

At the beginning of 1979, all parties to the Rhodesian conflict were committed to alternatives away from the negotiating table. For any possible mediators, "Rhodesia had seemingly inscribed itself on the permanent agenda of the world's political-ethnic conundrums—Northern Ireland, Cyprus, the Middle East, South Africa—unamenable to human persuasion or reason" (Davidow 1984, 13). Yet, by the end of the year an agreement between all parties would be reached at Lancaster House, and after a harrowing cease-fire and election, Zimbabwe would be granted independence in April 1980. This chapter chronicles the events of 1979 as they pertained to resolving the conflict in Zimbabwe and describes in detail the Lancaster House negotiations. The next chapter analyzes why the British were able to succeed in bringing the Zimbabwean revolution to an end in 1980 and compares the British mediation in 1979 to previous efforts.

As summarized in Chapter 4, Smith and Muzorewa were committed to seeing through their strategy of an internal settlement. Smith and the white military establishment had no illusions about Muzorewa and Sithole's ability to end the war. The promise these black leaders had held out—that the internal settlement would lead to widespread desertion among the guerrillas and a collapse of the revolution—had been recognized by many whites for the pipe dream it was. Muzorewa, however, firmly believed reports from his people that guerrilla discontent was rampant and that many guerrillas were ready to desert to his side (Muzorewa 1987, interview by author). On the other front, the wooing of Nkomo from Mugabe seemed most unlikely in January 1979. Muzorewa and Sithole were committed to going it alone in the belief that they could triumph without Nkomo's aid (and without risking his competition within a larger coalition). ZAPU had itself become more radicalized, and with the shooting down of the Viscount plane, Nkomo had burned his bridges to the interim settlement.

What remained was the prospect of international recognition of the new government that would emerge after elections in Zimbabwe-Rhodesia and the hope that such recognition would lead to an increase in aid that might improve Salisbury's position. Without such recognition, however, the situation of the Rhodesian side was desperate. The military, intelligence, and economic arms of the white government saw the situation clearly: it would be a matter of time before they faced outright defeat (Flower 1987, interview with author).

On the Patriotic Front side, ZANU was convinced that victory was certain. Their only doubts were about the time span necessary to finish the job and how the final victory would take place. Robert Mugabe had finished his job of consolidating his leadership and was committed to the further intensification of the guerrilla war and bringing down the white government by force. ZANLA's training bases in Mozambique had grown tremendously; they were able to render much of Zimbabwe ungovernable and had succeeded in bringing the war to Salisbury for the first time.

Joshua Nkomo and ZAPU, however, were playing a different game. Nkomo favored a negotiated transition to majority rule but knew that a settlement was unlikely to hold without Mugabe. On the other hand, by casting his lot with Mugabe, he ran the real risk of being a junior partner in a coalition with a much larger partner who might decide to fight alone. ZAPU's strategy called for a buildup of conventional war-fighting capabilities in order to compensate for their numerical disadvantages *within* the partnership. ZAPU's military strategy, based on Soviet advice, assumed that ZANU would fatally weaken the Salisbury regime through guerrilla warfare *without being capable of dealing it a final death blow* (ZAPU Delegate A. 1987, interview with author). Basing their experience on the Angolan civil war, ZAPU believed that a last-minute change of strategy to a conventional blitzkrieg tank and plane attack would be necessary to bring down the Salisbury regime. Such action by ZAPU would also provide them with bargaining leverage with ZANU in a liberated Zimbabwe. The ZAPU dilemma can be summarized as this: they saw that no coalition could win without ZANU but realized that ZANU might be strong enough to win on their own. Therefore, cooperation was risky for a junior partner that had real limits on its base of support.

## The Change in Circumstances

Two elections—one in Rhodesia and one in Britain—opened a slight window of opportunity for a new mediation attempt to end the civil war. The first election in April 1979, in which Bishop Muzorewa was elected prime minister of Zimbabwe-Rhodesia, provided leverage for the British.

The Muzorewa government desperately needed the lifting of sanctions and could make a case that the British conditions for independence had been met and therefore recognition should be granted. The British were given an opportunity to forge a solution to the war that would not include the Patriotic Front, an opportunity recognized by all of the parties. Despite the assertions of Vance and Owen that neither of the mediating countries would legitimize the outcome of the April election, none of the Zimbabwean parties was convinced.

Doubts were multiplied when Margaret Thatcher was elected prime minister of Great Britain in June. The Conservative party platform had advocated the lifting of sanctions against Rhodesia; both Thatcher and Francis Pym, a leading candidate for foreign secretary, had echoed that sentiment, and, finally, Lord Boyd, a Conservative who had been sent to observe the Zimbabwe election, returned to Britain and contended that the elections were free and fair and represented the preferences of Zimbabweans. White Rhodesians believed that the Conservatives would turn things around. The Front Line presidents were so convinced that Thatcher would recognize Muzorewa that they contemplated an escalation of the war (Jaster 1983; Martin and Johnson 1981).

As I argued earlier, the first possibility that the war in Zimbabwe would escalate came from the attempts of the Rhodesian military to widen the scope of conflict. For three years the presidents of Zambia and Mozambique had refused to accept Ian Smith's escalatory gambit. Kaunda and Machel both believed that internationalization of the conflict would lead to events beyond the control of local actors. As discussed in the previous chapter, Kaunda was becoming increasingly desperate for relief from the war. This desperation prompted Kaunda to search unilaterally for avenues to terminate the Zimbabwean revolution. Kaunda's actions rekindled internecine squabbling between him and the other Front Line presidents. In October 1978, Zambia, in a move that Kaunda claimed was necessary for his nation to survive, reopened its border to Rhodesia, prompting stern criticism from Machel and Nyerere (Thompson 1981, 62).

The burden of bearing the high costs of the war, combined with the real possibility that the British and Americans would recognize Muzorewa, drove the Front Line presidents to entertain a Cuban proposal that would have escalated the war and prompted large-scale intervention. The particular incident occurred in June 1979. The combination of the failure of the United States and Britain to reach a negotiated settlement the previous year, the internal settlement between Smith and Muzorewa, and the election of Margaret Thatcher led many to believe that a peaceful termination of the civil war in Rhodesia was a chimera.

At this time, as a measure "to forestall world recognition of the Muzorewa government,"

> Cuba proposed that Nkomo and Mugabe should announce the formation
> of an independent Zimbabwe government in one of the guerrilla-
> controlled areas of Rhodesia near the Mozambique border and that
> this should be done at an elaborate ceremony, with foreign journalists
> and both ZIPRA and ZANLA [the military wings of ZAPU and
> ZANU] troop units in attendance. To guard against Rhodesian or
> South African attempts to disrupt the ceremony, Mozambique's armed
> forces were to be fully mobilized, and a mechanized Mozambican
> battalion, complete with artillery and anti-aircraft weapons, would
> enter Rhodesia at the time of the investiture. (Jaster 1983, 10)

As Jaster remarks, "the most astonishing element of this episode is
the apparent acquiescence in it of the Three Front Line leaders: Machel,
Kaunda, and Neto" (Jaster 1983, 10). Certainly, Kaunda and Machel
realized that this would most likely "prompt the entry of South African
troops into the war." In this particular case, Nkomo and Mugabe vetoed
the plan. Jaster attributes Mugabe's reluctance to an unwillingness to
take a leadership position under Nkomo and Mugabe's fear of an
escalated internationalized war (Jaster 1983, 10). Nkomo dismissed
the plan immediately: "I thought to myself this is crazy. Why would I
want to get myself killed?" (Nkomo 1987, interview with author).

## *British Policy, June to August 1979*

After winning the prime minister's office and appointing Lord
Carrington as foreign secretary, Margaret Thatcher backed off her
stand for recognition of Muzorewa. Carrington argued persuasively
that recognition would not end the war; it would alienate Britain from
the Commonwealth and have disastrous consequences for Britain's
interests in Africa, especially its burgeoning trade with Nigeria. Others
in the Foreign and Commonwealth Office provided the clinching
argument: the situation was ripe for one *final* attempt to reach an all-
sides settlement *provided that Britain was prepared to act boldly and
seize the initiative.* Their case was deceptively simple: the combination
of a losing military situation for the Muzorewa regime and the leverage
of what would become known as "the second-class solution"—the
recognition of Muzorewa—provided an opportunity to solve the crisis.
One final initiative by Britain would prove to the Commonwealth that
the British had at least tried to bring in the Patriotic Front. If the
conference failed because of rebel intransigence, no one could fault
Britain and Thatcher. Britain would incur risks only in the unforeseen
development that the conference actually led to a settlement.

   To put this last point into perspective, Robin Renwick, one of the
architects of the Lancaster House Conference, estimated that at the
beginning of the conference there was a 1 in 100 chance of a settlement.

Upon reaching agreement in December, he estimated that the chances of the agreement actually ending the war were 1 in 20. This makes for a fascinating premise, if one imagines an adviser telling Thatcher, "There is a 1 percent chance of this conference succeeding and Britain incurring high risks. However, in the unlikely event it does succeed, we then incur a 95 percent chance that our troops and the Commonwealth troops we commit to the cease-fire will be involved in a bloody morass, from which extrication might prove extremely difficult."

Thatcher decided in June 1979 to proceed with the initiative. British officials had studied the past failures of mediation and concluded that the previous proposals had *substantial* flaws that *in and of themselves* sufficed to sabotage any possible agreement. In the case of the Kissinger effort, the fatal flaw concerned Kissinger's "package deal," in particular, the provisions on white control of Defence and Law and white veto over the Council of State and the Council of Ministers (Renwick 1981a, 7). In the Anglo-American initiative, the stipulation that during the transition period the armed forces would be based on the guerrilla armies precluded white acceptance. Any new initiative would have to take from the previous talks a core of a settlement, yet avoid these specific problems.

The British also felt that Owen and Vance had underestimated Muzorewa and had driven him into Smith's clutches. Their study of past efforts led to a strong belief that Smith would fight any proposed agreement, and, therefore, it would be crucial to isolate him from the rest of the Salisbury delegates. On the Patriotic Front side, the British believed that Mugabe would also fight any settlement. But the British recognized that Mugabe's reluctance did not stem from ideology or principle. As one diplomat stated, "Mugabe was convinced that he could win outright and he feared risking the gains he had already won. Mugabe was convinced that he would win an election, but was unsure he would have a chance to win an election. He believed in armed struggle, *because of Smith*" (British Diplomat A. 1987, interview with author). To pressure Mugabe, the British once again needed the help of the Front Line presidents. As for Nkomo, he "didn't need a lot of pressure—he was the weak link in the Patriotic Front. Lancaster House was his last chance" (British Diplomat A. 1987, interview with author).

The British recognized that both sides, if left to their own devices, would never reach agreement. The British would therefore have to decide in advance what the most polarizing issues were and then present to the participants what they believed to be the only acceptable solution. Such a strategy approximates arbitration, where a third party lays down the law after hearing the positions of both sides. As argued in the last chapter, for a third party to pursue such a strategy when the settlement will be self-enforcing requires leverage, firm control by a dictatorial chairman, and some kind of legitimation. The difficulty lay in the contradictions of the requirements: How could Britain use other actors, especially the Front Line States, the Commonwealth, and the United States, for leverage and legitimacy without forfeiting control? As Renwick wrote later, "It was central to the new approach that this should be a purely British initiative. But it was no less essential to the chances of success to seek to attract the widest possible international support" (Renwick 1981a, 12).

In July, the British sent an emissary, Lord Harlech, to meet with the Commonwealth African presidents. In canvassing their opinions he made clear that the British *had not decided* on a course of action and that the advice of the presidents was crucial. He "found general criticism of the new constitution and a conviction that a solution must stem from Britain as the constitutionally responsible authority" (Renwick 1981a, 13). The British decided to formulate a new set of proposals and use the Commonwealth Meeting of Heads of State in Lusaka in August as the opportunity to unveil their plans. It was important that the British not play their hand prematurely, however, since many assumed that they would not take a bold stance against the Rhodesian elections. By appearing to be undecided, they would give the illusion of being persuaded by the Commonwealth leaders. This was a powerful bargaining tack: if the Commonwealth leaders knew that Thatcher was committed to a new initiative, they would pressure her for more concessions. Since the Commonwealth heads assumed Thatcher had no intention of seeking an all-parties solution, they would be grateful if Thatcher took any stand at all against the Muzorewa regime. The British aim was to be given free rein over the running of a new constitutional conference, with that conference publicized as a *Commonwealth* decision. In this way the British desire for sole control would not be compromised and they would also receive the legitimating stamp of the Front Line States, the Patriotic Front's closest allies.[1]

The British plan was put into action in August at the Commonwealth meeting in Lusaka. Most of the heads of state there assumed that the future of Zimbabwe would be a heated topic for debate, and few were prepared for Margaret Thatcher to examine the problem with an open mind. But after she gave a speech that signaled her willingness to consider new approaches to the Zimbabwean problem, Carrington and others went to work. Under the foreign secretary's supervision, a Commonwealth working party consisting of Kaunda, Nyerere, Jamaican prime minister Michael Manley, Commonwealth secretary general Sridath Ramphal, Australian prime minister Malcolm Fraser, and Nigerian foreign minister Major General Henry Adefope hammered out a joint Commonwealth position on Rhodesia:

The resultant communiqué, approved by all the heads of government, affirmed their commitment to genuine majority rule, noted that the internal settlement constitution was defective in certain important respects and accepted that it was the British government's responsibility to bring Zimbabwe to legal independence. It recognized that the search for a lasting settlement involve all the parties to the conflict and appropriate safeguards for minorities; that the government formed under the independence constitution must be chosen through free and fair elections properly supervised under British government authority and with Commonwealth observers present; and that it was the British government's intention to call a constitutional conference to which all the parties would be invited. (Renwick 1981a, 14)

Renwick argues that "the recognition that it was Britain's responsibility to propose a solution was an essential element of the Lusaka communiqué. No less important was the commitment to fresh elections. These were the natural corollary of a new constitution and the key to offering all the parties an alternative to continuing the war" (Renwick 1981a, 14).

The different Zimbabwean parties had different reasons for wanting to attend the Lancaster House Conference, and the British tailored their informal invitations accordingly. In the words of one Salisbury delegate, the British "needed different ruses to get people there and then different carrots and sticks on the different groups" (UANC Delegate A. 1987, interview with author). The Muzorewa regime was motivated first by the desire of recognition and the ending of economic sanctions. They had been assured by the British that if the conference failed on account of the Patriotic Front, Britain would grant formal recognition. Although the white Rhodesians might have been skeptical of such a promise in the past, they felt they could trust the Conservatives and Thatcher to hold up their end of the bargain. Furthermore, the white military's position had worsened and they needed recognition.

The Patriotic Front was aware of the military situation and therefore was extremely hesitant to attend the conference. They were certain that, although the costs would be great, victory was a matter of time. Coupled with their deep distrust of Thatcher and Carrington, the Patriotic Front felt that little could be gained from further talks. It was up to the Front Line leaders, especially Machel and Kaunda, who felt that they could no longer absorb the costs of the struggle,[2] to put an ultimatum to Mugabe and Nkomo:

If the PF refused to take part in the Lancaster House negotiations, the Front-Line States would withdraw their support of the PF and close down the war. At the same time, the PF was reassured that, if the Conference failed because of Britain or Muzorewa, the Front-Line States would support fully a renewal of the armed conflict. (Jaster 1983, 12)

After being so informed, Nkomo and Mugabe agreed to attend. But before doing so they committed a tactical blunder: they issued a statement that they would attend only under the condition that they would be negotiating not with the Salisbury regime but rather with the British government as the decolonizing agent. Although such a statement was intended to save face for the Patriotic Front's decision to attend the meetings, it would forfeit control of the supply of information to the British at the conference. The Patriotic Front would never know to what extent the British and the Salisbury regime were colluding. Moreover, the Patriotic Front would be totally dependent on the British to supply the views and information of the Salisbury regime.

## *The Players on the Eve of the Meetings*

The election of Muzorewa and the formation of the new coalition between Muzorewa and Smith led to a larger realignment of key players in the government such as Peter Walls and Ken Flower. These whites had embraced the Muzorewa faction as the only hope for saving Rhodesia from elimination. At the time the invitation to Lancaster House was tendered, Muzorewa knew that he needed to carry the Rhodesian Front with him, but he also knew, as did Flower, that Ian Smith would not compromise under any circumstances. Muzorewa's solution therefore was to try to convince David Smith, a leading Rhodesian Front politician and much respected minister of finance, to join the Salisbury delegation as the representative of the Rhodesian Front. David Smith, however, refused to go to Lancaster House unless Ian Smith was included in the delegation. Muzorewa acceded to the demand, so on the eve of Lancaster House there were four discernable factions in the Salisbury coalition: Muzorewa and his party's faction, Walls and the government faction, Ian Smith and the Rhodesian Front faction, and Sithole and the internal opposition to Muzorewa.

The four factions had different positions on issues and concerns. Muzorewa had not received diplomatic recognition from a single state. Moreover, his government was also in trouble. Much of his own political party had defected from him during the summer months, and there was much dissatisfaction among white Rhodesians at his inability to induce guerrillas into the amnesty program. His acceptance to attend Lancaster House was an attempt to bolster himself internationally and domestically. Peter Walls and Ken Flower, those individuals most concerned with security, had recognized that the country desperately needed a settlement and believed that Muzorewa could win an election. Ian Smith, on the other hand, had decided against any concessions. His strategy going into Lancaster House was to stonewall any changes in the new constitution in the hope of forcing Thatcher and the conservatives to recognize Muzorewa. He preferred no settlement to a settlement that would alter the constitution and allow the Patriotic Front the opportunity to govern the country (Smith 1987, interview with author). Sithole, on the other hand, while not eager to see the Patriotic Front included in any deal, was anxious for new elections and a second opportunity to become prime minister. The key "swing" vote was David Smith. On the one hand Smith, as finance minister, recognized that a settlement was crucial if the Rhodesian economy was to avoid total collapse. On the other hand, as a loyal Rhodesian Front member, he had never challenged Ian Smith.

As for their counterparts at the bargaining table, the Patriotic Front was probably at its most unified. Yet, there were important differences between ZANU and ZAPU going into the conference. These differences were not based on issues but rather on the desirability of a settlement. Much has been made about the differing degrees of radicalness in the parties, but in fact on most policy matters there was broad agreement, especially on issues of equality and redistribution. On the ZANU side, however, Robert Mugabe was deeply suspicious of any settlement and feared that the conference was an attempt to strip ZANU of what it had gained on the battlefields. Moreover, he was absolutely convinced that ZANU would win outright in the next three years. Before the conference started, however, the commander of the ZANLA guerrillas, Josiah Tongogara, told other ZANU members that the conference could bring the results they wanted—power through the ballot box without the sacrifice of more lives. At a dinner before the conference, Tongogara told another ZANU delegate that "if there are elections, free and fair, we are sure to win them; no one else has comparable machinery to what we have" (Mubako 1987, interview with author).

Nkomo, on the other hand, entered Lancaster House with an almost fatalistic attitude. Before Lancaster House began, Nkomo and Mugabe had met with the Front Line presidents and, with the leaders of the Nonaligned Movement (NAM) in Havana. Whatever was said in these talks had a sobering effect on Nkomo. One ZAPU delegate at Lancaster House described the mood of the delegation immediately before the start of the conference:

> When we came to the conference, and here I mean ZAPU, we were told by our leadership that the war was over. We must not bluff ourselves that we were going back to the bush after the conference. The agreement at Lusaka was heavily weighted to ending the war. Colleagues were struck by how stage managed the conference was by the British. The PF didn't get near to anyone at Lusaka. The ploy that the British used was that the Queen was going to be assassinated by the Rhodesians, thus security was held by the British—not the Zambians—and they kept the PF out of the way. In a real sense

Lancaster House was redundant, no real negotiations took place, the real negotiations were done at Lusaka. This is exaggeration, but not much. The meeting of NAM in Cuba between Lusaka and Lancaster is where the PF tried to unravel Lusaka, but that failed.

I remember the first meeting of our delegation when Nkomo arrived fresh from Havana. He told us, "When this conference is over we're going home. The Front Line States are not going to support us as previously. Confidentially, we don't have any cards. The chances of us saying we don't accept this are nil. It's based on a fantasy. We're not going back to the bush." (ZAPU Delegate A. 1987, interview with author)

Clearly, Kaunda had impressed the necessity of an agreement on Nkomo. At that point, Nkomo hoped that a settlement could be reached but also acceded to his military commanders to formulate a military alternative if the conference failed. The alternative involved the move to a conventional war-fighting strategy that would escalate the war (Nkomo 1984; Cilliers 1985; ZAPU Delegate A. 1987, interview with author). One delegate described Nkomo's decision:

There was a plan for escalation. It involved sending a massive strike of tanks over the border and seizing airfields so that we could fight the war internally in a much more conventional fashion. ZIPRA saw a longer war than ZANLA, and saw that the outcome would involve a massive war needing the training of pilots and tank drivers. An eloquent expression of this is in ZIPRA's criticism of ZANLA. ZIPRA depended much more on heavy reconnaissance and low-key slow development. But you have to understand that escalation would have been an act of desperation, not strategy. Nkomo had just returned from Cuba and at our first briefing said, "This is the reality. Zambia and Mozambique are not going to keep on supporting us. Either we go for an agreement or the whole tenor of the struggle will change with a whole new military structure and strategy, with the disadvantage that the state will be nominally black. Therefore, negotiating is going to be tough and we have to accept a lot." (ZAPU Delegate A. 1987, interview with author)

The British had a clear idea of what they wanted going into the talks. Lord Carrington's strategy for the Lancaster House meetings emphasized four factors. First, Carrington would use what he called the second-class solution—British recognition of Muzorewa and removal of sanctions—as a carrot with Muzorewa and as a stick with the PF. As stated earlier, the British had hinted to Muzorewa that if the PF was responsible for the failure to reach a settlement, Muzorewa would gain recognition. The attractiveness of the second-class solution is that it established a bargaining game whereby the first party to walk away from the table would lose; the game, therefore, had a dynamic built into it, so both parties feared being the first to repudiate the negotiations. To put the utmost pressure on the Patriotic Front, the British would turn first on each issue to the Salisbury delegation and then, armed with their acceptance, would put matters to the Patriotic Front on a take-it-or-leave-it basis.

Second, Carrington realized that, although this first factor was powerful leverage, it was not enough. It was crucial that both parties believed that they could win a fair election. If any party believed that it could not win, it would have reason to walk away from a settlement. Moreover, the parties had to believe that the British would run fair elections and that both parties would abide by the results, regardless of their outcome.

Third, the British had determined beforehand that within the two delegations, they would have to work to isolate those members who were opposed to a settlement: Ian Smith and Robert Mugabe.

Fourth, Carrington realized that Britain lacked sufficient leverage with the Patriotic Front and therefore needed the help of the Front Line presidents to pressure Mugabe and Nkomo, especially Mugabe.

The British also faced the problem of avoiding another experience such as Geneva. Carrington and his staff put together a tactical plan that emphasized the use of ultimatums, an agenda that would address the problems of the constitution before moving on to the other items, and, finally, a strong emphasis on the seriousness with which the British were approaching the exercise. It was crucial that the participants believed that the British were committed to seeing an end to the conflict and that if the conference failed there would be no more attempts to settle the war at the negotiating table. Indeed, one British diplomat went so far as to tell Mugabe at the beginning of the conference that "you won't like the proceedings here because we are going to be tough on everyone including you, because we are serious. Something is going to change at the end of this conference" (British Diplomat A. 1987, interview with author).

The tactical plan relied on the following components: (1) a strong conception of a feasible outcome; (2) what the *Economist* called Carrington's ability to "huff and puff and fudge": the strong imposition of deadlines into the meetings combined with making necessary concessions when conditions arose; (3) a step-by-step approach to the major issues in the hope of building and sustaining momentum toward an agreement; and (4) the use of a single negotiating text (this draws on Davidow 1984, 107–114).

The British wanted to keep the influence of other international actors to a minimum during the proceedings. This was a particularly difficult business. As stated earlier, Carrington knew that in certain instances he might have to call on the help of the Front Line States or the Commonwealth to pressure Mugabe. On the other hand, the British did not want any other international actor putting forward its own initiatives that might contradict the British efforts. Since Carrington had decided to take a hardball approach to the negotiations, he did not want to let other actors go to bat for either side. The other difficult problem was South Africa, which had the potential to veto any agreement reached at the conference. But unlike previous episodes, the election of Muzorewa had given the British direct leverage with Salisbury, so that the route to Rhodesian cooperation no longer ran through Pretoria. At Lancaster House, the British wanted South African acquiescence, *not their help*. But it was still a problem, which the British "dealt with by assurances to them; by raising their fears of being sucked in deeper in an escalating conflict; and by convincing them that Muzorewa could win" (British Diplomat A. 1987, interview with author).

## Lancaster House

At the introductory session of the meetings, the delegations set the tone for what would follow. Emphasizing that the conference had the backing of the Commonwealth, Carrington stressed that Britain was determined to carry out its role as decolonizer. He made it clear that the conference was a "constitutional" conference; that since the constitution was the most important issue and cause of the war, it would have to be addressed first: "It is essential to the prospects of success that we should first seek agreement on our destination—which is the independence constitution. If that can be achieved it will be necessary to decide the arrangements to give effect to that agreement." Moreover, he stated that "it is illusory to think that any settlement can fully satisfy the requirements of either side."

Carrington also stated themes that would recur throughout the meetings: (1) that Britain was acting on a mandate of the Commonwealth; (2) that the British were serious about asserting their decolonizing responsibilities; (3) that the constitution was the key to the settlement, and that only when that was solved would the conference proceed to discussions about arrangements; (4) that Britain had long experience as a decolonizing power, which enabled the British negotiators to deal with the sticky issues involved in the conference; (5) that agreement would demand compromises by all parties; (6) that independence did not mean that one side would win but that all sides would have an equal chance to win an election; and (7) that the British proposals would form the basis of the working document—other parties' suggestions would be considered but only insofar as they dealt with the British document.

Hoping to establish an atmosphere of reconciliation, the British threw a cocktail party for the delegations on the first night of the meetings. The Patriotic Front declined, issuing a press statement to the effect that they did not associate with "murderers and thieves" (Keesing's, 30165).

## The Constitution

From the start, Carrington's dictatorial role was evident. He made clear that the only working document would be the British proposals he put forth. While welcoming any revisions to these proposals, Carrington emphasized that no other documents would be discussed. This restriction immediately raised the ire of Mugabe, who complained about Carrington's aristocratic style and what he thought was Carrington's attempt to bully the PF. Early on, however, Mugabe was thoroughly chastened by Nyerere, who was in London at the time: "This is a British conference. Carrington is a British chairman. So don't waste your time telling him how to run it" (quoted in Jaster 1983, 14).

The agenda of the conference was decided in the first meetings. Both the Patriotic Front and the British put forth proposals. The British plan consisted of three issues: (1) proposals for a new constitution, (2) the plan for a transition period before elections, and (3) the arrangements for the cease-fire. The Patriotic Front's proposal envisioned first discussing the transitional period—arrangements and a temporary constitution—and then moving on to the topics of the independence constitution and cease-fire. The first split occurred in the Muzorewa delegation on September 12, when Ian Smith backed the Patriotic Front's agenda, a move that baffled the Patriotic Front (*Daily News* [Dar es Salaam], September 13, 1979, in Baumhogger 1984, 1052). Smith's reason, however, was similar to the guerrillas': before he agreed on one piece of the deal, he wanted to see the whole package.

Carrington argued forcefully that the constitution be settled first: "The only way to end the war is to remove the reasons for it. . . . The approach of the British Government has been to discuss the best way to achieve a solution with their friends and allies and the parties involved. It was clear from these discussions that the root of the problem lay in the constitution. If the conference could agree on the constitution, it would remove the causes of the war, once agreement on the constitution was settled, agreement on other matters could come more easily" (United Kingdom 1979, minutes of first plenary).[3] Muzorewa seemed to bridle under the suggestions that the constitution was inadequate and insisted that "the people of Rhodesia had already decided on the constitution." Carrington prevailed, however, as neither side wanted to waste negotiating capital so early in the proceedings.

The three sides tabled proposals for the new constitution. The British proposal basically accepted most of the formalities of the new constitution of Zimbabwe-Rhodesia but eliminated the discriminatory provisions that Smith had forced on Muzorewa, most importantly the blocking mechanism of the whites in government. The British proposals still contained important safeguards for protecting minority interests. The most important of these safeguards was an extensive bill of rights guaranteeing individual freedoms, an undetermined number of white seats in a 100-person legislature for a period of seven years, remuneration for any land that might be redistributed, and the honoring of pension rights for white public officials.

The Patriotic Front spent the early meetings insisting that no agreement on the constitution could be reached until the arrangements for the transition were known. In Mugabe's words, it was essential to spell out the transitional arrangements to ensure that "progress towards independence was irreversible." On this matter there could be no compromise on Britain's part. The British had learned from Geneva that there would be no end in sight to the conference if the parties were allowed to renegotiate clauses at later dates in the proceedings. The British insisted that all matters having to do with the transition and cease-fire would be addressed, but only after agreement was reached on the constitution.

Having lost the procedural battle, the Patriotic Front took aim at the specific components of the constitution. At the sixth plenary session, Mugabe reproached the British on minority representation in Parliament:

> The British proposals variously call this minority "European" and "white." The Patriotic Front certainly wants to see everyone in Zimbabwe represented in the legislature, but I am puzzled that the British Government should want the new republic to start off with a constitution which divided the people. All people who live in Zimbabwe should consider themselves as citizens of that country. Is it possible to call a section of the community European? Surely there can be no such thing as a European in Africa? Similarly the term "white" could cause problems. Is the conference being asked to work out a chart of shades of colour and then agree the percentage by which each shade should be represented? This is a racial approach and repugnant to our delegation.
>
> *Carrington*: It was accepted that the ideal solution is that the people should think of themselves as citizens of Zimbabwe rather than black or white, Shona or Matabele. The crux of the issue is how this is to be achieved. The political realities of the past cannot be ignored. Nor can the hopes and fears of the people.
>
> *Mugabe*: I wish to underline the fact that the war of liberation has been waged to destroy the racial basis on which society in my country has been constructed. The minority has acquired certain rights and privileges to the exclusion of the majority. The war has been waged against this exploitation. The British want us now to retain vestiges of that system. (United Kingdom 1979, minutes of sixth plenary)

Ian Gilmour, Carrington's second in command, then answered that it had been agreed at Lusaka that it would be in Zimbabwe's best interest for the whites to stay and that the provisions in the constitution would be necessary for them to remain. He also pointed out that the civil war had made it necessary for the arrangements only on a temporary basis. The plenary came close to dissolving into open rebellion as members of the Patriotic Front battered the British arguments on racial and regional representation. At the end of the meeting the discussion turned to the guarantee of civil servant pensions. Edison Zvobgo, Mugabe's press officer, pointed out that such civil servants "might be regarded as public officers by some people, but by others as mercenaries." Mugabe went a step further: "If this is to be a retrospective blessing by the British Government for treasonable conduct, this should be clearly stated." When no progress was made at the next plenary on September 18, it was agreed that it might be best for the conference to work in bilateral meetings away from the negotiating table. The British would negotiate separately with each team.

The first showdown of the conference within the delegations came in the Salisbury team. In meetings from September 19 to 21, Ian Smith argued vociferously against the dilution of the white safeguards and insisted that any constitution had to have a blocking mechanism for the whites. Muzorewa and others supported the compromises put forth by the British. The African members of the delegation had never had any fondness for the white veto, and Carrington and his aides had made it clear to the white members of the delegation that, while protective measures would be placed in the constitution, the blocking mechanism had to go. If not, Carrington added, the country would never gain recognition.

In a bilateral meeting on the nineteenth, Carrington presented the Salisbury delegation with specific numbers. Twenty seats out of a 100-person Parliament would be reserved for whites, and seventy votes would be necessary to amend the constitution. Eight of the twelve-man Salisbury delegation, including David Smith, spoke in favor of changing the constitution. Ian Smith, however, refused to back down and for more than an hour argued with Carrington that the mechanisms were necessary "to maintain white confidence and morale." On the morning of the twentieth in a meeting of the four white delegates, Smith found that he had no support. The key apparently was a telegram from General Peter Walls that underscored the need for a quick agreement.

This first showdown came to an end on the morning of September 21. For two and a half hours Ian Smith argued his position. He had backed off his insistence on the white veto; his insistence now was based on "'maintaining standards,' by retaining the dominant position of white officials in the commissions for defence, the public service, the Army and the police" (*Observer*, September 23, 1979, in

Baumhogger 1984, 1059). One Muzorewa delegate said that Smith's arguments were not "practical, but philosophic in nature" (UANC Delegate A. 1987, interview with author). At this meeting, David Smith, "who had never been prepared to slug it out with Smith," did so. According to one delegate, David Smith, after listening to Ian Smith go on, finally stood up and said, "enough is enough." Muzorewa then called for a secret vote on whether to accept the constitution: the tally was 11 to 1 in favor. That evening the Salisbury delegation publicly announced their acceptance of the new constitution. But they also tried to pressure Carrington by insisting that sanctions be removed, since they had fulfilled their part of the bargain ("Statement by the Government of Zimbabwe Rhodesia," in Baumhogger 1984, 1060).

Carrington then turned to the Patriotic Front, which held out for two weeks in disagreement with the British proposals. The PF had accepted the twenty-seat representation for whites but still raised objections over land, pensions, citizenship, protected rights, and form of constitutional government. On October 1, a British diplomat, Derek Day, briefed representatives of the Front Line presidents on the stalled talks. Later that day, these same representatives met with Mugabe and Nkomo to relay Front Line dissatisfaction with the progress of the negotiations. The representatives emphasized that because the Front had accepted the difficult issue of special representation for the whites, the other less important issues should not halt the proceedings.

The tenor of the meetings became quite heated as the British and the Patriotic Front clashed when the plenaries resumed on October 2. The Patriotic Front attempted to go through the constitution on a point-by point-basis. While Carrington addressed their concerns, Muzorewa objected that the use of the plenary session to do so was not a particularly useful procedure, but he consented to be "happy and sit and look on." Repeatedly, the Patriotic Front tried to engage the Salisbury delegation in debate, but Muzorewa and his aides stonewalled. Mugabe finally exploded:

> I wonder whether further discussion is in fact worthwhile. The Salisbury delegation has made it known they consider it to be worthless. . . . Points of difference have emerged which I thought the Salisbury delegation might listen and react to. It is important for the conference as a whole to understand where the areas of agreement and disagreement are. (United Kingdom 1979, minutes of eighth plenary)

At this point, Carrington interceded that the plenary was for the Patriotic Front to put their case across to Muzorewa. He added that he thought Muzorewa was aware of the points of difference. As for the complete picture, the Salisbury delegation "had accepted in principle the British proposals" and the Patriotic Front had not. Carrington then asked whether they still wished to present their arguments to the Salisbury delegation.

When Mugabe complained that the bilateral sessions were incorrect procedure that prevented the sides from negotiating with each other, Carrington shot back at him: "At the start of the Conference Mr. Mugabe, Mr. Nkomo and delegation had expressed the desire to negotiate only with the British side." When the Patriotic Front left the session, Mugabe and Nkomo gave their first joint press conference since the talks started on September 10 and accused the British of having made a secret deal with the Salisbury delegation.

On the next day, October 3, the British tabled the revised constitution in specific detail. It failed to grant any concessions to the Patriotic Front. Within two days, Muzorewa had granted his delegation's acceptance. On October 6, Ian Smith flew back to Salisbury to rally Rhodesian Front support for his rejection of the constitution. While at home, Smith raised the issue of whether the constitutional changes had to be ratified by the Rhodesian Parliament. The British, in conjunction with the Salisbury delegation, immediately squashed this possibility by contacting the highest-ranking judge in Rhodesia, who gave an impromptu ruling that ratification was out of line in view of the circumstances.

On October 9, the Patriotic Front again tried to stick by their positions. Carrington's responses on that day are revealing of the British intention to arbitrate and not mediate a settlement. For example, in responding to Patriotic Front demands for an executive presidency, Carrington states, "The British Government *reached its decision* only after very careful consideration of all the arguments." Other statements read like a judge's decree: "The Patriotic Front say . . . the British Government does not take that view"; "There can be no question of the British Government or Parliament accepting such a provision"; "The Patriotic Front have also reiterated their objections to the principle of dual citizenship. In our view their fears are misplaced"; "The British Government regards it as essential that the Declaration of Rights be specially entrenched"; "The British Government cannot accept those changes" [regarding land]; [on public service,] "The British Government regards it as eminently reasonable that. . . . "

When the Patriotic Front suggested "agreeing to disagree" and moving on to discuss the transitional arrangements, Carrington put his foot down: Considerations of transitional matters could not be taken before the constitution was settled. It was not good enough to "agree to disagree" and leave it. There must be agreement. The British government had taken into account all sides and had presented a constitution as "the only basis on which it is now possible to reach full agreement at this conference." Matters would not be allowed to be reopened now or in the future. Carrington finished by reasserting Britain's duty to *arbitrate*: "When the Conference cannot agree, when the parties cannot agree, we have an obligation to make clear what in our mind is fair and reasonable and we have done so" (United Kingdom 1979, minutes of eleventh plenary). Carrington then asked the Patriotic Front to provide a "definitive reply in two days" as to whether they would accept the constitution as presented by the British, and left to attend the annual Conservative party convention in Blackpool.

Within the PF delegation there was intense debate on what to do. They had reached the point where they could swallow all of the concessions that Carrington demanded, save one: what to do about land. One ZAPU delegate stated what was mentioned in many interviews: "The land issue was the hardest to accept, because it involved such visceral feelings and our mobilization had depended on land, thus we decided we had to make some kind of stand." But what kind of stand? Hard-liners, including Mugabe, threatened to walk out of the conference. Tongogara warned that Mozambique would take away ZANLA bases. Mugabe insisted, and Nkomo told him if ZANU walked, they walked alone. The Patriotic Front would have to break: Zambia would take away ZAPU's bases.

Two days later at the next plenary session, the Patriotic Front refused to respond. Carrington publicly set another deadline. According to Jeffrey Davidow, Carrington also approached the PF in a bilateral session and presented them with a British offer to cover some of the expense of reimbursing farmers for land redistribution. This offer "was pocketed by the Patriotic Front's leaders, and did not lead to an immediate change in their stance" (Davidow 1984, 62).

The intransigence of the PF prompted both a search by third actors for some kind of face-saving measure for Mugabe and Nkomo and a hard line from the British. On October 15, Carrington publicly stated that the conference, with or without the participation of the Patriotic Front, would resume the next morning to begin talks on the transition period. He added that until the guerrillas had accepted the constitution, he would be forced to move on with only the Salisbury delegation. At this, Shridath Ramphal, the secretary-general of the Commonwealth, publicly rebuked Carrington: the British mandate from the Lusaka meeting was for an "all-parties" conference. Kenneth Kaunda backed Ramphal, calling Carrington's actions "not helpful" and "negative." The Front Line presidents in a special summit session backed the Patriotic Front, as did Nigeria's President Shagari. On the other side of the issue, South Africa sent its foreign minister, Pik Botha, to London to pressure Carrington into getting on with things and recognizing Muzorewa's government.

Between October 15 and 18, the United States, in response to initiatives by Ramphal and Carrington, gave ambiguous support for a fund that would help Zimbabwe bear the economic burden of pensions and compensation for land. In the words of one ZANU delegate: "With the United States offer of aid we had something we could sell to the people. The Front Line States told us, 'You have a promise from the United States; if you feel like you have something you can sell to the electorate, then take it'" (Mubako 1987, interview with author). On the eighteenth, the Patriotic Front announced that, pending their satisfaction with the transitional arrangements, "there will not be need to revert to discussion on the constitution" ("Statement by PF," in Baumhogger 1984, 1113).

*The Transitional Arrangements*

Turning to the details of the transition period, Carrington insisted that it would be handled with the existing Rhodesian military and police forces under direct British supervision with no role for any UN officials or peacekeeping force, and in a two-month period. The British wanted to keep their risk to a minimum, which the plan bears out. First, the British had no intention of giving their or anyone else's troops the job of stepping between the two armed adversaries. They went to great pains to emphasize that any cease-fire would have to be largely self-enforcing. Instead of peacekeeping forces, the British plan called for a small contingent of Commonwealth troops (no more than 300) to monitor the cease-fire. Because the British knew that the Salisbury regime would balk at United Nations involvement, they had ruled out such a possibility. Second, Britain, while willing to take over power during the interim, wanted to minimize commitment of resources so therefore decided that a British governor would use the existing police and bureaucracies to run the country. Finally, the time element was crucial for maintaining the illusion that the election was "up for grabs." As one British official said, "We felt most strongly about a short transition period. If anyone found out who lost before the election, then it was all over" (British Diplomat A. 1987, interview with author).

On October 19, Carrington presented his general view on the transition. Once again donning the mantle of legitimacy vested at Lusaka, he demanded that both parties accept the principle that "there had to be free and fair elections, properly supervised under the British Government's authority, with Commonwealth observers present." Nkomo immediately asked for clarification on the term "British Government's authority." Carrington replied that "this refers to our responsibility for the conduct and supervision of the elections." Mugabe then answered that the Patriotic Front had their own proposals and would need to wait to see the specifics of the British plan. Muzorewa announced that the Patriotic Front proposals were absolutely unacceptable, and that after all, "free and fair elections have already been held in Zimbabwe Rhodesia" (United Kingdom 1979, minutes of thirteenth plenary).

The weekend of October 20 and 21 led to public posturing by both antagonists. Muzorewa stated that he would not consider stepping down during the election; the Patriotic Front argued that Muzorewa would "have to be removed and his armed forces dismantled." Mugabe, during a televised interview, denied that the Patriotic Front had accepted British authority to run the election and stated that the British could not be expected to be impartial. His press spokesman, Edison Zvobgo, went so far as to say that when the Patriotic Front gained power they would seize the land and refuse to compensate the landholders.

These statements led to fireworks at the October 22 plenary meeting. Carrington began by reading Mugabe's and Zvobgo's comments and demanded that Mugabe "clear up these two issues":

*Mugabe:* The Conference is in session in order to discuss Conference business, and not statements made to the press. My delegation's position is represented by what is said at the Conference. What is said outside is not the business of the Conference.

*Carrington:* The Conference has been convened on the basis of the agreement at Lusaka—that there should be free and fair elections under the British Government's authority. You said specifically on television that you did not accept that. This obviously puts the Conference in a very serious position.

*Mugabe:* If this is the position of the Patriotic Front, we will say so. My saying it on television does not mean that it constitutes an official Patriotic Front position. My delegation's proposals on the interim period are quite clear. They put over a different point of view on the supervision of elections. My understanding was that the parties present at the Conference were free to agree on something different from what is suggested in the British proposals. (United Kingdom 1979, minutes of fourteenth plenary)

Carrington then referred to Zvobgo's remarks and said, "It is difficult to have a conference where agreements are made, only for spokesmen outside to disagree on them." To which, Nkomo replied, "Your responsibility is Conference business, not press matters. My delegation does not question what is said by others outside the Conference."

Carrington then spelled out the British proposals on the transition:

1. Elections would be held with all parties free to participate. The elections would be held under the following circumstances:
   a) "Administration of the election will be scrupulously fair and

impartial."
 b) "Peaceful political activity will be freely conducted."
 c) "All . . . will have free and uncensored access to all the public media."
 2. "It will be the constitutional responsibility of the British Government, as recognized in the Lusaka communique, to ensure that these requirements are met." During the two-month transitional period there would be:
 a) A British governor with executive and legislative authority;
 b) An Election Commissioner and staff appointed by the British to supervise the elections;
 c) Commonwealth observers;
 d) An Election Council to satisfy parties that elections are fair and impartial and to make recommendations to the Commissioner and Governor on any election matter; and
 e) No registration of voters and a party-list method of voting.[4]
 3. "The Governor's instructions will require him to do all things necessary to secure compliance with the conditions for free and fair elections. The Commanders of the security forces will be responsible to him."
 4. "The Governor will assume authority over the civil police. They will be responsible, under his supervision, for the maintenance of law and order."
 5. "There will be agreement . . . regarding a cease-fire."
 6. "After elections result are finalized and a government formed, independence will be granted." (Extracted from Document CC(79)32, Conference Paper, "British Proposals for Implementing the Independence Constitution," in United Kingdom 1979, minutes of fourteenth plenary)

Carrington added:

I do not believe that the eventual outcome of this Conference can conceivably be regarded as a victory for one side or for the other. It is our concern that it should be a victory for the people of Rhodesia and of the neighboring countries.
 As I said at the beginning of the conference, the crucial question before us is whether you are prepared to settle your differences by political means. (United Kingdom 1979, minutes of fourteenth plenary)

The measures brought a strong response from Nkomo questioning Carrington's mandate from the Lusaka conference: "My delegation appreciates the role of the Commonwealth catalyst in bringing about the Conference. I do not, however, believe that the Commonwealth Conference prescribed how this Conference should run. If it had, there would be no need for a Conference." Then switching from a confrontational mode to one of problem solving, Nkomo emphasized that Patriotic Front proposals had been designed to minimize the suffering of the Zimbabwean people and to afford security to all concerned. He concluded by suggesting that a six-month interim may be the optimal amount of time.

While Carrington was wrapping up the session by asking if anything further needed to be said, a parting shot was leveled by ZAPU delegate George Silundika: "Is the British paper being tabled merely for reaction or for negotiation?" Carrington, ever opaque, replied that the British proposals were on the table "for discussion."

The plan was equally onerous to both Muzorewa and the PF. For Muzorewa, "the advent of a British governor with full legislative and executive power could only mean the relinquishment of power by the bishop and his cabinet, a bitter pill for a newly elected government" (Davidow 1984, 69). Mugabe and Nkomo objected on four grounds. First, relying on the existing police to keep the peace offered no protection whatsoever. They felt that only a police force composed of both Salisbury and Patriotic Front officers would work. Second, becuase the transition government did not incorporate any of the liberation movement's political or military personnel, the guerrillas were not granted legitimacy or equality. Their minimal demand was equal recognition. Their maximum position demanded a full integration of the armed forces with the guerrillas forming the core of the army. Third, the PF felt that the short time period was insufficient: they wanted the opportunity to move mass numbers of people from their refugee centers back into Zimbabwe. Fourth, the Patriotic Front, fearing that the Salisbury regime would try to rig the elections, demanded a full registration of voters—a long arduous task that would take longer than two months.

At the fifteenth plenary meeting on October 25, Bishop Muzorewa sought clarification on a number of issues. The essence of his questions was a desire to know whether parties would have to denounce violence before being permitted to compete in the elections. He furthermore wanted assurance "that the process of law will be invoked against those persons who attempt to undermine and subvert the election by unlawful means" and demanded that political detainees held by the Patriotic Front in Zambia and Mozambique be released. The bishop objected that some Commonwealth countries were biased against his government and should not be allowed to observe the election. He then requested that his questions be taken up in a *bilateral* session and finished by referring to what he regarded as a serious omission in the British proposals: "May I ask you bluntly, Mr. Chairman, when are sanctions going to be lifted?"

Before Carrington could take up the last question, Mugabe expressed his pique over the procedure of negotiation in bilateral sessions. Carrington fended off Mugabe's objections by agreeing "that the conference should proceed in plenary session as far as possible," but that it would be wrong to refuse a bilateral meeting if requested by one of the delegations. Carrington then promised Muzorewa prompt answers to his questions. This time it was Muzorewa's turn to be indignant: "My delegation and I are running a country. We have been in London too long and are losing patience. To achieve progress I want my delegation's questions answered today in plenary session, together with a bilateral meeting" (United Kingdom 1979, minutes of fifteenth plenary).

Later that afternoon, Carrington reassured Muzorewa that all parties would have to uphold the cease-fire and that those who violated it would be ruled ineligible to compete in the elections. Carrington determined that all detainees would be released, and to Muzorewa's concern about sanctions, he responded that "the British Government will lift sanctions as soon as there is a return to legality in Rhodesia" (United Kingdom 1979, minutes of sixteenth plenary).

Carrington, as he did during the discussions on the constitution, sought Muzorewa's acceptance before that of the Patriotic Front. For tactical reasons Carrington needed Salisbury's approval to keep pressure on Mugabe and Nkomo. This time, however, the British were not as confident of the outcome. As Jeffrey Davidow has argued, "Obtaining from Muzorewa his agreement to step aside and transfer power to a British governor proved to be the single most difficult task confronting Carrington" (Davidow 1984, 69). This point was emphasized by one of the British diplomats at Lancaster House: "To ask a government to get out of the way and let you run it is a tough business" (British Diplomat A. 1987, interview with author). In the case of Muzorewa and the request that he stand down, the British confronted a split delegation. On the one hand, Ian Smith chose the issue to make one last stand: he argued that if Muzorewa gave in, then the path would be clear for a Patriotic Front takeover of the government. On the other hand, Sithole, as leader of the opposition, wanted new elections and saw that if Muzorewa stepped down, it would increase his chances of electoral success. Muzorewa's own deputies were adamantly against the concession. Their concern stemmed from their own interests, for if Muzorewa lost power, then they would lose power. Since the proposals were put as a package, however, there was much that appealed to the white members of Muzorewa's faction, especially Peter Walls, who found appealing the provisions calling for reliance on the existing security forces.

Unlike the experience of the Salisbury delegation in accepting the constitution, the decision on whether Muzorewa would stand down was his alone. The British worked on two tracks. The first appealed to the bishop's ethics and tried to convince him that stepping down was the "right" thing to do, that it was necessary to give everyone an equal chance to lead a new Zimbabwe. The second track aimed at Muzorewa's interests and attempted to convince him that his loss of position would be temporary, that he would win another election and regain his position in a matter of months (Carrington 1987, interview with author). Finally, one has to take into account Muzorewa's realization that there was a real possibility that the PF might not, in Davidow's words, "gag and swallow" the transition conditions. If so, the door would be open for British recognition, but only if Muzorewa first accepted the British terms. The British privately were telling the bishop that acceptance of the transition by the Front was unlikely. On the October 28, when a response was requested by the British, Muzorewa, after a night of prayer, acceded to their demands to step down. From interviews with him and others in his delegation, I am convinced that he did this as the "fair" thing to do. But I am as equally convinced that Muzorewa was completely certain that he would be reelected and that relinquishing his leadership spot would be temporary.

During the time Muzorewa deliberated, Lord Carrington had sent his minister for African affairs, Richard Luce, to visit the Front Line presidents. While the move was in part to inform them of the proceedings, it was also undertaken in order to build up a reserve of legitimacy for the British proposals. This legitimacy was obtained just in time for the eight plenary sessions held between October 26 and November 1. In plenary on October 26, the Patriotic Front presented a stinging analysis of Britain's plans for the interim period. Their anger focused on the British choice of using existing police and administrators, who, the Patriotic Front argued, could not possibly be impartial. For the guerrillas the plan was a recipe for violence and bloodshed. Because Britain had often referred in the past plenaries to their history of effective decolonization as evidence of their abilities and good intentions, the Patriotic Front concluded their statement with historical references of their own:

> This plan is another example of the kind of disastrous policy pursued by Britain in a number of her former dependencies. Once again Britain has refused to face and solve the problems and tensions of the territories concerned, with the result, as for instance in Cyprus and Palestine, that they have moved into independence with a legacy of permanent instability, widespread suffering and bloodshed, affecting not only the countries themselves but also the international community. The British delegation has throughout this conference, whenever they have found themselves having to support a proposal which is insupportable in logic, stressed the need for reconciliation. In their plan for the interim period they appear to have abandoned this position; they are quite clearly determined to maintain the status quo. (Conference Paper CC(79)39, "Patriotic Front Analysis of British Proposals for the Interim Period," United Kingdom 1979, seventeenth plenary)

Having criticized the British plan, the Front then repeated their proposals: a six-month period before the election; security forces and police made up of both the regime's and the PF's forces; a United Nations peacekeeping force and police force; an electoral commission; and an interim government formed on a power-sharing basis with equal numbers of Patriotic Front leaders on one side and British and Salisbury leaders on the other. Their attack was met with intransigence. Carrington insisted that the Lusaka conference had established the appropriate parameters for solving the conflict. At this point, the Patriotic Front's only alternative was to question the British mandate to settle the conflict:

*Nkomo*: In view of your statement my delegation considers it necessary to appeal to the Commonwealth countries quoted by the Chairman to state exactly what was meant in the Lusaka Communiqué. It is important for the Commonwealth to state clearly what its position is in this matter.

*Carrington*: I myself was in Lusaka during the discussions and the drafting of the Communiqué and the 39 Heads of Government had agreed there that the elections should be held under British Government authority.

*Mugabe*: Why are you not prepared to go beyond the terms of the Lusaka Communiqué? The document agreed at Lusaka should not be regarded as immutable. If it does not allow sufficient basis for peace, and if my delegation's recommendations enhance or amplify what has been agreed at Lusaka are you going to object merely on the grounds that the Lusaka Communiqué has given certain terms of reference—terms which I do not consider binding on you?

*Carrington*: Both before and at Lusaka there was discussion of how to proceed. Other solutions had been put forward over the years and had failed. That is why it was decided that it should be the British Government's responsibility. This is a matter of principle. If proposals are put forward outside the Lusaka Communiqué which do not constitute matters of principle, and which would improve what has been agreed at Lusaka, I will be happy to consider them. But the principle is something on which the British Government will stand absolutely and resolutely firm.

*Nkomo*: I would like to suggest that the interpretation of British authority in the Lusaka Communique differs from that offered in the British proposals. Those who are interested in seeing peace and security in Zimbabwe will strive to enhance what was done in Lusaka.

*Carrington*: There can be no question of any departure from the fundamental basis on which the Lusaka Agreement was signed. My government has in recent days been in touch with a great many Commonwealth leaders and, as far as I know, not one has disputed this. (United Kingdom 1979, minutes of seventeenth plenary)

At the eighteenth plenary on October 27, Ian Gilmour, acting on behalf of Lord Carrington, responded point by point to the Front's proposals. The result was a heated discussion between Gilmour and various members of the Front's delegation but no concessions on the British part. This prompted Nkomo and Mugabe to test the British mandate. On October 28, they met with Michael Manley, Jamaican prime minister and one of the authors of the Lusaka Communiqué, and Shridath Ramphal. This meeting was preparatory to a showdown on the British handling of the negotiations. While the Commonwealth set up a special meeting in London for October 30 to discuss a Patriotic Front call for change in the British plan, the Front also went to the public with their case. Edison Zvobgo told the press: "After our talks today it is fairly clear that our position is regarded as very sound by the Commonwealth. Does Britain really expect Nkomo and Mugabe to sleep in Salisbury guarded by Bishop Muzorewa's men? We might not even see the end of an election. Why should they not just kill us?" (*Guardian*, October 29, 1979).

The next evening as high commissioners and representatives of thirty-nine Commonwealth states were seeking a mandate from their superiors for a vote on Tuesday, Carrington and Manley met with Margaret Thatcher. It was conveyed that many Commonwealth leaders felt that the Patriotic Front's concerns were legitimate, a sentiment also signaled to Carrington by the U.S. ambassador to Great Britain, Kingman Brewster, on behalf of the Carter administration. Carrington indicated that privately the British were willing to bend on some issues.

The next day, the Patriotic Front was denied a public victory over Carrington. After listening to Ramphal and the Commonwealth's Committee on Southern Africa, the representatives of the thirty-nine states failed to endorse Patriotic Front demands for UN participation and refused to condemn the negotiating efforts of the British. In a very lukewarm statement, the diplomats "expressed concern" rather than criticism. The only point on which there was general agreement was that the two-month election period was too short and that there should probably be a strengthening of the Commonwealth observer team to the elections.

While Carrington had maintained the mandate of the Commonwealth, it had been made clear to him that the British would have to give up ground to the Patriotic Front. To give the reader a sense of the chasm that separated the two parties, the following is a long exchange from the twenty-fourth plenary, on November 1, two days *after* the special Commonwealth meeting (Carrington began by discussing when the governor would be sent and the time frame for the cease-fire and transition, and then reiterating that elections would be under British authority with Commonwealth *observers*):

*Mugabe*: It is clear that the British Government adamantly refuses to accept any of my delegation's arguments or proposals, no matter how rational. This causes some concern, if not real frustration. We are beginning to wonder what purpose the Conference is meant to serve if it is not designed to lead to the capitulation of the Patriotic Front. . . .

When the Conference started we made clear our view that it was to establish peace: the peace process should entail the transitional arrangements proposed by my delegation. There has been a liberation struggle in Zimbabwe since 1966; my delegation assumed the responsibility of decolonizing the country and in doing so we have established formidable forces. Significant advances have been made, such as the acceptance of the principle of majority rule and the holding of this Conference. Mine is a party to be reckoned with, which holds definite positions from which we can not be moved if the intention is to force us to capitulate. We are still ready, however, to reach a solution to achieve full sovereignty for the people and peace honourable for all parties. We have built an army and police force which we want to see given a definite role alongside the forces of the other side during the interim period and afterwards.

My delegation has therefore proposed the integration of forces; we have proposed a Transitional Defence Committee comprising representatives of the Patriotic Front, the Rhodesian regime and Britain. This would have the function firstly of liaison between the Governing Council and the Ceasefire Supervisory Committee, both of which my side proposed, and secondly of starting the process of building the new Zimbabwe army—a process which should commence during the interim period.

My delegation has also proposed a Transitional Police Committee with representatives in equal numbers from the two sides, who would be appointed by the Governing Council and function under its authority. Its main proposed functions would be to supervise and maintain public order; to provide liaison between the Governing Council and the UN civil police force which my delegation proposed; and to commence the building of the Zimbabwe police force.

My delegation also proposed a UN Peace Keeping force alongside the Transitional Defence Committee. Peace has to be maintained; therefore, despite the proposed integration of forces, conflict might develop necessitating a third party. We therefore proposed UN involvement, both as regards the armed forces and the police. My delegation does not understand the rationale for the British refusal to accept UN involvement. The Rhodesian situation has long been a matter of concern to the international community and is regarded as a threat to international peace and security. There have been acts of aggression on neighboring states, and South Africa has also made threats.

I would like to conclude by expressing again my anxiety that the British Government has relegated our forces to the role of mere observers of the ceasefire. The role of ensuring the security of the state in the interim period has been restricted to the Rhodesian forces as they stand; this is discrimination and bias. Why has Britain chosen to use the institutions of the regime and to refuse equal participation of those of my delegation? We can not accept a position of inferiority in a situation where we are moving towards victory—although victory may take time.

My delegation wants peace and are prepared to take an equal position. We are not prepared to lay down our arms, however, if we lose political status. This is a crucial area and I ask the Chairman to re-examine the British position in the light of my delegation's principles and proposals. I am not saying that the Patriotic Front has to be assisted to power but rather that we have to have similar conditions to those accorded to the other side, whether administrative, military, political or legal.

*Carrington*: When my delegation put forward proposals on the interim period, we took into account the views of both delegations. The proposals put forward have, in our view, been a compromise which should be acceptable to both the other delegations but which mean that both sides have to make concessions. I think the concessions made by Bishop Muzorewa's delegation have been considerable; some of those asked of Mr. Mugabe and Mr. Nkomo are also considerable. My delegation seeks a peaceful settlement and the achievement of a fair compromise.

In essence the difficulty is that Mr. Nkomo's and Mr. Mugabe's approach to the interim period is totally different from that of the British Government. Mr. Mugabe's and Mr. Nkomo's delegation seem to be harking back to a large extent to a variation of the Anglo/American Proposals of 1977. Objectively considered, these were extremely elaborate and entailed a large degree of negotiation and difficulty on nearly every issue. In my judgement, they failed because they were too elaborate.

When the present British Government took office and decided to seek a fair solution, it endeavored to learn by past mistakes. Genuine efforts had been made but all had failed. The chief reason the Anglo American Proposals failed was that they were too elaborate. My Government therefore thought it right to propose something as simple and speedy as possible. Elaborate arrangements, like those in the Patriotic Front paper, would be almost impossible to negotiate. . . .

We do not believe that it is possible to integrate the forces in the short period concerned and in the context of elections. We believe it better that the Governor should assume responsibility and use instruments at his disposal fairly and impartially under instructions from the British Government.

I understand the difficulties faced by both visiting delegations. My government believes that our proposals are the only way to proceed in the present very difficult circumstances and very late hour at which the conference is being held. I therefore find it difficult to accept Mr. Mugabe's delegation's arguments, however logical they may be in the abstract. . . .

*Tongogara*: My delegation would find it extremely difficult to explain the British proposals to our forces; they are a recipe for the continuation of fighting rather than for peace.

*Gilmour*: The mechanics of the cease-fire can be discussed the following week—I agree that is a vital part of the Conference. (United Kingdom 1979, minutes of twenty-fourth plenary)

At this point in the plenary, George Silundika, a ZAPU delegate, well respected by ZANU, initiated a line of questioning that led to the final compromise. Although the British did not immediately pick up on Silundika's point, it is clear that while others at this plenary were in a confrontational mode, he was seeking a way out of the deadlock:

> *Silundika*: The British delegation's statements on the role of the military forces lack clarity. In paragraph 9 of paper CC(79)49 it is stated that the "essential task of the military forces of both sides will be to maintain that ceasefire." In another paper, however, CC(79)46, paragraph 6 it is said that the Governor will assume authority over the defence forces and their commanders will report to him. What would they report about? The ceasefire? In any case that does not apply to the forces of the Patriotic Front. I want clarification; do the British delegation perhaps mean that the military forces of the Patriotic Front and Rhodesian regime will have an equal status in law and neither will perform functions greater than those of the other? Such wording might provide the basis for better discussion. . . .

> *Nkomo*: The Conference is considering a war situation which involves two forces, those of the Patriotic Front and of the Rhodesian regime and the British are saying that free and fair elections can take place with one being regarded as a security force and the other mainly to observe the ceasefire. The British are in effect asking my delegation to accept that the Patriotic Front forces have been defeated by the Rhodesian forces and asking them to surrender. If the British cannot accept the Patriotic Front forces they should freeze the two forces and bring in another from outside.

> *Gilmour*: The British are under no illusion about the war and we are not asking for a surrender. We are asking Mr. Mugabe's and Mr. Nkomo's delegation to agree to compete peacefully for power and are trying to create conditions under which this can be done.

> *Willie Masururwa* (ZAPU): The terms being offered by the British amount to capitulation terms. The British are the arbitrators and I ask what criteria have been used to determine which of the two forces will be used to maintain law and order in the interim period. (United Kingdom 1979, minutes of twenty-fourth plenary)

The conference, now going into its eighth week, was starting to unravel. Both the British and the Patriotic Front turned to a brinksmanship style of bargaining. At the end of plenary on November 2, the British had asked for a definitive answer from both parties by November 5 on the full fourty-two-point proposals for the transition period. November 5 was a significant deadline, because the British Parliament that week was to begin debate on whether to continue sanctions against Rhodesia. When the deadline came, Muzorewa accepted fully the British proposals. The Patriotic Front refused to commit themselves and gave the British a list of concerns that they wanted addressed. That Muzorewa had accepted and the Front had not, put enormous pressure on Carrington and Thatcher from the Conservative party to recognize Muzorewa's government and to lift sanctions. When another plenary session on November 6 failed to elicit PF acceptance, Carrington decided to up the ante the next day.

As the twenty-eighth plenary began on November 7, Carrington informed both delegations that the British had introduced into Parliament an enabling bill that would set in motion the necessary paperwork for Rhodesia to be returned to British authority. Although this inflamed the Front, Carrington refused to relent. At the end of the brief plenary, Carrington demanded an answer to the transitional arrangements the next day. Carrington added that if he did not receive one, he did not know how he could continue the conference. One piece of news that Carrington had not reported to the Patriotic Front was that Ian Gilmour was also to inform Parliament that, while most sanctions would remain in force, the Thatcher government had no intention of renewing them.

The Patriotic Front did not attend the plenary that had been planned for the next day, November 8, and Carrington did not receive an answer. Carrington took the opportunity to castigate the Patriotic Front in public. The Patriotic Front claimed that it was a misunderstanding caused by the failure of their request for postponement to reach Carrington. In lieu of the plenary meeting, Mugabe and Nkomo had met with Kenneth Kaunda, who had flown to London in hopes of breaking the deadlock. Kaunda's concern had been intensified because of a series of Rhodesian attacks on ZAPU bases in Zambia and economic and transportation targets within that country, purportedly to minimize ZAPU infiltration into Zimbabwe in anticipation of an election. Zambia, already reeling from three such attacks in October, was dealt a further blow when the Muzorewa government, on November 5, decided to use food as a weapon and halt maize shipments into Zambia.

From November 8 to 10, in plenary sessions, the British and Patriotic Front castigated each other for their stubbornness. The Patriotic Front suspected that the British and Muzorewa had cut a secret deal and realized more than ever their information disadvantage. Nkomo, after a long rambling statement about the lack of understanding and common language between his delegation and the British, stated that the PF desired to know directly from the Salisbury delegation how they felt about issues:

> It is necessary for each of the delegations to get to know what the others are thinking. If we had not wished to discuss matters with the Salisbury delegation we would not have come . . . the present method of operating makes it difficult for my delegation to find out what the Salisbury delegation wants. If my delegation could let the Salisbury delegation see what our aims are they might be able to agree.

*Mundawarara* (Muzorewa aide): My delegation has already finished with this part of the conference. We therefore have nothing to contribute to discussions . . . it might be helpful at this stage for the Chairman to hold bilateral meetings with the Patriotic Front delegation.

*Nkomo*: The problem has arisen because the Salisbury delegation has accepted the British proposals. My own delegation has means of meeting some of the issues within the British proposals. It is essential that these be discussed. It is fitting, and indeed vital, that those who have agreed to the British proposals understand the Patriotic Front delegation's objectives. (United Kingdom 1979, minutes of thirtieth plenary)

Carrington shrugged that it was up to the Salisbury delegation to choose how they would be involved. George Nyandoro, a Muzorewa aide, summed up the feeling of the Salisbury side by throwing back in the face of Nkomo that the Muzorewa delegation had previously wanted meetings with the PF and that they had refused.[5]

While the bickering continued between the delegations, Carrington, Kaunda, and Thatcher thrashed out possible compromise agreements. First, Carrington decided and made public that there would be a Commonwealth monitoring force of around 1,200 soldiers to supervise the cease-fire. Although Carrington had been loath to discuss the cease-fire before an agreement on the transition, the sharing of this information would make it easier for the PF to understand what was coming if the negotiations proceeded. Second, the British would lengthen the interim period from two months to twelve to thirteen weeks. Because part of the Front's objections to a short interim period was their concern to resettle refugees in camps in Mozambique and Zambia, the British government would undertake assistance in helping such resettlement.

The Kaunda intervention helped to bring the parties together. In plenary on November 14, Carrington and Mugabe discussed areas of agreement and disagreement. The Patriotic Front had accepted a British governor who would rely on the existing Rhodesian administration, an election council and British election commissioner, and a party list system of voting. Areas of disagreement included the full registration of voters, the nature of the police force, the length of the transition, the formation of a cease-fire commission, and the composition of the peacekeeping force. Carrington then spelled out the compromises the British would make: the lengthening of the cease-fire an addition of more than 100 staff members to the election commissioner, and a Commonwealth monitoring force rather than a peacekeeping force. Carrington flatly vetoed a cease-fire commission: "The role of the military forces on both sides will be to maintain the ceasefire, for which they will be equally responsible to the Governor" (United

Kingdom 1979, minutes of thirty-third plenary).

A series of bilateral meetings between the British and the Patriotic Front went late into the night of November 14. The Front had accepted all of the British proposals but hedged because they believed that the language of the agreements still provided differentiated status to the two armies. Harking back to George Silundika's probes about the intent of British wording about the role of the armed forces, a compromise was finally reached.

The next day in plenary, Mugabe read a statement that was quickly agreed to by Carrington: "In the light of the discussions we have had as a result of President Kaunda's proposals to the Prime Minister, if you are prepared to include the Patriotic Front forces in paragraph 13 of the British paper, we are able to agree to the interim proposals, conditional on a successful outcome of the negotiations on the ceasefire" (conference paper CC(79)76, November 15, 1979, United Kingdom 1979, thirty-fourth plenary). The added sentence read, "The Patriotic Front's forces will also be required to comply with the directions of the Governor" (conference addendum 1, November 15, 1979, United Kingdom 1979). The final concession was a symbolic one. The sentence formally granted Nkomo and Mugabe what they had been fighting for—the acknowledgment that they were equal to the existing administration. And while Silas Mundawarara, acting on behalf of Muzorewa, squawked that the Salisbury regime did not recognize the change, his implied threat was not credible. The negotiations moved on to the cease-fire.

*The Cease-fire*

Carrington felt that the problems of reaching an agreement on the cease-fire would be greater than those encountered during the previous negotiations. But he also felt that his strategy of proceeding issue by issue was paying off and was providing the momentum he had hoped to achieve. On November 16, the British tabled their general proposals. The next plenary session fell into the pattern of the previous two months: the Patriotic Front tabled their own proposals, Mugabe and Nkomo expressed displeasure at how the British were running the conference, and then Carrington asserted that "a conclusion is needed within a few days" (United Kingdom 1979, minutes of thirty-fifth plenary).

The Patriotic Front proposals once again differed dramatically from the British outline. First, they envisioned the demarcation of different parts of the country to be under the control of the guerrillas and other parts under the Rhodesian security forces. The British rejected this out of hand because such a process would "result in our discussions being prolonged indefinitely, with little prospect of agreement ever being reached." The heart of the Front's plan called for a peacekeeping force that would enforce the cease-fire. The British argued that the cease-fire had to be self-enforcing with the responsibility for maintaining the peace with the respective armies. Finally, the Front believed that during the cease-fire a start should be made in integrating the armies and police forces. The British countered that the interim period would be used for all concerned to get their electoral message across and not to begin the making of a new Zimbabwe.

The Patriotic Front once more felt at a disadvantage: the Salisbury regime had not tabled their own proposals. Because of this the Front once again suspected collusion between the British and Muzorewa. Moreover, the British were running the conference as they had for the previous ten weeks:

> *Nkomo*: We are talking about a war involving some 100,000 armed men and women scattered all over the country; we are not talking about a few bands of guerrillas. . . . The British proposals seem to be designed to put the Patriotic Front forces on one side and the Rhodesian forces on the other with a referee in the middle to keep both where they are. Supposing that this happened, what would be done with the two armed forces by the party which won the election? Would the winning side eliminate the other? The question before the conference is one of life and death. . . . We have to be certain that any agreed plan will bring about conciliation between the two fighting forces and among the people: anything short of that is unacceptable. (United Kingdom 1979, minutes of thirty-fifth plenary)

When Ian Gilmour suggested that detailed discussions on the arrangements should proceed and that the best way to do so would be through bilaterals, Nkomo erupted:

> In the case of bilateral discussions, my delegation will not know what the Salisbury delegation has said to the British, and equally the Salisbury delegation would not know what my delegation has had to say. It is important for each delegation to know what transpired between the other two. Otherwise it will look to my delegation like an orchestrated way of reaching agreement. This has happened during the discussion on the constitution and on the interim agreements, and now a similar procedure was contemplated for the much more crucial ceasefire discussions. Perhaps when Mr. Day was in Salisbury the British had concluded a deal there. Have the British brought us to London merely to orchestrate matters? (United Kingdom 1979, minutes of thirty-fifth plenary)

On November 22, Carrington tabled the full proposals for the cease-fire. The most important feature of the plan was that it would take place in two stages. First, the Salisbury troops would be deployed to their main bases. Second, when the monitors had reported that the troops were at their bases, the Patriotic Front guerrillas would have to gather at assembly points throughout the country, where they would then be fed and monitored by the Commonwealth force. The time span for these two stages was seven to ten days.

Carrington, at the same plenary where he submitted the full proposals, also took time to respond to events taking place in the region at that moment. On November 16, South Africa had announced that it would not accept "chaos" in Rhodesia. Between November 16 and 19, Rhodesia bombed five road bridges in Zambia and destroyed the last remaining rail bridge that linked Zambia to the outside world. The destruction of all transport routes out of Zambia put the country on the edge of economic collapse. Kaunda countered by mobilizing his country for war. The East German and Soviet embassies in Lusaka took rare action and officially warned South Africa to keep their forces out of Zimbabwe if the Patriotic Front came to power.

At the time, Rhodesia's motives were thought to be a search for leverage on Kaunda to force him to put greater pressure on the Patriotic Front. In fact, the bombings had not been ordered by Salisbury's military commanders. Rather, the actions were undertaken by lesser officers temporarily out from beneath the control of their elders, who were preoccupied at Lancaster House. For these junior officers, the destruction of economic targets did not constitute a major escalation: the bombings were a way of turning on the heat at Lancaster House (Flower 1987, interview with author). For Kaunda, however, the action was at the threshold of crossing a tacit limit that could change the conduct and scope of the war.

Carrington issued two ultimatums at the November 22 plenary. First, he demanded that both sides accept the British cease-fire proposals by November 26. Second, he urged that "as an immediate measure to reduce the danger of a further escalation of the conflict . . . an agreement should immediately be concluded in order to avoid any further increase in tension between Rhodesia and Zambia." The agreement would include Rhodesian word that cross-border operations into Zambia would cease and Patriotic Front word that there would be no more further movement of personnel from Zambia into Rhodesia. Carrington stated that he had already received cooperation from President Kaunda, who had been in touch with Margaret Thatcher that day, and that he expected word from both delegations on this proposal by the following morning.

The plenary quickly dissolved into heated argument. Mugabe and Nkomo were irate that Carrington was drawing a similarity between the two forces and their actions. As to Carrington's deadline on the cease-fire, Mugabe demanded that the Salisbury delegation publicly state their unwillingness to talk directly with the Front or the talks would not proceed. Tongogara, in a more problem-solving way, expressed his frustration with not talking directly with the Salisbury delegation, because "these are the two forces in conflict; my delegation cannot secure an agreement with Britain." He then added that it would prove difficult in the future for the two sides to sit down and talk in Salisbury if they were not prepared to talk in London. The conference ended when Mugabe and Nkomo pulled their delegations, Nkomo warning Carrington "not to come the following Monday and expect an answer from my delegation without discussions—the chairman will not get one" (United Kingdom 1979, minutes of thirty-seventh plenary). The two rebel leaders gave an impromptu press conference, "still shaking with anger. . . . Asked what will happen when the Monday deadline comes, so far as the Patriotic Front is concerned, Mr. Mugabe said there could be no question of toeing the line. Lord Carrington, he said, 'can go to hell'" (*Guardian*, November 23, 1979).

Carrington's ultimatum prompted Mugabe to fly to Dar es Salaam to meet the Front Line presidents, where Mugabe publicly stated that he would not allow his soldiers slaughtered on the way to the assembly points and "General Walls gaining at Lancaster House what he failed to achieve on the battlefield" (quoted in Smith and Simpson 1981, 139). The intensity of the meeting in Dar es Salaam, as well as the brutal "give and take" among the participants, was reminiscent of Kissinger's meeting with Ian Smith three years before:

> "I am not going to stand for my forces being herded like cattle into these detention centres at the mercy of the Rhodesian army and air force. My army could be destroyed within days," Mugabe said.
>
> Nyerere and Machel, like Kaunda before them, urged conciliation, if not instant concessions from the Front. Machel is reliably reported to have told Mugabe: "We hear what you are saying, but we know you will hear us when we say the war must end." At the end of a long meeting, Mugabe remarked only: "We will be going back to London to negotiate." (Smith and Simpson 1981, 141)

After the meeting in Dar es Salaam, the Front Line presidents, through their representatives in London, lobbied Carrington hard on three issues: the length of the cease-fire, the need for close monitoring of the Rhodesian forces, and the need for particularly close watch on the Rhodesian air force to prevent them from bombing the assembly points. Carrington grudgingly met these two latter demands but refused to concede a longer cease-fire period.

This was the only time where Carrington's emphasis on arbitration had to yield to a softer approach. What is intriguing is that while Carrington and his staff and the Patriotic Front's legal advisers were playing a hard bargaining game on the issues of the cease-fire, an informal coalition was formed between the Patriotic Front's military leaders and the British Military advisers, who both felt that the stakes were too important to leave negotiating to the civilians. One ZAPU delegate remarked, "The only give and take negotiations were over the military transition and cease-fire.... There were negotiations then only because the British military were frightened; they had to listen if we said you can't do something in 24 hours, for example.... Everyone was interested in saving lives and it was a matter of finding the best way of doing things" (ZAPU Delegate A. 1987, interview with author). Simbi Mubako, ZANU's member of the Patriotic Front's legal team, went so far as to mention Tongogara's role in moderating the cease-fire negotiations:

> I remember him saying [about the number and location of the assembly points], "This is not a point on which to break the conference." You see the military people knew the situation on the ground; they knew what they could live with; what they could get away with. For example, he knew that so many would be able to be kept out of the assembly points and he knew that we could send the majibas [teenage scouts] into the assembly points and keep our best fighters out and in the villages to work on the election. The lawyers were much more theoretical because we didn't know what could happen on the ground."
> (Mubako 1987, interview with author)

An important piece of information that was shared between Tongogara and the British was that he could reach any of his troops by relay in four days (Davidow 1984, 81-82). This dramatically undercut the Front's bargaining position on the need for a long cease-fire period. Moreover, at this time Tongogara began consultations with Peter Walls and Ken Flower over military arrangements. According to the personal notes of Richard Moose, then U.S. assistant secretary of state for African affairs, Robin Renwick went so far as to call Tongogara's cooperation with Walls "impressive." David Owen even speculated on "the possibility of a coalition involving Muzorewa and Tongogara" (Moose 1979).

The PF gave partial acceptance on December 6 but made full approval conditional on the longer cease-fire period and additional assembly points. Just when agreement seemed imminent, the PF's conditional acceptance threatened to bring down the whole settlement. The conference had become "bogged down over precisely how, where, and when the war would end" (Smith and Simpson 1981, 148).

Carrington was forced to cash in on the momentum that had built to this point by reporting to the press that a settlement was only days away and that, given all that had been accomplished so far, the Patriotic Front could not possibly turn their backs from the negotiation. Relying on brinksmanship, Carrington then named Lord Soames governor of Zimbabwe and dispatched him to Salisbury. Both moves provoked the

PF's most belligerent responses to date, with Mugabe's press secretary, Edison Zvobgo, informing the British press that Lord Carrington "can go to hell," and that "Thatcher can jump in the Thames." Zvobgo concluded the impromptu press conference by "brandishing the British maps [of the assembly points] and giving a shake of his head into camera for each of the television networks there: 'The answer, Lord Carrington, is NO . . . NO . . . NO'" (Smith and Simpson 1981, 150).

The British, with Mozambican and U.S. help, put the screws to Mugabe. In response to British requests, the United States decided that it would lift sanctions against Rhodesia. On December 14, the U.S. State Department sent a confidential cable to its embassies in the Front Line States. It ordered the embassies to give a letter to the Front Line presidents informing them of the impending decision to remove sanctions: "What we want to happen is for your guy to pick up the phone and call Josh and/or Robert. It will be clear from text of letter that U.S. cannot retain sanctions. This being the case it greatly preferable that the President be able to lift in the context of an agreement" (U.S. Department of State 1979).

Just when the edifice was about to collapse, Samora Machel came to Carrington's rescue. Samora Machel passed a message to his chief aide in London, Fernand Honwana, to give to Mugabe. Honwana informed Mugabe that the war was over and that "if he [Mugabe] did not sign the agreement, he would be welcomed back to Mozambique and given a beach villa where he could write his memoirs" (Davidow 1984, 89). After a final face-saving gesture by the British in granting the Front an additional assembly point, the Lancaster House accords were signed on December 21, the 102nd day of the conference.

## The End and Beginning

The signatures at Lancaster House only signaled a commitment to a peaceful transition. The next two months would be more harrowing for the participants than any other time in the conflict. In the words of Lord Soames, the British governor, "It was a tinderbox, but, happily, no one struck a match" (Newhouse 1983, 78). The fuel for the fire was everywhere. In the first two weeks of the cease-fire, 22,000 guerrillas marched to assembly points. ZANU and, especially, ZAPU kept most of their best fighters out of the camps as a fail-safe measure in case the country exploded. The British, fearing the possibility of a coup from disgruntled white soldiers or a reneging on the cease-fire by the Salisbury regime, went out of their way to be tough on ZANU in order to appease Muzorewa and Walls. In a not very subtle move, the South African army moved three divisions to the Zimbabwean border as a reminder of what they would do in the event of "chaos." Amidst threats by the British that they would disqualify ZANU because of intimidation, Mugabe feared that his suspicions of a double-cross might come true.

Two of the three individuals who were moderating influences on ZANU at Lancaster House were unable to play that role during the election campaign. Tongogara, in advance of the ZANU delegation, had flown to Mozambique a week earlier than the signing in London to ready his troops for the cease-fire. While in Mozambique, he died in an automobile accident, which amidst rumors of assassination brought everyone's nerves to the edge. Then Mugabe, before leaving London, announced that ZANU would run on its own in the election and not in coalition with ZAPU. This stunned Nkomo, as his strategy throughout the previous two years had been predicated on coming to power in conjunction with Mugabe. But Mugabe, confident of victory on his own, discarded his less powerful partner.

British pressure kept building on ZANU until Mugabe had a direct talk with Soames. The talk was prompted in part by two assassination attempts against Mugabe. Soames privately reassured him that no party would be disqualified from the election.[6] Britain's public posturing against ZANU, however, prompted Julius Nyerere two weeks before the scheduled elections at the end of February to say that he would recognize the winner only if it was Mugabe. This greatly angered Soames and his staff, because the whole election period and cease-fire hinged on the believability of a free and fair election any of the parties could win and whose results all parties would respect. Nyerere's statement threatened the confidence of the white Rhodesians, because it was an implicit threat that if ZANU did not win the election, the war would continue.

At Lancaster House, the British had an idea of a feasible settlement but when the conference succeeded, they were really not prepared for stepping into the breach. A member of Soames's staff described the transition as "a gigantic game of bluff, keeping just enough Rhodesians obeying the Governor long enough to pull it off." Britain's formal status of decolonizer became crucial at this point, for enough white Rhodesians in the administration saw the British presence and authority as legitimate.

After the election on February 27, 28, and 29, but before the announcement of the election results on March 4, the British, knowing that Mugabe was to win, contacted Machel and arranged a meeting in Mozambique between Mugabe, Flower, and Walls. Machel's aide, Fernand Honwana, "understood that if Mugabe won, he would need the British and a modus vivendi with Walls." At the meeting, Mugabe offered Walls the command of the new Zimbabwean army, a job he accepted.

On 4 March 1980, the election results were announced. Mugabe and ZANU had won fifty-seven out of 100 seats, Nkomo had gained twenty seats, and Muzorewa three. To a stunned nation, Soames, Mugabe, and Walls went on television that evening. Soames began by announcing his duty to hand over power in an orderly fashion. He was followed by Peter Walls, who appealed "to you all for calm, for peace. No hatred. No bitterness." The last speaker was Robert Mugabe: "Let us join together. Let us show respect for the winners and the losers. . . . There is no intention on our part to victimize the minority. We will ensure there is a place for everyone in this country. I want a broadly based government to include whites and Nkomo" (quoted in Flower 1987, 267–268). On April 18, 1980, Zimbabwe was granted formal independence from Great Britain.

## Notes

1. By not publicizing her intention to call a new conference on Rhodesia, Thatcher also protected herself from any sniping from members of her own Conservative party (Carrington 1987, interview with author).

2. For an attempt to quantify the costs of the war for the Front Line States, see Thompson (1985, 75–86).

3. When quoting the minutes of the meetings at Lancaster House, I have transformed the words of the participants into the active voice. At Lancaster House two sets of minutes were taken—one set by the British as the formal minutes and another set by ZAPU. One PF delegate who read both sets of minutes described them as roughly equivalent, with the exception of the discussions of the land issue. The ZAPU minutes were apparently destroyed when the Zimbabwean government seized ZAPU's records in 1983.

4. A party-list method of voting calls for the voter to vote for a political party and not for a specific candidate. The political parties create lists of candidates in order of their importance to the party. The number of votes the party gains determines how many candidates on the list are chosen.

5. Unknown to most at the meetings, including their partners, Nkomo and two of his military commanders met in private with Peter Walls and Ken Flower. The meeting, called by Nkomo, was an attempt to convince the Salisbury delegation that the transition and cease-fire were too important to leave to the British. The Rhodesians listened attentively but refused to accommodate the ZAPU leader.

6. This seems to have been the only point in the mediation effort where an important division within the mediator threatened the whole process. ZANU and Mugabe feared—with good reason—that the British were trying to sabotage Mugabe's chances for victory. The British in the first six weeks of the campaign clearly leaned on ZANU more than they did on any other party. I received two versions from different British diplomats about the reasons for this. One line, the "official" line, portrays the British as bullying ZANU in order to placate the Rhodesians and keep them (the Rhodesians) in line. A different line, put to me by two different British diplomats, was that Anthony Duff, acting on his own, believing that ZANU would be a disaster if it won power, instigated a wrecking campaign against Mugabe. In this latter story,

Soames, who originally went along with the idea of pressuring ZANU to coddle the Rhodesians, learned about the true extent of Duff's actions, became furious, chastised Duff, and made peace with Mugabe. One piece of evidence that supports this version is in Flower's autobiography, where Flower has in his notes from Lancaster House the record of a conversation he had with Duff in the middle of December. At that point, Duff confided to Flower that he was convinced that the internal solution—Muzorewa—was the only "practicable solution." Later in his notes Flower writes of an idea that Duff was bandying about : "We might find it difficult, if not impossible, to reject the PF. Another possibility emerging is the 'Mark one-and-a-half' solution as referred to recently by Sir Anthony Duff, whereby one faction of the PF competes peacefully, in which regard Nkomo's placatory approach as published in the *Herald* is significant" (Flower 1987, Appendix—"Notes taken by D-G CIO in connection with the Lancaster House conference, London, September–December, 1979," 314–316).

# 6

# Comparing Success
# and Failure

*For another thing, the date of a change, like that of a harvest,*
*might have its influence upon the kind of fruit you get.*
                                                      —Jules Romains

In this chapter, I discuss the successful British mediation at Lancaster House in light of earlier discussions regarding how civil war can be settled through negotiation. In doing so, I draw explicit comparisons to the other subcases of attempted mediation in Zimbabwe. My argument is that, in terms of ripeness for resolution as defined by Zartman, the conflict in September 1979 should not have led to settlement. The war failed to meet criteria of hurting stalemate and parity. Qualified confirmation is given to the variables of reversal of fortune and perceptions of a worse moment lying in the future if negotiations were to fail. A comparison with previous episodes, however, shows that these variables were present at an earlier junction, which suggests other factors at work at Lancaster House. In particular, I argue that changes internal to the fighting groups, changes in the mediation effort, and the ability of the new mediator to learn from past failures led to the success at Lancaster House. In this chapter, I also examine the key alternatives to the participants away from the bargaining table and explore why the conflict did not escalate. From a comparison of the four most identifiable instances where the conflict could have led to a regional or larger war, I discuss the interrelationship between decisionmaking concerning likelihood of settlement and decisionmaking concerning escalation. Having discussed the findings of the Zimbabwean cases, I turn in the final chapter to a refinement and elaboration of the concept of ripeness and resolution of conflict.

## The Question of Ripeness

What made Lancaster House different from the other attempted settlements? The most obvious place to look for an answer is the tide of the war. This answer suggests that unlike previous attempts, the military situation in 1979 made the conflict "ripe for resolution."[1] Recalling our discussion in Chapter 1, William Zartman argues that there are moments in conflict when third parties can intervene and bring a conflict to an end and that such moments depend on three conditions. A crisis is ripe when (1) there exists a situation perceived by actors as deadlock and deadline; (2) "unilateral solutions are blocked and joint solutions become conceivable"; and (3) the party that previously had the upper hand in the conflict has slipped and the underdog has gained in strength. Both sides perceive that the conflict is a "hurting stalemate." Each antagonist believes it is unable to win the conflict by itself and that such a state of affairs will last into the indefinite future with each side still possessing the ability to make the other hurt. At the same time, each party perceives "a moment when things will significantly get worse if they have not gotten better in ways that negotiation seeks to define" (Zartman 1983, 353; 1985).

Was the situation leading up to Lancaster House a hurting stalemate? This description fails to capture accurately the course of the war in September 1979. The participants, those directly and indirectly involved, had different perceptions about the military situation at that point. For the Rhodesians, the situation was worse than a stalemate: they were facing a desperate crisis due to the combined economic and military damage to the country. As Ken Flower described it, "We needed a settlement, any kind of settlement. We were losing the war" (Flower 1987, interview with author). For the Patriotic Front, the leaders believed that victory was inevitable; the only remaining question concerned the costs of that victory. Nkomo and Tongogara favored winning at the negotiating table rather than on the battlefield. Mugabe, however, remained skeptical about a settlement throughout Lancaster House and feared that the agreement was a way for General Peter Walls to win at the table what he could not win on the battlefield.

For the Front Line States, the war had different effects. The country that took the most punishment from the war was Zambia, with Mozambique close behind. Kaunda and Machel wanted a settlement because the costs of the war had taken too much of a toll. In Kaunda's case, no one questioned his desperation and his credibility about shutting down ZAPU if the war continued. In Machel's case, however, there was some doubt in ZANU whether he would really carry out his threat of relinquishing support and guerrilla bases (Mubako 1987, interview with author). The Front Line country hurt the least in the war, Tanzania, could afford for its leader, Julius Nyerere, to be less compromising, as evidenced by his threat to ignore the results of the election if the PF did not win.

If the conflict was not believed to be stalemated, was it at least the case that the participants perceived the consequences of no agreement as leading to a worse situation for all? Lancaster House gives qualified support to this factor. At the beginning of the Lancaster House Conference, the British tried to inculcate the belief that if no agreement was reached at the conference, the situation would be markedly worse. This was done mostly by impressing on the delegations that this was likely to be the last attempt to negotiate a settlement, that this was the last chance for the participants to end the war. Within the delegations some of the individuals did fear the consequences of not reaching an agreement. Yet others welcomed not reaching an agreement.

The various political leaders—Muzorewa, Smith, Mugabe, and Nkomo—perceived differently the costs of no agreement. For Smith, no agreement was his first priority: his fear of the Patriotic Front in power was greater than his fear of continuing the war. This stemmed from two sources. His ideology, which I have discussed earlier, mostly accounts for his preference, but also a small part must be attributed to his belief that if the Salisbury delegation were to hold out, then Thatcher eventually would be forced to recognize the Muzorewa government. For Mugabe, it is also the case that he did not perceive a moment that would be worse if the conference were to fail. When it was clear in December that all of the other parties had jumped aboard the settlement, Mugabe then saw that to continue fighting would be a difficult undertaking. But Mugabe's worst nightmare was his troops being slaughtered at the assembly points during the cease-fire, which he believed was a possible outcome of any settlement. This, he felt, would be worse than the price of no agreement. For Muzorewa, the evidence is unclear: he wanted peace for his country, so that it could be said that he saw the failure of reaching agreement as leading to a time when matters would be worse. But this does not capture accurately his belief about the consequences of no agreement: he honestly believed that the Patriotic Front forces were desperate and would abandon Mugabe and Nkomo if the war were to continue (Muzorewa 1987, interview with author).

The only political leader who clearly feared the consequences of no settlement was Joshua Nkomo. He believed that the situation would be worse, in part because he took steps to fulfill the prophecy. He, of all the leaders at Lancaster House, was convinced that this was the last chance to settle the matter at the negotiating table. Indeed, he bound himself to seeking a peaceful settlement by ordering his military advisers to prepare for the escalation of the conflict to conventional war, if the conference failed. His advisers admitted that this would have been a move made out of desperation and not out of rational calculation.

The military leaders of the different delegations came much closer to having the sense that Zartman describes. I mentioned Ken Flower's sentiment above. Tongogara also feared the consequences of no settlement at Lancaster House, because he dreaded the possibility of fighting a guerrilla war without bases in Mozambique. While some of the ZANU leaders questioned the credibility of the Mozambican threat, Tongogara either felt it was credible or had no desire to find out whether it was.

Zartman's insight comes into play after agreement was reached. Once the parties were locked into the settlement implementation, the costs of breakdown rose dramatically. If either side grossly violated the agreement, all hell would break loose. What had heretofore been a guerrilla struggle would see pitched battles between thousands of soldiers; South Africa, which had kept a minimum distance, probably would have intervened, if only as a rescue mission for white Rhodesians. The British would find themselves nominally administering a country in an all-out conventional war, with the few troops they had in great jeopardy. The British plan can best be likened to transforming the conflict into a one-shot game of chicken: there may have been incentives to cheat and seek advantage of the cease-fire, but the costs of total breakdown were prohibitive. The cease-fire built into the plan the consequence of dramatic escalation were either side to breach it. This aspect of the plan was recognized in a conversation that one British official had with Tongogara before he left for Zimbabwe in December: "Tongogara told me immediately before he left Lancaster House that this was very risky for them. I told him that it was equally risky for us and for Walls, but that if we did not carry it through the country would be reduced to ashes. And South Africa will come over the border to take the whites out, leaving as much destruction as they can, to which Tongogara agreed" (British Diplomat A. 1987, interview with author).

Did the agreement come at a time when the fortunes of the players were reversed; that is, was the weaker party surpassing the other? In the flow of the war, I have argued that such a moment came earlier, back in 1974. The effect then was to instill more fear into the whites and more confidence into the blacks, with the net effect of making the contest extremely difficult to settle at that juncture. If we take Zartman's proposition in a broader sense, however, and think of such moments as simple reversals of fortune rather than single turning points in the conflict, we may get a more powerful proposition. Militarily, by early 1979, the blacks had the upper hand, and the Salisbury government was weaker. The election of Thatcher, however, *threatened* to reverse the situation. It provided incentive for both parties to settle at that point, in part because it was not the *first* major reversal in the war. The participants had been sobered by the conflict and did not act as previously: the underdog did not become overly confident or the stronger party overly fearful.

It was not until 1979 and the emergence of Muzorewa as leader that the Salisbury regime understood the advantage of negotiating from temporary strength. Ian Smith, for instance, never understood this. The Rhodesian military would give Smith tactical strength in the belief that he would use such moments to bargain. Instead, he always confused temporary strength with long-term power, which prevented him from settling the conflict (Flower 1987, interview with author).

I would like to take issue with another of Zartman's points. He argues that the role of the mediator is to put forward a second-track solution when it is shown that the actor's first preferences are unattainable. Although the British did craft a second-track solution that met the needs of both sides, Zartman's proposition misses the proper causal sequence in the Zimbabwean case. At Lancaster House, the British succeeded precisely by holding out the possibility to the Salisbury regime that their first preference was attainable, if the Front did not accept the settlement. Compliance by the Salisbury delegation was produced all along the way by the incentive of possibly gaining their unilateral goal rather than from their belief that their unilateral preference was unattainable.

This brings us to one last point vis à vis Zartman and Lancaster House. Inherent in Zartman's analysis is that a rough parity has to exist between parties before a settlement can be reached.[2] Indeed, he goes so far as to say that there are times when an active third party may have to provide resources to one of the sides so as to provide parity. The Zimbabwean case fails to bear this out and cautions against it. In September 1979, there was not a rough parity between the Salisbury regime and the Patriotic Front. British leverage stemmed from the fact that the white regime was falling and the British had the capability to breathe new life into their battle with the guerrillas. Had the British, in the belief that actors only bargain from strength or from parity, recognized the Muzorewa government and lifted sanctions *first*, they would have forfeited their only leverage.

This goes back to a point made earlier in the chapter. Most actors who find themselves bargaining during war believe that they need to be made stronger before negotiating seriously. A third party that undertakes to equip or aid one side in order to provide parity not only risks becoming involved in a war it would rather avoid, but that party's actions may also be the impetus for the underdog to think that, with the new influx of resources, it can win. The Rhodesian struggle was lengthened precisely because Ian Smith took every temporary victory as an indicator that he could avoid compromise. A safer maxim to employ for a third-party mediator is if the actors are unequal in strength, then one should use the *prospect* of strengthening the weaker actor as leverage on both parties to reach an agreement. To summarize so far, I have argued that Lancaster House, though leading to a settlement of the Rhodesian war, was not ripe for resolution given the factors that Zartman emphasizes. It is useful at this point to examine Table 6.1, which compares the four mediation efforts as they pertain to Zartman's variables.

Table 6.1  Ripeness and Resolution in Rhodesia, 1974–1980

| | International Mediation Attempts | | | |
|---|---|---|---|---|
| | Détente 1974–1975 | Geneva 1976 | Anglo-American 1977–1978 | Lancaster House 1979–1980 |
| Hurting stalemate | no | no | no | no |
| Worse moment ahead (Nationalists/ Rhodesians) | mixed/ yes | no/ mixed | no/ no | mixed/ mixed |
| Reversal of fortune | yes | no | no | yes |
| Parity | no | yes | no | no |

Not one of the cases fits Zartman's criteria for ripeness, although the Kaunda/Vorster "détente" exercise in 1974–1975 compares favorably with Lancaster House. At a minimum, we can say that at least *some* of the participants in the conflict must perceive that the conflict, if not resolved, will grow fundamentally worse, and that some kind of reversal of fortune may play a role in establishing the objective circumstances necessary for settlement. But Table 6.1 also suggests that because another case also fits these qualifications, we should compare the cases on other dimensions.

## Internal Politics and Negotiation

In Chapter 1, I argued for the centrality of politics internal to actors in determining decisions on settlement. Political actors, whether states or revolutionary parties, are coalitions of individuals with different values, preferences, and resources. Through group decisionmaking, leaders argue and debate what is "rational" for the group: its objective situation, the character of the opponent, the minimal demands to be met, its alternatives, etc. Coalitions of diverse actors form to push one alternative over another.

Table 6.2 summarizes three factors internal to the parties distinguished by mediating attempt. The first category simply lists those leaders who had "last say" on any decision in the particular negotiations. One obvious change—but again, in no sense trivial—is that at Lancaster House Ian Smith no longer negotiated for the Salisbury regime.

The second category measures the solidity of the leader-follower relationship within the parties, that is, whether the movement is consolidated behind the leader so that the leader can be confident of "leading"—making a choice that he or she expects others to obey. From Table 6.2 we can see that at Lancaster House the liberation groups had for the first time two leaders who had consolidated their leadership and had established a reservoir of authority from which they could draw. While this had always been true for Nkomo and ZAPU, it is only at Lancaster House that Mugabe was clearly the leader of ZANU. Whereas in previous mediation attempts Mugabe could not seek settlement for fear of risking a mutiny from his soldiers, at Lancaster House, Tongogara, the commander of ZANLA, actively pushed Mugabe for settlement.

Finally, the third category in the table examines whether the movement spoke with one voice. In the case of the liberation movement, there was not a single instance when the parties truly put the interests of the movement above their own parties. The Patriotic Front was at its most unified at Lancaster House, but Nkomo and Mugabe had different interests, sponsors, and constituencies. In the case of the Salisbury side, Ian Smith for years had been the dominant voice in Rhodesian politics. In negotiations, what Smith said, Smith delivered. It was only at Lancaster House that Smith's say became one among a cacophony of voices: Muzorewa, Walls, Flower, David Smith, among others.

How did these three factors influence the negotiations at Lancaster House? I have argued earlier that in 1979 not all of the major actors wanted a settlement. On the Rhodesian side, a coalition emerged between Bishop Muzorewa, David Smith, and General Peter Walls that favored a settlement and overcame the opposition of Ian Smith, who admitted that his strategy was predicated on refusing to compromise and seeing if the Thatcher government could have been pushed into recognizing the Muzorewa regime. Failing such recognition, Smith was committed to a fight to the bitter end (Smith 1987, interview with author). On the liberation side, Robert Mugabe did not favor a settlement but Joshua Nkomo did. The British were able to play on this split and to use pressure from Samora Machel to push Mugabe toward settlement. The wild card that the British had not counted on was ZANLA's General Josiah Tongogara, who emerged as the most powerful and persistent voice for settlement within the ZANU camp.

Table 6.2 Internal Political Changes in Rhodesia 1974–1980

| | International Mediation Attempts | | | |
|---|---|---|---|---|
| | Victoria Falls 1974–1975 | Geneva 1976 | Anglo-American 1977–1978 | Lancaster House 1979–1980 |
| Negotiator(s): | | | | |
| Nationalists | Nkomo Muzorewa Sithole | Nkomo Mugabe Muzorewa Sithole | Nkomo Mugabe | Nkomo Mugabe |
| Rhodesians | Smith | Smith | Smith | Muzorewa |
| Consolidated leadership? (Nationalists/ Rhodesians) | no/ yes | no/ yes | no/ yes | yes/ yes |
| One voice? (Nationalists/ Rhodesians) | no/ yes | no/ yes | no/ yes | no/ no |

The point here is that in the Zimbabwe negotiations the British recognized that some individuals were opposed to settlement and would have to be isolated from their team members. This points to the two faces of unity in negotiations. On the one side, unity on the part of the negotiating sides is necessary to ensure that any agreement reached will be carried out.   On the other hand, a certain amount of disunity within the negotiating sides allows the mediator to craft bargains and elicit compromises.   The dilemma, however, lies in what options the loser in any coalition may have when isolated from team members. For example, the Lancaster House outcome would have been dramatically different if Ian Smith had had support in segments of the Rhodesian military and had decided to fight the accords.

The example of Ian Smith is important because his objections to genuine majority rule in Rhodesia were philosophical and not practical in nature. In such cases negotiation is impossible, because nothing can be done to change preferences or belay concerns.  Interests are not at stake; principles are.  Whereas one can craft compromises that protect interests or offset possible tangible material losses, it is impossible to negotiate points of principle.

In 1976, Kissinger's attempt failed essentially because he was unable to create an alternative that met the needs of both the whites and the blacks. Much of the failure on Kissinger's part is attributable to his self-confessed strategy of isolating "the ideological radicals" (read ZANU, Mugabe, and Machel), who Kissinger believed would never accept a negotiated compromise. The irony was that the true ideological radical who would not compromise was Ian Smith. One of the main differences that explains the successful termination of the conflict at Lancaster House was the fact that Ian Smith no longer negotiated on behalf of the Salisbury regime.

Another related difference in the negotiating episodes concerns the consolidation of leadership as an internal property of the parties in conflict. During the Vorster/Kaunda détente episode, it was not clear if anyone spoke for ZANU. There was much confusion concerning the roles of Ndabaningi Sithole and Robert Mugabe. Even if a settlement could have been reached that included a leader from ZANU, it is not at all clear that the military wing of the party would have honored any agreement. Indeed, Sithole lost much political capital at this time by pursuing negotiations. Robert Mugabe's triumph in ZANU is attributed precisely to his refusal to negotiate during this period. By the time of Geneva in October 1976, Mugabe was still consolidating his leadership and could not have afforded to take a conciliatory line even if he had so desired (which he did not). At Lancaster House, Mugabe (in conjunction with Tongogara) was firmly in control of ZANU and could make bold moves toward a settlement.

Some of the important changes at Lancaster House concerned the internal properties of the actors. Although a mediator should not ignore objective circumstances and the course of the conflict in trying to forge a settlement, the analysis here suggests that a would-be mediator must be keen to factors within the actors and how they can contribute to making a crisis ripe for resolution. The next section examines the British mediation at Lancaster House and compares it with the prior attempts to solve the conflict.

## British Mediation at Lancaster House

The success of the British at Lancaster House was produced through their political skill at taking advantage of the opportunity to manipulate each side into an agreement containing features odious to both sides, even though strong voices on both sides spoke against settlement. The opportunity consisted of four components that came together at one time: First, the military and economic situation had deteriorated to such a point that the whites were losing and would face political elimination in the future. Second, the election of Muzorewa in Rhodesia weakened those within the Salisbury coalition that were adamantly against settlement, namely Ian Smith and the Rhodesian Front, and strengthened the faction that favored a settlement to forestall elimination, in particular, Peter Walls, David Smith, and Ken Flower. Third, Muzorewa's election handed the British direct leverage with Salisbury: the British, instead of dismissing the change in "Rhobabwe," partially acknowledged and embraced it in order to press for a settlement that would win international acceptance. By not rejecting outright Muzorewa's election, they enhanced the belief that they might recognize the new government. By only partially embracing Muzorewa, they kept in their possession the carrot of full recognition, which could be used to win commitments from the Salisbury delegation at Lancaster House. An important component of this opportunity was that the British were free to negotiate a settlement that was not dictated by South Africa and that therefore could include Mugabe and ZANU.  Finally, the war continued to take a large toll on the guerrillas' patrons, Kenneth Kaunda and Samora Machel, who were therefore willing to pressure the Patriotic Front into accepting a settlement, if they were assured it was a fair settlement.

The objective changes should be seen as operating on four different levels: (1) on the fortunes of different actors in coalitions, (2) on the direct resources of the players, (3) on the indirect resources of the players through their allies, and (4) on the resources of the mediator.

These objective changes would not have led in and of themselves to a settlement. Rather, they provided a very slight opportunity for Carrington and the British government to manipulate the parties to agreement. Carrington's performance at Lancaster House was a textbook example of what William Riker calls heresthetic: the art of "structuring the world so you can win." The British were able to establish a bargaining game that could lead to settlement.  They manipulated the agenda and rules of the negotiations to push the parties to the outcome the British desired, and were able to play on the perceptions of the players to produce the desired tactical effects they needed.

To produce a settlement, the British were able to create a game whereby the first player to leave the table would lose. There was powerful incentive to avoid being the player that "wrecked" the conference. This aspect of the Lancaster House Conference was first observed by the *Economist* before the proceedings started when it wrote that "both delegations face traps the avoidance of which could just condemn this conference to 'succeed'" (quoted in Davidow 1984, 46). The strategy that the British employed has been labeled the "second-class option."

There were many instances of the British doing the tactical "right thing." The first example, and the key one for what followed, was their manipulation of the parties at Lusaka. The British goals going into the conference were to get the backing of the Front Line States and a mandate from the Commonwealth heads of state that would provide the legitimacy for the dictatorial way they intended to run the conference. The dilemma was simple: how to get such backing without ceding participation to any of the supporters. By recognizing the dilemma, the British were able to see their way out of it; what was crucial was to hold private the information that they had already concluded—that the internal settlement was flawed and that they therefore intended to call an all-parties conference. If such information remained hidden,[3] the appearance of British concession to calling a new conference would overjoy all present. If such information leaked out, the terms of the debate at Lusaka would change: having already given word that they would call a conference, questions would naturally arise on the details. The result at Lusaka was that Britain would call the conference, with minimal constraint on their action.

That the tactic succeeded was evident after the fact to all concerned, especially the Patriotic Front. Robert Mugabe, in an interview during the heat of the conference in November, described what the Commonwealth leaders failed to see at Lusaka:

> We are in difficulty here because of the Commonwealth decision—I must make that quite clear. The Commonwealth communique in Lusaka has landed us in a lot of difficulties, because the British Government is now using that as if it was the Mount of Sinai where they derived a new law, and they justify their stand on the fact that they had this mandate from Lusaka. You see, the Lusaka communique did not remove the British from the orbit of the internal settlement. It criticized the internal constitution and said it had serious defects. In my opinion they should never have made reference to that constitution. They should have condemned it outright because it was the work of an illegal regime. Britain should have been urged to work on a new basis fair to all parties. (*West Africa*, November 19, 1979, in Baumhogger 1984, 1146)

Yet, even Mugabe was hoodwinked by the British tactic. He goes on to say, "True, it was good that they [the Commonwealth] urged Britain to convene a conference of all the parties. But Britain took advantage of the situation." Such an admission reveals that Mugabe believed that whatever alms the British had given to that point were the result of Commonwealth pressure, and therefore his criticism of the Commonwealth leaders was muted.

The next tactical considerations concerned the agenda and the decision to proceed on a step-by-step basis. The British chose to deal with the constitution first in the belief that because that was the reason for the war, it had to be confronted first. The British felt that if agreement was reached on the constitution, there would be greater pressure on the parties to settle the later issues of the transition and cease-fire. As Renwick wrote later, "The attainment of majority rule was what the war was supposed to be about. If it were possible to achieve an independence constitution which, indisputably, provided for that, the conflict would be reduced to the dimensions of a struggle for power; and the pressure would be greater on the parties for that competition to be settled by other means" (Renwick 1981a, 16).[4]

The British, by immediately confronting the problem of the constitution, brought out the latent splits in the two parties. On the Salisbury side, the framing of the issue immediately divorced Smith from the Salisbury delegation. Had any of the whites been partial to backing Smith, they would have realized that if Muzorewa had not accepted the proposed elimination of the white veto, he would have lost all credibility with blacks in Zimbabwe. The whites had a stake in Muzorewa's political future, so that even if they were inclined to keeping the blocking mechanisms, there were also cross-pressures for them to concede on the issue.

Smith recognized this aspect of the issue after the fact. In an analysis that would delight William Riker, Smith

> claimed that the British had "succeeded in dividing our Government of National Unity by putting the black members of the delegation in an impossible situation." The plan reduced the safeguards of the white population and gave these to the blacks. If the blacks refused to reduce white safeguards, the country's opponents would use this to sway the black electorate into believing the Bishop had rejected increased opportunities for blacks. For the internal black parties this would be equivalent to committing political suicide. The Bishop's delegation had thus been put in an impossible situation, Mr. Smith said. (As reported in the *Daily Telegraph*, October 8, 1979)

On the Patriotic Front side, the acceptance of the constitution put heavy strains on their alliance. The British still held out as a possibility that Nkomo might defect from Mugabe. Although in the end Mugabe deserted Nkomo for the elections, the possibility of having to walk out of the conference without Nkomo was something Mugabe did not want to contemplate. For one, Mugabe would not only have to bear the brunt of the approbation of the Front Line States alone, but he had to consider the reaction of some of his officers, especially Tongogara, who also counseled compromise. The constitution brought these tensions to a head when Mugabe threatened to leave over the land issue.

Equally important to the choice of beginning with the constitution was the British decision not to divulge their plans for the other issues before the issue on the table was resolved. Given the number of concessions by both sides and the magnitude of the concessions, had the British proposals been common knowledge at the beginning of the conference, or before the conference, both parties would have balked. Moreover, by revealing only a part of their proposals, the British could selectively drop information to the parties to accentuate the chances of their approval. For example, fearing that the Salisbury delegation might waver in accepting the transitional arrangements, the British could drop hints about favorable aspects of their plan for the cease-fire, thus further inducing them to agree on the immediate issue of the interim period: a process that Davidow refers to "as giving them a peek at the goodies." This tactical revelation of information worked in another way as well. During the negotiations over the constitution, the British informed the Salisbury delegation of their transitional plans in order to convince Muzorewa that there was a good likelihood that the Patriotic Front would not accept the transition proposals.

Carrington also understood the value of time pressure in keeping a sense that the conference was progressing. He constantly chided the participants to give him responses as quickly as possible, often setting deadlines to enforce his pressure. Over the course of the proceedings, the efficacy of Carrington's deadlines eroded. The first set of deadlines on the constitution was effective because Carrington gave the impression of being willing to forge ahead on a settlement without the Patriotic Front. After agreement was reached on the constitution, this threat lacked credibility, so Carrington found himself constantly extending deadlines after responses were not forthcoming. Carrington then found himself relying more and more on moves away from the table to pressure the Front: submitting the Enabling Act to Parliament, informing Parliament that sanctions would not be renewed, sending Soames to Rhodesia.

Carrington had tremendous control of information at Lancaster House. This was given to him partly by the Patriotic Front's mistake of demanding that they would bargain only with the British and not with the Salisbury delegation. The advantages accrued to the British were obvious. For one, the British were able to make commitments or assurances to either side (often contradictory—some beyond the bounds of plenary diplomacy) that would have been impossible if they had simply overseen direct talks between the parties. One example concerns promises about personnel. During the negotiations over the constitution, questions arose from the Patriotic Front over personnel from the Salisbury regime who would have to be kept on if the PF came to power. In open plenary session, the British stuck to the line that most of the administration would have to be kept and that only top-ranking officials could be replaced. They also emphasized that the exception to the first-tier officers was the highest judge in the land, who could not be dismissed. This prompted a strong opposition from the guerrillas: the current chief justice had a reputation for racism and had sent many guerrillas to the gallows. While the British had to stand in public for his retainment, they privately told the Front that they had assurances that he would retire voluntarily if the Front took over. This was information that could not be used publicly: much of the conference the British spent convincing Muzorewa that he would win. A statement that implied that the Front *might* win, and that the highest judge in the land was already considering the implications of such a victory, would have undercut the British selling job to the bishop. By presenting it privately to the Front, of course, the guerrillas had no way of gaging the veracity of the British claim. It may or may not be true, but if the negotiations had been head to head, the promise would never have been given.

Reportedly, some of the information the British gathered came from wiretapping the rooms of the delegates (Davidow 1984, 128). If the British were able to use such information, it would help explain Carrington's successful brinksmanship diplomacy. For one, it would give Carrington a sense of how far he could push the participants and when he would have to make concessions. He would also gain a much better sense of internal politics within the parties. I am cautious, however, about granting too much power to this information. Individuals from different delegations told a similar story: at Lancaster House they assumed their rooms would be bugged and acted with this in mind. If this was the case, and we may never know,[5] the value of such information is obviously reduced. Indeed, such an assumption would lead to strategic manipulation on the part of the delegates as to what they wanted the British to know.

The other key part that information played concerned the revelation of player types. As described in Chapter 1, a key problem in revolutionary situations is the determination of whether one's opponent is a limited player or an all-out player. A third party can be useful in supplying such information by vouching for a player, but, as was pointed out, the third party should not reveal such information too soon. The British held this information throughout the election period, thus contributing to an overall sense of danger. This danger worked to caution the antagonists and contributed to upholding the cease-fire. When the election was over, however, the British realized that the time was right for revealing the true nature of the players. The key passing of information came when the British orchestrated the meeting between Walls, Flower, and the Mozambicans. At this meeting, the whites learned of Mugabe's victory, but also his intention of keeping them on and the fact that he would counsel reconciliation among the peoples of Zimbabwe.

## British Mediation in Comparative Perspective

Table 6.3 compares the four different mediation attempts on several important dimensions: (1) the mediators themselves, (2) their leverage, (3) the extent of problem solving that was carried out, (4) whether the mediators relied on tactical pressure and whether such pressure had its intended effect, (5) the mediators' goals, and (6) whether those goals placed a limit on the solution, (7) whether the mediators learned from past efforts, and (8) the main lessons they derived from those experiences.

One large advantage that Carrington had at Lancaster House was the benefit of control and coordination that came from being the sole mediator. In the three previous efforts, mediation was more difficult simply because there were more fingers in the pie. The Kissinger/ Geneva efforts were undermined in part because Callaghan put together a possible solution, Kissinger sold it to Rhodesia and the Front Line presidents, and Ivor Richard had to run the transitional conference. By that time, Richard was in the dark about promises that were made to the different parties and could not rely on U.S. leverage because of the 1976 election.[6] During the Anglo-American initiatives, Carter's unilateral promise to Nyerere over the composition of the Rhodesian army nearly sank the efforts of Britain and the United States and privately infuriated the British Foreign and Commonwealth Office. Later, while David Owen was feeling immense political pressure at home, he not only had to defend his position, but also take heat for many of Andrew Young's undiplomatic off-the-cuff quips.

At Lancaster House, Carrington insisted on full control, not because of learning from the Rhodesian cases but rather from an experience he had in 1971. As chief negotiator for NATO in their dealings with Malta over base rights, Carrington frequently found representatives of NATO's member states undermining his position—officially, the NATO position. In what has become a classic case study in the ability of the weak to extract concessions from the strong, an infuriated Carrington found deal after deal sabotaged because of the inability of NATO to speak in one voice.[7] In 1979, he made it clear that if he were to undertake the Rhodesian problem, he would have to have sole authority (Carrington 1987, interview with author). The difficulty of this position, as described in Chapter 5, was to get the benefits of international support for leverage without sacrificing any control.[8]

### Strategic Leverage

Earlier in this book, when I discussed Owen's and Carrington's strategy of arbitration, I pointed out that the requirements of such a strategy are

Table 6.3  International Mediation in Rhodesia, 1974–1980

| | International Mediation Attempts | | | |
|---|---|---|---|---|
| | Détente 1974–1975 | Geneva 1976 | Anglo-American 1977–1978 | Lancaster House 1979–1980 |
| Mediator(s) | Kaunda Vorster | Kissinger Richard Vorster | Owen Vance | Carrington |
| Leverage on Nationalists, Rhodesians | Front Line States South Africa | Front Line States South Africa U.S. | Front Line States South Africa U.S. | Common-wealth FLS |
| Problem solving | no | no | yes | yes |
| Tactical pressure on Nationalists Rhodesians | no no | yes no | no no | yes yes |
| Mediators' goals | Regional stability: "Conservative black regime" | Superpower reputation: "Isolate the radicals" | African reputation: "Progressive foreign policy" | Problem Solving: "Get Rhodesia off our backs" |
| Limits on solution? | yes | yes | yes | no |
| Learning? | —— | Limited | Extensive | Extensive |
| Lessons | —— | Détente plan sound; all that's needed U.S. push. | Need for details and problem solving; blacks will not accept white veto or control of police and security. | S.A. not helpful; need for internation-al assistance without sacri-ficing control; what whites will not accept; need to split Smith from Muzorewa; constitution first; keep tight rein on confer-ence; use dead-lines; stress final attempt |

difficult to meet. How did the British at Lancaster House gather the leverage that would be necessary for pushing the parties to settlement? In the case of the Salisbury delegation, the British made use of a promise to recognize the Muzorewa government in order to induce cooperation. In each stage of the conflict the Salisbury delegation accepted Carrington's terms in the hope that the Patriotic Front would walk away from the table. That Carrington's terms had to meet the minimum needs of the delegation is important but does not explain Salisbury's incentive to accept them. Carrington held out the big prize—recognition and lifting of sanctions. His actions, and those of his boss, Margaret Thatcher, from the time that they took office, communicated a warmth for the changes that had taken place in Rhodesia. This partial embrace of the Muzorewa administration, combined with the fact that it was a Conservative government in Britain, heightened the expectations of the Rhodesians for recognition.

As far as British leverage with the Patriotic Front was concerned, the key was the Lusaka meeting of the heads of Commonwealth nations that took place in August 1979. At that time, Britain was able to forge a consensus on a solution to the Rhodesian conflict and on a mechanism for reaching that solution. The result of the meeting was that Britain could claim both legitimacy and support based on Commonwealth approval and that it could count on the help of the Front Line presidents in pressuring the Patriotic Front to compromise. As Table 6.3 shows, every previous effort relied on the Front Line presidents. As the patrons of the guerrillas, as leaders who provided sanctuary and supplies, the presidents carried strong leverage over the Front. One dimension that the table does not draw out is that if, in the previous three attempts, the Front had doubted the credibility of Kaunda or Machel to carry out the threat to cut off aid to the fighters, at Lancaster House fewer doubts existed. Nkomo made it clear that Kaunda had reached his limit; Machel's threat to cut off ZANU was doubted by some in the party but was credible as far as Tongogara was concerned.

Table 6.3 brings out an important advantage that the British had over previous mediation efforts: they did not have to rely on South Africa as their leverage for forcing Salisbury to settle. In the Kaunda/ Vorster effort, the Kissinger attempt, and the early stages of the Owen/ Vance initiatives, it was believed that the path to Salisbury's compromise was through South Africa. For a time this was partly true: South Africa held Rhodesia's lifeline and could sever it at any moment. On at least two occasions in 1974 and 1976, the South Africans did pressure Smith to make compromises. The price of South African help in bringing a settlement to Rhodesia was that any outcome there had to be satisfactory to the South Africans, and this meant a government led by anyone but Mugabe. The goal of a settlement that included Mugabe—the only settlement that could end the war—and the goal of the South Africans were completely incompatible. Moreover, after November 1976, one discerns in Ian Smith's demeanor a real disbelief that South Africa would see his regime fall.

The biggest benefit that accrued to Britain from the election of Muzorewa was that they then had direct leverage with Salisbury and could bypass the Pretoria route. The election of Margaret Thatcher delivered Rhodesia into British hands: the whites and Muzorewa believed that Thatcher could deliver anything she promised. In this instance two changes—one internal to one antagonist and one internal to the would-be mediator—created leverage where there was none before and created the circumstances to make the conflict resolvable.

*Tactical Leverage*

Tactical leverage refers to bargaining techniques that help move parties to agreements in the day-to-day course of negotiating. Such techniques include agenda setting, the single-text method, the use of moves away from the table to pressure the participants, the setting of deadlines, and the control of information. I have already outlined the British ability to use such techniques at Lancaster House, but it is informative to compare the mediation in 1979 with earlier efforts.

As I described in Chapter 2, there was almost a näiveté on the part of Kaunda and Vorster that all that was needed was to bring the sides together and they would hammer out an agreement. Going into the talks at Victoria Falls, there was not even an agenda, let alone a comprehensive plan to bring the parties to settlement. In 1976, Kissinger did use the deadline of the U.S. election to pressure Ian Smith. When the deadline came, however, and Carter defeated Ford, Smith left the Geneva talks and the Rhodesian position hardened. In terms of day-to-day running of the Geneva conference, Ivor Richard, because Kissinger had not provided a plan for the talks, found himself with four parties who had no prior agreement on any matter. Such a situation prompted him to rely on "keeping the talks going at any cost." This contrasts dramatically with Carrington at Lancaster House, who had the luxury of pressuring to keep the talks as short as possible. He could use deadlines and moves away from the table, because he had planned for such measures. The helter-skelter process that brought Geneva together precluded anything but "muddling through." Finally, there were great differences between Geneva and Lancaster House as far as British control of information was concerned. Richard was much more forthcoming about different positions, with the British often making common knowledge what unfurled in bilateral sessions. By Lancaster House, the British were quite close-lipped and used information as the resource and commodity that it is.

*Problem Solving*

Along with the leverage that Carrington and the British had at Lancaster House, it was equally important to create a solution that both parties would prefer to fighting. It was imperative for them to have a solution that both parties could embrace. After the détente experience and the Geneva conference, the British learned that the biggest single myth that could be invoked at any time was that "Rhodesia's problems are for Rhodesians to settle." There was a steady progression in the negotiating episodes from the Kaunda/Vorster attempt, which relied on the participants hammering out some kind of agreement, to Lancaster House, where the British, in a sense, dictated a solution to the participants. By the time of Lancaster House, the British were not mediators in the classic sense of the word. Rather, they were arbitrators. Going into the negotiations, the British had decided from their reading of past negotiations that there were points on which the PF and the Salisbury delegation were not going to agree and that it would be incumbent on them as mediators to decide what were fair solutions to the negotiations. This is not to imply that the British crafted the solutions without regard to the needs of the participants. The British had studied the previous proposals going back to the Kissinger mediation and the Anglo-American initiatives and had a sense of an outcome that would satisfy all concerned, a point I will discuss shortly at further length.

*The Goals of the Third Parties*

A comparison of the different mediation exercises shows that the goals of the mediators placed limits on possible settlements. In 1974–1975, the goal of South Africa for a stable, conservative black regime in South Africa, along with Kenneth Kaunda's favoritism for Joshua Nkomo, meant that a solution in Rhodesia would preclude ZANU. In 1976, Henry Kissinger's desire to craft a solution that would exclude "the ideological radicals" won the support of Vorster and South Africa's powerful leverage on Ian Smith but precluded any settlement with Mugabe and ZANU. In 1978, one of the chief goals of Jimmy Carter's foreign policy was to strengthen his ties to black Africa and the Third World in general. This goal took priority over the specific goal of ending the Rhodesian conflict and prompted him to include Julius Nyerere's demand that the armed forces during the transition period in

Zimbabwe be composed solely of Patriotic Front troops, a demand that the whites would never accept. In this instance, Carter's larger goal of enhancing his reputation with the OAU and Nigeria prompted him to include a demand that would endanger the hopes of settlement in Rhodesia.

By contrast, in 1979 the British were willing to accept any party coming to power in Rhodesia, as long as they did so through the ballot box. The British preferred that Muzorewa or Nkomo win, but they could live with Mugabe if he was the choice of the Zimbabwean people. The overriding interest of the British can be described simply as getting the Rhodesian problem "off of their backs," once and for all.

*Learning*

The key variable that linked changes in the "objective" military situation with changes in the internal parties was the British ability to use bargaining leverages within the parties and between the parties. What enabled them to do so with such precision and forethought was the extensive cumulative knowledge they had gained from the prior settlement attempts.

After the first attempt at Victoria Falls, the different mediators slowly learned the positions of all the players, their minimum demands, the limits of their leverage, struggles within groups and how they pertained to the conflict, and which individuals simply would never settle. Kissinger, for example, gained limited knowledge from the détente exercise. Primarily he believed that all that was needed was the force of U.S. prestige (and his personal presence) to bring the conflict to resolution. He had accepted the bases of the détente plan and felt that Mugabe and Machel were ideological radicals who would never accept settlement. He chose to ignore British advice that Ian Smith would never negotiate in good faith. The result was that Kissinger did gain the public commitment to majority rule by Smith but in doing so undercut any forthcoming attempt to terminate the conflict.

In 1976, Kissinger made a distinction between those who could be negotiated with and those who, because their objections were ideological, could not be negotiated with. My research in the Zimbabwe case supports Kissinger's distinction but suggests that determining who fits what category can be determined only through experience and certainly cannot be predicted on the basis of a priori judgments. For Henry Kissinger, the distinction meant that Robert Mugabe and Samora Machel could not be negotiated with. In reality, Ian Smith could not be negotiated with, and it was only when he was isolated by many in the white government was a settlement possible.

The British experience at Geneva produced a number of lessons that Owen and Vance attempted to utilize.  First, Richard's effort had shown the multilayered complexity of the problem and that much thinking was needed on the different facets of the settlement.  It was obvious that Rhodesia's problems were *not* "for Rhodesians to figure out." The experience also led the British to view Mugabe as an individual whose ideology did not preclude negotiation.  They also were impressed by Samora Machel's "pragmatism." From the Kissinger proposals they had learned that the blacks would never accept white control of police, security, or the judiciary.  While Vance and Owen continued to believe that the route to Salisbury was through South Africa, Owen, in particular, gradually soured on South Africa as leverage.

By Lancaster House, the British had compiled information that directly affected their choice of strategies and tactics.  Their learning was extensive and was divided into knowledge about the actors, politics within the actors, possible solutions, bargaining tactics, and sources of leverage.  Their main lessons included:

1. South Africa could not be counted on as leverage against the Salisbury regime; they accepted the internal settlement and would not work for any solution that included Mugabe;
2. Any mediation effort would have to aim at isolating Ian Smith from Bishop Muzorewa; the problem of the Anglo-American accords is that the effort drove Muzorewa into Smith's camp;
3. Mugabe was hostile to settlement because of Smith's past intransigence; it would be necessary to use Nkomo as pressure against Mugabe;
4. The terms of settlement were limited: the whites would never accept guerrilla forces constituting the interim army or police force, nor would they accept United Nations involvement, and the blacks would never accept a white blocking mechanism or future control over police and security;
5. Although international support was crucial, it had to be gained without forfeiting control;
6. The key to the settlement was the constitution and not the transitional arrangements; any conference should deal with the constitution first and then proceed to other issues;
7. The two parties were so far apart that the British would have to dictate a solution; and
8. At all costs another Geneva experience had to be avoided, a tight rein was needed, deadlines would have to be imposed, only one text would be used, and information had to be tightly controlled.

What made such learning so impressive is that the goals of the actors and what they were willing to accept often changed over the course of the struggle. This harks back to Chapter 1 and our assumption that settlement terms that are available early in a conflict will become foreclosed if the conflict continues. For example, looking back at the 1974–1975 period of early negotiations, the blacks (including Mugabe) were willing to accept a five-year transition to majority rule if Smith accepted the principle of one person–one vote. The intransigence of Smith led within a year to a much shorter acceptable transition period of two years. By 1976, further intransigence led to immediate majority rule as the only acceptable goal on the part of the blacks. Given that the demands of the participants were fluid, the British had to be able to update constantly the information at their disposal. Thus, although Owen and Vance had failed, the efforts of these two mediators kept abreast of the different actors and changes in circumstances. Such efforts formed an invaluable trove of information when Carrington and the British one last time attempted to solve the problem in 1979.

## Why No Escalation?

All of the information in the world would not have made a difference in 1979 had the war escalated with large-scale intervention of foreign troops. The lack of escalation has to be attributed to the amount of attention that international actors gave to trying to solve the conflict and to the effort of many who were involved to keep negotiation alive as a possibility.

From 1974 to 1979, the violence intensified in Zimbabwe and the war expanded into the neighboring countries of Zambia, Botswana, and Mozambique. At no point, however, did the conflict cross a barrier where the war entered a new "higher" stage. It is important to spell out the precise meaning of my claim. What constitutes an escalation in war is not always clear and depends on the interpretation of the actors. Sometimes the escalatory threshold is not defined until after a possible escalatory act occurs. A good example comes from the Zimbabwe case. Before the Rhodesians undertook massive raids into Mozambique and Zambia, one could only guess whether such action would lead to a counterreaction that might prompt the intervention of other actors or a change in the course of the war. It was certainly the intent of the Rhodesians to prompt a reaction from the Front Line presidents that would change the course of the war. But it was not until the raids occurred, and those presidents reacted in a defensive manner, that such raids were accepted as not constituting an escalation. The Front Line presidents chose not to acknowledge this as a move that was "out of bounds" or that promised to change the course of the war.

The Zimbabwean conflict suggests that in war there are both

clearly defined escalatory thresholds and ambiguous escalatory thresholds. In the former, the contestants, through expressed warnings, establish beforehand that a particular act is escalatory. In the latter case, the threshold may not be established and emerges after the fact. Or the threshold may arise out of one actor's probing to find the opponent's threshold. Table 6.4 shows that in the Zimbabwean case the participants recognized three clearly defined escalatory thresholds: (1) the introduction of Cuban or Warsaw Pact troops into the fray; (2) an offensive counterattack by Zambia or Mozambique in retaliation for Rhodesia's punishing raids into their countries, and (3) a change by either of the revolutionary armies to a conventional war-fighting strategy within Rhodesia. There were three ambiguous thresholds that arose in the course of the fighting: (1) Rhodesian raids against Zimbabwean refugee and guerrilla camps in Zambia, Botswana, and Mozambique, (2) Rhodesian attacks against economic targets in Zambia and Mozambique, and (3) hot-pursuit raids by Zambia and Mozambique into Rhodesia after Rhodesian attacks. While the first ambiguous threshold was clarified early on by Front Line passive defense, it is interesting to note that the last two thresholds arose in the last six weeks of the war.[9]

The reason that an escalatory threshold was never crossed stemmed from the fact that the parties had opportunities to settle the conflict through negotiation. The corollary to this is that escalation was at its highest probability when the actors believed that their ability to negotiate was foreclosed. A comparison of the three instances where escalation was seriously considered highlights this process.

Table 6.4  Escalation Thresholds in Rhodesia, 1976–1979

Mutually Understood Thresholds

| Eastern Bloc/Cuban intervention | Offensive counter-attack by Zambia or Mozambique | Guerrilla armies change to conventional war-fighting strategy |
|---|---|---|

Ambiguous Thresholds

| Rhodesian raids against Patriotic Front camps in Front Line States | Economic targets in Front Line States | Front Line hot pursuit after Rhodesian raids |
|---|---|---|

The first attempt to escalate the war was in the form of a gambit by the Rhodesian forces. Through a series of punishing forays into Zambia and Mozambique from 1976 to 1978, they hoped that the Front Line States would respond by seeking Cuban or Warsaw Pact assistance, which the Rhodesians hoped would bring South Africa and the United States into the war on their side. By turning the revolution into a regional or larger war, the Rhodesians hoped to forestall majority rule. The gambit, however, received no takers. The Front Line States recognized Smith's motives and refused to take the bait. Their responses were of a defensive nature and included a willingness to suffer losses instead of broadening the conflict. Their unwillingness to take the escalatory counteraction can be interpreted only in light of their belief that a settlement was a possibility and that there were opportunities to end the conflict with a satisfactory outcome short of a larger war.

Evidence exists that both Kaunda and Machel were aware of the high stakes involved and, more important, understood Rhodesia's strategy and realized that they had more to lose than gain from escalation of the war. They therefore purposely tempered their responses. As Alexander George notes, this form of escalation control is adopted when "one or both sides feel that the costs and risks of stepping up their intervention are likely to be excessive in relation to the benefits to be attained thereby" (George 1983a, 391). In the face of punishing Rhodesian raids into their countries, Kaunda and Machel adopted "a policy of inaction" (Smoke 1977, 172). Throughout the period, these leaders did not retaliate, and when Zambia was finally forced to seek outside assistance after the 1978 bombing outside of Lusaka, they requested only defensive antiaircraft weaponry from the Soviet Union. Moreover, because the Front Line States controlled the flow of weapons to the guerrillas inside Zimbabwe, they could veto any weapon systems or outside involvement that could lead to escalation (Napper 1983, 166). Therefore, during this phase in the conflict, not only did the Front Line presidents refuse to escalate the conflict, they also actively policed the guerrillas' activities to ensure escalation did not take place.

In Richard Smoke's book *War: Controlling Escalation*, the policy of inaction is mentioned only in passing with reference to Turkey's refusal to respond to Russian occupation of key cities during the Crimean War. In that instance, Smoke argues, the keys to pursuing the policy were the ability to tolerate the economic costs imposed by the provoking side as well as the lack of domestic opinion demanding retribution (Smoke 1977, 172). Both factors were present for a time in the case of Kaunda and Machel. But in the Zimbabwean case, one must also add that such a policy was attractive only as long as a possibility of a negotiated settlement existed. Evidence for these propositions can be found from examining the one incident when the FLPs seemed ready to internationalize the conflict.

In June 1979, the attitude of the Front Line presidents to the escalatory option changed. As described in Chapter 6, Cuba had put forth a proposal that would have most likely led to massive South African intervention in the Rhodesian war. From all evidence, the Front Line presidents were willing to acquiesce to the plan. The leaders' acquiescence can be understood by the following factors as discussed by Smoke: (1) Zambia and Mozambique had suffered devastating destruction and staggering economic costs and (2) in the case of Zambia, there was widespread domestic dissatisfaction at bearing the brunt of the Rhodesian civil war. But equally important was the perception that the Western powers, particularly Britain, had "abandoned the search for a settlement involving all the parties to the conflict, including the guerrillas, and would instead support Smith's internal settlement" (Jaster 1983, 9). In essence, the Front Line presidents were being pushed into an act that they had tried to avoid, because they perceived that their opportunity to negotiate a fair settlement had been eliminated.

At the time, the Patriotic Front vetoed the plan. In the words of Nkomo, "I thought, this is utter nonsense, utter foolishness. Why would I want to get myself killed?" (Nkomo 1987, interview with author). Yet, three months later Nkomo approved of a military plan that would have called for a massive conventional strike into Rhodesia, a move that would have changed dramatically the military situation and certainly would have prompted a South African response. That Nkomo did so was a reflection of his belief that Lancaster House was the last opportunity for a negotiated settlement. If the conference failed, he would have no option but to make the strategic escalatory move. And because the plan needed a lead time, Nkomo and ZAPU locked themselves into the plan. But this was not in any sense a move that Nkomo or ZAPU preferred. As one adviser put it, "Escalation would have been an act of desperation, not strategy. . . . Nkomo had just returned from Cuba and at our first briefing said, 'This is the reality . . . either we go for an agreement or the whole tenor of the struggle will change with whole new military structure and strategy with the disadvantages that the Rhodesian state would be nominally black'" (ZAPU Delegate A. 1987, interview with author).

This points to a two-sided aspect of escalation and opportunities to negotiate. On the one hand, as long as opportunities existed to settle the conflict, then escalation was not seriously considered as an option. On the other hand, when the opportunity to negotiate seemed foreclosed, the pressure to escalate increased tremendously. When escalation might have occurred, it forcefully drove the actors to make the necessary compromises to settle. Part of the Lancaster success has to be attributed to the belief on the part of the Front Line presidents and Nkomo that this was the last chance to settle the conflict at the table, a sentiment the British tried to foster. If Lancaster House had failed, however, and the conflict had erupted into a regional or larger war, it would have been in part because major actors believed that negotiation was foreclosed.

Finally, it is significant that two of the ambiguous thresholds were crossed in the last two months of the conflict. The first threshold concerned a series of Rhodesian attacks on transport lines in Mozambique and Zambia, which began in mid-October and by the end of November threatened to strangle the economic livelihood of Zambia. Kaunda responded by putting his country on war mobilization in November, a response that further led to the perception that a larger war would break out if settlement was not reached. In this case, however, the Rhodesian authorities were not instigating the bombings in order to sabotage an agreement; rather, middle-ranking officers thought such moves would be more likely to bring about an agreement.

The second ambiguous threshold was crossed in the third week of October after a stinging Mozambican defeat of a Rhodesian attack on a ZANLA base in Mozambique. As the Rhodesians retreated, the Mozambicans harassed the Rhodesians as they crossed the border into Rhodesia and followed them for a short time in "hot pursuit." Two points stand out. First, unlike the purposive escalatory attempts, it is likely that as with the Rhodesian "bridge bombings," the pursuit was not ordered at the highest levels. Second, the Rhodesian authorities, who learned of the Mozambican action, did not treat the pursuit as constituting a new action that should justify an escalatory counterresponse. This makes sense given that the Mozambican action occurred less than a week after agreement on a constitution at Lancaster House and before the conference had bogged down during the transitional talks. Were an Ian Smith still in command, such an action undoubtedly would have prompted a severe punishment. However, Bishop Muzorewa, and, more important, Peter Walls, wanted a settlement and chose not to treat the pursuit as something out of the ordinary.

## The Dog That Didn't Bark

One question that arises for any student of the Zimbabwe conflict concerns something that did not happen: If South Africa's main goal in Zimbabwe was to prevent Mugabe from winning, why did it not intervene? The British explanation is that they had made the costs clear to the South Africans, and such costs were prohibitive against their intervention. This explanation suffices for the election period. But why didn't South Africa enter in force when Mugabe won? A convincing explanation is offered by Moorcraft. First, while the emergence of P.W. Botha in 1977 as the successor to John Vorster signaled the victory of the hard–line foreign policy faction in the South African government, by 1980 the transition had not filtered through the foreign policy and intelligence apparatuses. At the policy-making level, the hard-liners had triumphed; at the policy implementation level, the moderates fought a holding action. The South African intelligence community had accepted completely the British estimates that Muzorewa would win; indeed, they had contributed to his campaign to help the prophesy come about. In this explanation, the intelligence failure had foreclosed alternative responses in the case of Mugabe's victory. When it came, the South Africans were unprepared.

## Final Thoughts:
### Contingency and the Risks of Peacemaking

A school of interpretation within political science that has become trendy over the last ten years attributes overwhelming causal power to big "structures": the "world system," "states," historical patterns of "class relations."[10] What is immediately apparent to any student of the Zimbabwean revolution is how incredibly contingent the outcome was on the choices and actions of individuals.[11] For Robert Mugabe to place 17,000 of his soldiers in holding camps while the Rhodesian army had freedom of movement was an incredible gamble; for the whites of Rhodesia to put their future well-being into a piece of paper called a constitution was likewise a bet for heavy stakes. This book has been devoted to explaining how peace came to Zimbabwe, but had a battalion of white commandos mutinied against the Lancaster agreement and attacked a holding camp, all hell would have broken loose. If the cease-fire had broken into conventional fighting, South Africa, which had played a limited role in the fray, probably would have jumped in. Great Britain would have found itself smack in the middle of a conventional war, and the task of this book might have been to explain how *not* to mediate a civil war.[12]

Beyond noting the contingency of the outcome, one obvious proposition from the Zimbabwean experience was not captured in my analysis: peacemaking is a risky business. It is risky for leaders in the conflict who take conciliatory positions, for those mediators who attempt to resolve the conflict, and for all concerned when and if an agreement is reached. With the exception of Mugabe, all of the major black leaders in the 1970s suffered political setbacks from their willingness to negotiate a settlement with Ian Smith. When the settlement was reached, the Patriotic Front gambled that the British would abide by the results of free elections. The Front furthermore had to gamble that the white military would not use their advantage during the cease-fire to slaughter the Front's troops that were gathered at holding camps throughout the country. On the part of the British, there was the real risk that the Commonwealth monitoring troops would be caught in a civil war if the cease-fire failed to hold. For white Rhodesians, there were risks that the aftermath of the agreement would unleash a reign of terror against them.

In a tribute that captured the element of risk taking in the decision for peace, the Commonwealth election committee concluded its report on the elections in 1980: "In the end, the essential triumph has been that of the people of Zimbabwe themselves. Transmuting their suffering, their faith in the processes of peace has exceeded their courage in war" (quoted in Martin and Johnson 1981, 334).

## Notes

1. I would like to put to rest a simple explanation for why Lancaster House succeeded where other attempts failed. In a seminar where I presented this chapter, one individual raised the thought that a threshold of casualties had been reached that had not been reached before, implying that everyone had had enough blood spilled to prompt a settlement. This can be dismissed rather quickly through comparison with other civil wars. It was estimated that between 30,000 and 40,000 people died in the Zimbabwean civil war. If this level of casualties was a threshold, we should expect similar wars to have this threshold. The overall level of casualties in Zimbabwe, however, was *small* compared with the Algerian revolution, in which nearly a million people died (Horne 1987, 537–538), or the American Civil War, when over 650,000 soldiers died (McPherson 1988, 824).

2. This point is also asserted by Modelski (1964).

3. Anthony Duff, one of the coarchitects of the Lancaster effort, confided to Ken Flower that the British had come to a decision on not recognizing the Salisbury regime and using recognition as leverage as early as May 7, 1979, a full three months before Lusaka (Flower 1987, 317).

4. Renwick's quote suggests that the British did not start from the common assumption that civil war, as a war fought over who will rule, cannot be settled through compromise. This makes sense when one realizes that much of politics is over who will rule and that many solutions have been found for this problem.

5. When I asked Carrington about the allegations of wiretapping, he responded, "No comment. I can't even begin to get into that" (Carrington 1987, interview with author). Flower, in his autobiography, states that Muzorewa at one point feared an uprising from his own ministers based on evidence Muzorewa had received from taping his own delegation (Flower 1987, 311).

6. Michael Handel has criticized Kissinger's shuttle style of diplomacy in the Middle East for many of the faults displayed in the Rhodesian episode: "There are many dangers in Henry Kissinger's 'lonely cowboy' shuttle diplomacy. Too much revolves around his own personality, and too many 'understandings, tacit agreements,' as well as formal agreements, can collapse with his departure" (Handel 1978, 18).

7. The Malta case is discussed in Wriggens (1976). David Abernethy suggests that a historical precedent of Carrington's demand for dictatorial power is Lord Mountbatten's insistence on having sole and ultimate authority over the negotiations of India's decolonization.

8. In my discussions with various British diplomats, all expressed a fundamental ambivilence over the help they received from the Commonwealth and Front Line presidents. While the British needed them to pressure the Patriotic Front, they resented their efforts on behalf of the Front. In talking with five different British officials, I found a remarkable consistency of opinion: all of them felt that Nyerere was impossible to count on—his mercurial temperament often meant that he did not keep his word on promises and often could not deliver his part of bargains. Likewise, they held a negative view of Shridath Ramphal, the secretary-general of the Commonwealth, whom they described as a nuisance, motivated by his desire for publicity as much as any intrinsic concern for the parties in the negotiations. On the other hand, every single official that I talked with had nothing but praise for Samora Machel and his deputy, Fernand Honwana. The British found these two remarkably reliant and pragmatic and made clear that they were absolutely instrumental to the agreements in London. One indicator of the respect that these two Mozambicans had gained from Margaret Thatcher was that upon Machel's and Honwana's tragic death in 1985, she personally went to the Mozambican embassy in London to sign a book of condolences, a very rare action for a British head of state. The relationship between these two countries has flourished since 1979. British soldiers now train Mozambican troops (who use Soviet weapons) in their fight against the MNR insurgency. The current president of Mozambique, Chissano, has gone so far as to discuss with Thatcher the possibility of Mozambique being allowed to join the Commonwealth.

9. It could be argued that one ambiguous threshold concerned the role of South African troops in Rhodesia. From 1968 on, South Africa provided equipment and small numbers of troops (about 2,000 in the late 1960s and early 1970s). After 1977, the numbers of troops grew, but one senses that the nationalists and the Front Line presidents always assumed that such assistance would be provided by South Africa. It would have taken a massive conventional invasion operation by South Africa to have clearly crossed the tacit threshold among the parties.

10. For a summary of such work see Tilly (1984).

11. For a critique of the tendency of political science to ignore the contingent nature of our findings, see Almond and Genco (1976). James McPherson (1988) makes contingency central to his discussion of why the American Civil War ended as it did.

12. A comparison to the efforts of the Indian government to mediate a settlement in Sri Lanka in 1987 is instructive. After forging an agreement between the Sri Lankan government and Tamil rebels in Sri Lanka, India committed itself as guarantor of the agreement and sent approximately 50,000 troops into Sri Lanka for "peacekeeping." The agreement was rejected by

some Tamil and Sinhalese groups. India found itself in a shooting war with the Tamil guerrillas, their soldiers became an occupation force in Sri Lanka, and they suffered more than 1,150 dead before withdrawing in 1990.

# 7

# Refining Ripeness

The notion that some conflicts are more ripe than others for resolution has much intuitive appeal. This stems from our desire to know when mediation can be effective for ending conflicts, as well as our hope that outside actors can contribute to bringing about the ripeness of a conflict. The possible fruitfulness of ripeness as a concept is twofold: as indicator or signal of an objective situation and as a malleable process that can be affected by the acts of individuals within or outside the conflict. William Zartman has pioneered the search for a concept of explanatory, predictive, and prescriptive utility and has given us a first cut of what ripeness might look like. My purpose in this book has been to concentrate on international mediation in the Zimbabwean civil war from 1974 to 1980 to see if Zartman's theory of ripeness accurately captures what led to the successful resolution of that conflict. I would like to suggest that Lancaster House forms what is called a critical case: if a theory of ripeness is to work, then it has to work in this instance. By subjecting the concept of ripeness to such empirical rigor I am taking a second step toward realizing the possible utility of the concept: refinement through the development of more contextually dependent generalizations. I have also attempted to add a significant component—internal politics of the parties involved, which I believed to be missing from Zartman's first notions about ripeness. This chapter presents how the Zimbabwean case should inform a more rigorous theory of ripeness and suggests new questions for investigation and specific hypotheses for testing. First I will use the Zimbabwe case to qualify specific components of Zartman's theory, and then put forward additional changes based on the study of internal politics in the Zimbabwean conflict.

### Ripeness: A Qualification of a Concept

It is necessary to review briefly Zartman's notion of ripeness and conflict resolution: Zartman argues that compelling opportunities arise for conflict resolution based on the *perceptions* of the main actors concerning their military situations. The crucial condition must be the mutual sense of hurting stalemate—a feeling that neither side can win and all will be dramatically worse off if the conflict is not ameliorated. The actors must also perceive a possible solution that will meet their minimum needs. Thus, a third party can attempt to shape the perceptions of the actors involved, and provide direct assistance to one party, but must also use its problem-solving ability to put forward a satisfactory compromise solution.

Based on the evidence of Lancaster House, the relationship between mutually hurting stalemate and ripeness needs to be amended. I argued that two of the major parties to the conflict did not perceive the situation as a mutually hurting stalemate. Robert Mugabe and ZANU believed that it was winning the war and that victory was inevitable. The Rhodesian military and intelligence believed that if something did not change, defeat was at hand. Thus, not all participants to a conflict need perceive a mutually hurting stalemate.

Yet some actors at Lancaster came close to the feeling that Zartman has described. Joshua Nkomo believed that a continuation of the war would prove very costly for all concerned and that victory would come through a prolonged, bloody war. Both the patrons of ZANU and ZAPU respectively—Samora Machel and Kenneth Kaunda—felt enormous pressure to bring about a settlement. The war had inflicted high costs on their countries and they viewed a quick military solution unlikely. All of these leaders pushed Mugabe for settlement, but Machel was clearly the key actor as far as Mugabe was concerned.

To save the centrality of a mutually hurting stalemate in the analysis, one could argue that Mugabe believed he could win outright. That belief, however, was conditioned on further aid from Machel. Machel threatened to hinder Mugabe's capability of winning the conflict, thus prompting Mugabe to see that his plight was indeed one of mutually hurting stalemate.

We could then say that it isn't necessary for the direct combatants to perceive a mutually hurting stalemate, if the perception exists at the patron level. But this conclusion is too sweeping and needs to be qualified in view of the context of the Zimbabwean war. Mozambique and Machel had a monopoly on the supply, training, and housing of Mugabe's troops. There were no alternatives for ZANU apart from Mozambique's active assistance. Such a monopoly was a product of the geography of the conflict. ZANU could not fight a war without Mozambique.

Second, for Machel's threat to cut off assistance to be effective, Mugabe had to believe that it was credible. Mugabe, if he wished, could have called Machel's threat and may have found that it was a bluff—that no matter what happened at the conference, Machel's support was guaranteed. Tongogara clearly had no desire to question Machel's sincerity, and one suspects that toward the end of Lancaster House neither did Mugabe. Nonetheless, the line of causality still exists: a threat by a patron must be found credible. Thus, we can say that the perception of a mutually hurting stalemate can be manifested at the patron level and be efficacious in bringing about settlement, if that patron holds a monopoly on assistance to its client and if that patron can persuade the client of the credibility of its threats.

However, another question immediately arises: Was the fact of Mozambique's hurting enough for it to pressure Mugabe? That is, was a mutually hurting stalemate for Machel sufficient for him to pressure Mugabe? Or was it the perception of a mutually hurting stalemate combined with the belief that Mugabe would win by the new rules of the game? Clearly, there is evidence throughout Lancaster House that Machel's impatience toward Mugabe stemmed from Machel's belief that free and fair elections would bring Mugabe to power in Zimbabwe. Would Machel have been so willing to pressure Mugabe without the belief in Mugabe's ability to win any election? In such a circumstance would Machel's threat have had the sincerity and force behind it for Mugabe to perceive it as credible?

In Zartman's formulation, ripeness is a product of actors believing that their most preferred outcome has been foreclosed, which prompts a willingness to look for compromise solutions. I would like to suggest that this need not be true for all cases. As I argued in Chapter 5, the Salisbury delegation entered into negotiations at Lancaster House because of the British lure of recognition and the possible achievement of their most preferred outcome. The incentive of winning unilaterally prompted Muzorewa et al. to compromise. Beyond the British lure of recognition, Muzorewa believed that he would win any election against Mugabe. On the Patriotic Front side, Nkomo was convinced in the end that any agreement would assure him victory from the ballot box, and as mentioned above Machel believed that Mugabe would win any election. I would like to suggest then that ripeness can come from the paradoxical situation in which both sides believe that a settlement will produce a victory for them.

In terms of differentiating among actors in conflict and their perceptions of hurting stalemate, the Zimbabwean case suggests that the military has a crucial swing vote in the peacemaking process. In the case of Rhodesia, the perceptions of possible defeat were evident in the military and security forces long before they took hold among the politicians of the Rhodesian Front. In the end, the military was convinced of the necessity of settlement and worked to isolate the intransigent Ian Smith. Within ZANU, the most important voice for settlement came from the head of the guerrilla forces, Josiah Tongogara. At crucial times of the Lancaster House Conference, Tongogara worked with the British and Rhodesian militaries in establishing a cease-fire. He firmly believed that if free and fair elections were held, ZANU would gain power. He consistently voiced his belief that Machel would cut off military support and render ZANU impotent. This provides a hypothesis for further testing: for a conflict to be ripe for resolution it is necessary for the military wings of both sides to support negotiation. The Zimbabwean example would also suggest that such support alone is not sufficient for settlement.

To summarize this section, the Zimbabwean case suggests that the notion of ripeness and conflict resolution should be amended as follows:

1. It is not necessary for all actors in a conflict to perceive a mutually hurting stalemate, although it is necessary for some actors to perceive it so.
2. The perception of a mutually hurting stalemate can be manifested at the patron level and be efficacious in bringing about settlement, if that patron holds a monopoly on assistance to its client, and if that patron can persuade the client of the credibility of its threats.
3. Ripeness, paradoxically, can come from a situation where both sides believe that a settlement will produce victory for them.
4. For a conflict to be ripe for resolution, it is necessary for the military wings of both sides to perceive a mutually hurting stalemate, but such perception alone is not sufficient to create a ripe situation for resolution.

## Ripeness and Internal Politics

In Chapter 1, I sought to add a separate component to the concept of ripeness: politics within groups in conflict and willingness to negotiate. The essence of this argument is that how groups are constituted greatly affects their willingness to negotiate. A principal contribution of this book is to show that ripeness comes in part from processes internal to groups in conflict.

In the Zimbabwean case, internal politics often played an important role in the success or failure of negotiations. During the détente exercise, the splits among the black nationalist groups and within those groups made a negotiated settlement an impossibility. Joshua Nkomo was the clear leader of ZAPU, but ZANU was split between Sithole and Mugabe, with neither leader representing the guerrillas in the field.

The attempted unity of ZAPU, ZANU, and the UANC (led by Bishop Abel Muzorewa) was a nonstarter: Muzorewa was chosen as spokesman because he was not threatening to ZAPU or ZANU. He had no power to deliver his own party, let alone the others. After the failure of Victoria Falls, Nkomo tried to negotiate separately with Smith. This brought him approbation from his competing Zimbabwean leaders, and also squandered some of his own power when the negotiations failed. For a year after the Smith-Nkomo talks, Nkomo had to appear the strident noncompromising revolutionary in order to regain lost support.

By 1976, the nationalist groups were each represented at the Geneva conference. Two had little military potential: Muzorewa and Sithole. ZAPU remained consolidated under Nkomo, but because of his renegade attempt to settle with Smith he could not be conciliatory. ZANU was neither consolidated behind Mugabe, nor did it have a unified military. Moreover, Mugabe's bid for leadership of ZANU rested on his unwillingness to negotiate. Thus the two parties with the guns were not in a position to settle the conflict.

The years of 1977–1978 were a period of flux, as the different parties sought to form coalitions in the hope of gaining or maintaining power. This search for coalition partners took precedence over the attempts by Vance and Owen to move the parties toward compromise. The result—a new Salisbury government—brought about one of the most important contributing factors in the subsequent ending of the conflict: Muzorewa and the Rhodesian military and intelligence service replaced Ian Smith as the principal negotiator for the regime. This change of leadership was necessary for a settlement to emerge; Ian Smith as leader of the Salisbury side would not compromise. His preferred action was to fight under worse and worse conditions, to choose war over settlement.

By Lancaster House, political configurations within the various groups pointed toward settlement. Within ZAPU, Joshua Nkomo had begun to feel pressure from more radical members of his party to escalate the war. He bound himself to this course of action if the conference proved fruitless. By doing so, he cast his lot to finding a compromise at Lancaster House—because if he did not, the ensuing escalation would jeopardize his own survival and his continuing leadership of ZAPU. Robert Mugabe had consolidated his leadership within ZANU, and, as important, Tongogara was the undisputed leader of ZANU's fighting forces. Tongogara, to the surprise of all concerned, favored settlement and provided Mugabe the liberty of choosing that option. Indeed, Mugabe probably at times calculated the continuing loyalty of his top general if Mugabe chose to continue fighting. On the Salisbury side, Muzorewa replaced Smith as spokesman, eliminating the most strident voice against negotiated settlement. All of these internal changes conspired to work for the success of Lancaster House.

## Ripeness: The Quest for Indicators

Surely, the usefulness of ripeness as a theoretical and practical tool depends on the clarity of its indicators. It is easy in retrospect to determine whether actors to a conflict perceived the situation to be a hurting stalemate. But as prescriptive theory, is it possible for third parties to recognize a situation of mutually hurting stalemate? What is the relationship between ripeness as a perception of the actors in conflict and ripeness as an objective situation dependent on the military equation of the time? To improve the usefulness of the concept, we need to bring more precision to it, so that ripeness becomes more than a tautology and subject to more rigorous definition than Justice Potter Stewart's description of pornography—"I know it when I see it."

Ideally, one would hope that there would exist some kind of direct link between objective military situations and subjective evaluation of such situations, but the Zimbabwe case shows the tenuousness of this relationship. When we focused on the objective military situation as of early 1975, we saw that there was ground for the actors to perceive a mutually hurting stalemate. From 1976 to 1979, the Rhodesian military warned Ian Smith of the desperate military position, to which Smith turned a deaf ear. In 1979, Bishop Abel Muzorewa believed that the guerrillas of ZANLA were ready to turn over their loyalty and fighting will to him.

One objective indicator for a ripe moment, argues Zartman, is a reversal in the military fortunes of the competing sides. In the Zimbabwean case there was an early reversal of fortune, in 1974, when the Mozambican border became sanctuary for ZANLA guerrillas. In the words of Moorcroft and McLaughlin (1982), "It is rare that the strategic initiative has passed so quickly in the course of a war." The net effects of the reversal, however, were to embolden the black guerrillas to eschew negotiation in favor of intensifying the war, while prompting the white political leadership to avoid negotiation in the hopes of regaining the upper hand in the conflict. In 1979, the election of Margaret Thatcher in England threatened to reverse the military situation in Zimbabwe-Rhodesia: recognition would mean a strengthened nominally black regime fighting on more equal footing with the Patriotic Front. This threatened reversal did prompt a more sober evaluation among some in the Patriotic Front, and the veto of a plan to escalate the war. Likewise among the whites the possibility of recognition prompted moves toward settlement. In this case the threatened reversal was enough to push the sides toward settlement. If the British had acted to recognize, however, and had actually reversed the situation on the ground, escalation and protracted war would have likely resulted.

Thus, changes in fortune on the battlefield may bring about a ripe moment whereby the side previously winning is sobered into negotiation, while the former underdog, being strengthened, will contemplate negotiation. On the other hand, when fortunes reverse, the previous winning side's fear of settlement may grow, and the former underdog may become confident and eschew negotiation.

I would like to argue that a perspective that focuses on the internal composition of groups and their willingness to settle provides a visible indicator of ripeness: changes in leadership. But under what circumstances does a change of leadership provide opportunity for settlement? Under what circumstances does a change of leadership mitigate against a settlement?

From the Zimbabwe cases I would like to put forward some observations and hypotheses about leadership change and ripeness:

1. The mere fact of leadership change or strife adds fluidity to what may have been a logjammed conflict; possibilities for settlement are created that did not exist before.

2. There is little relationship between political positions of new leaders and their willingness to settle. That is, when hard-liners come to the fore, the likelihood of settlement is not necessarily lessened, and when soft-liners are brought to the fore, the likelihood of settlement need not increase. Under some circumstances, hard-liners are able to bring about a settlement because their position is more stable and they can deliver their movement. (This is somewhat akin to the Nixon/China phenomenon.)

3. The previous argument suggests that the power position of a new leader is more important than his or her position on issues: leaders who are confident of support and consolidated in their hold over their movements make compromise more likely. It is possible to suggest that leadership change increases chances of settlement but that leadership struggle does not. That is, leadership change that is consolidated at the time of the change can lead to settlement, whereas leadership struggle tends to caution; thus, ripeness occurs when a leadership change culminates a process of leadership consolidation that minimizes the leader's risks of settlement. In those instances where leadership change is not consolidated, leaders are unable to risk peacemaking initiatives.

4. An alternative to the argument above is that leadership change that is not consolidated can lead to ripeness if the new leader stakes his or her consolidation on attaining a settlement.

5. This leads to a more general proposition: leadership change can lead to settlement if such a settlement is in the practical political interests of the new leader.

6. For changes in leadership to prompt negotiation, the new leader must be backed by the military wing of the movement or government.

7. The perception of precipice—that the situation will soon be dramatically worse— need not come from the threat of the other side; it can come from leaders who fear losing control of their own forces. In such a situation, leaders may believe that without a settlement the purposive use of violence may degenerate into violence beyond their control. In such a case leaders may believe the time is ripe for settlement in order for them to retain power within their organizations.

# Sources

## Primary Sources

African National Council (Sithole). 1977. Minutes of the First Constitutional Settlement Talks. December 2. Crane Collection, Hoover Institution Archives, Stanford, California.

Baumhogger, G., ed. 1984. *The Struggle for Independence: Documents on the Recent Development of Zimbabwe (1975-1980)*, vols. 1–7. Hamburg: Institute of African Studies, Africa Documentation Center.

Minutes. 1978–1979. Rhodesia, External Working Party. National Archives, Harare, Zimbabwe.

Minutes. 1978 –1979. Rhodesia, Internal Working Party. National Archives, Harare, Zimbabwe.

Minutes. 1978. Meeting between Dr. David Owen, secretary of state for Commonwealth and Foreign Affairs and the Rev. Ndabaningi Sithole, president of ZANU, February 20–23, London. Transcript released by Sithole. Crane Collection, Hoover Institution Archives, Stanford, California.

Minutes. 1977. Meeting held on Thursday September 1st 1977 at Mirimba House, Salisbury, at 3:00 P.M. . . . between the Rev. Ndabaningi Sithole, his delegation and the British foreign secretary Dr. David Owen and the United States ambassador to the United Nations Mr. Andrew Young. Transcript released by Sithole. Crane Collection, Hoover Institution Archives, Stanford, California.

Moose, Richard. December 1979. "Points I Want to Make in the Secretary's Staff Meeting Concerning the Reactions of the People with Whom I Spoke Last Night." National Security Archives, Washington, D.C.

Mugabe, Robert. 1974. Report to the Catholic Commission on Peace and Justice. Salisbury, Rhodesia. December 17. Archives, Catholic Commission on Peace and Justice, Harare.

Nyangoni, C., and G. Nyandoro, eds. 1979. *Zimbabwe Independence Movements: Selected Documents*. London: Rex Collins.

Rhodesia, Central Statistical Office. 1980. *Rhodesia Monthly Migration and Tourist Statistics for January 1980*. Salisbury.

Rhodesia, Central Statistical Office. 1971. *1969 Population Census, Interim Report Volume I: The European, Asian and Coloured Populations*. Salisbury.

Rhodesia, Ministry of Finance. 1975. *Economic Survey of Rhodesia*. Salisbury.

Sithole, Ndabaningi. 1978. Letter to David Owen, February 19. Crane Collection, Hoover Institution Archives, Stanford, California.

United Kingdom. 1979. Constitutional Conference, Lancaster House, London: conference papers and summaries of proceedings. Unpublished documents. National Archives, Harare.

United Kingdom. 1977. Rhodesia: Proposals for a Settlement, Presented to Parliament by the Secretary of State for Foreign and Commonwealth Affairs by Command of Her Majesty. September. London: Her Majesty's Stationery Office.

U.S. Department of State. December 14, 1979. Outgoing Telegram. National Security Archives, Washington, D.C.

## Interviews

British Diplomat A., participant, Lancaster House. 1987. Interview by author, April 24, London. Notes.

British Diplomat B., participant, Owen-Vance Initiatives. 1987. Interview by author, June 5, London. Notes.

Carrington, Lord Peter, British foreign secretary, chairman of Lancaster House Conference. 1987. Interview by author, June 3, Brussels. Notes.

Flower, Ken, chief of Central Intelligence Organization, Rhodesia. 1987. Interview by author. May 21, Harare. Notes.

Masarurwa, Willie, ZAPU Revolutionary Council, press secretary at Lancaster House. 1987. Interview by author, May 11, Harare. Tape recording.

Mubako, Simbi, ZANU legal adviser at Geneva, Lancaster House. 1987. Interview by author, May 28, Harare. Notes.

Muzorewa, Abel, leader of ANC and prime minister of Zimbabwe-Rhodesia. 1987. Interview by author, May 6, Harare. Tape recording.

Nkomo, Joshua, leader of ZAPU. 1987. Interview by author, May 29, Bulawayo. Notes.

Richard, Ivor, chairman of Geneva Conference. 1987. Interview by author, June 4, London. Tape recording.

Smith, Ian, prime minister of Rhodesia. 1987. Interview by author, May 22, Harare. Tape recording.

UANC Delegate A., participant, Victoria Falls, Geneva, Lancaster House Conferences. 1987. Interview by author, May 19, Harare. Notes.

UANC Delegate B., participant, Geneva. 1987. Interview by author, May 4, Harare. Notes.

ZAPU Delegate A., participant, Geneva, Lancaster House Conferences. 1987. Interview by author, May 11, Harare. Notes.

ZAPU Delegate B., participant, Victoria Falls, Geneva, Lancaster House Conferences. 1987. Interview by author, May 13, Harare. Notes.

## Newspapers

*ARB* (*Africa Research Bulletin*). 1974–1980.
*Daily Telegraph* (London). 1979.
*Guardian* (Great Britain). 1979.
*Keesing's Archives*. 1974–1980.
*New York Times*. 1988.
*Times* (London). 1978–1980.

## Books and Articles

Abernethy, David. 1985. Reflections on a continent in crisis. In *African Crisis*

*Areas and U.S. Foreign Policy*, ed. G. Bender, J. Coleman, and R. Sklar, 321–339. Berkeley: University of California Press.

Adam, H., and K. Moodley. 1987. *South Africa Without Apartheid: Dismantling Racial Domination*. Berkeley: University of California Press.

Allison, Graham. 1969. Conceptual models and the Cuban missile crisis. *The American Political Science Review* 63 (September): 689–718.

Almond, G., and S. Genco. 1976. Clouds, clocks and the study of politics. *World Politics* 29 (July): 489–522.

Anglin, Douglas. 1975. Zambia and southern African "detente." *International Journal* 30 (Summer): 471–503.

Austin, Reginald. 1975. *Racism and Apartheid in Southern Africa, Rhodesia: A Book of Data*. Paris: UNESCO Press.

Azar, E., and J. Burton, eds. 1986. *The Theory and Practice of International Conflict Resolution*. Boulder: Lynne Rienner.

Bar-Simon-Tov, Y. 1980. *The Israeli-Egyptian War of Attrition, 1969–1970*. New York: Columbia University Press.

Bender, Gerald. 1978. *Angola Under the Portuguese: The Myth and the Reality*. Berkeley: University of California Press.

Berridge, G. R. 1987. *The Politics of the South Africa Run: European Shipping and Pretoria*. Oxford: Clarendon Press.

Blake, Robert. 1977. *A History of Rhodesia*. London: Eyre Methuen.

Bowman, Larry. 1973. *Politics in Rhodesia: White Power in an African State*. Cambridge, Mass.: Harvard University Press.

Burton, John. 1982. *Dear Survivors*. Boulder: Westview Press.

————. 1979. *Deviance, Terrorism and War: the Process of Solving Unresolved Social and Political Problems*. New York: St. Martin's.

Butterworth, R. L. 1976. *Managing Inter-State Conflict; 1945–1974*. Pittsburgh: University Center for International Studies.

Cabezas, Miguel. 1978. The coup-makers against Mugabe. *New African* (June): 60.

Caute, David. 1983. *Under the Skin: The Death of White Rhodesia*. New York: Penguin.

Cilliers, J. K. 1985. *Counter-insurgency in Rhodesia*. Sydney: Croom Helm.

Coker, Christopher. 1986. *The United States and South Africa, 1968–1985: Constructive Engagement and Its Critics*. Durham: Duke University Press.

Curle, Adam. 1970. *Making Peace*. London: Tavistock.

Davidow, Jeffrey. 1984. *A Peace in Southern Africa: The Lancaster House Conference on Rhodesia, 1979*. Boulder: Westview.

De Reuck, Anthony. 1984. The logic of conflict: Its origin, development, and resolution. In *Conflict in World Society*, ed. M. Banks, 96–111. New York: St. Martin's.

Diamond, Larry. 1987. Ethnicity and ethnic conflict. *Journal of Modern African Studies* 25: 117–128.

Diesing, Paul. 1966. Comments. In *Strategic Interaction and Conflict: Original Papers and Discussion*, ed. K. Archibald. Berkeley: Institute of International Studies, University of California.

Duner, Bertil. 1985. *Military Intervention in Civil Wars: The 1970s*. New York: St. Martin's.

El-Khawas, M., and B. Cohen. 1975. *The Kissinger Study of Southern Africa*. Nottingham: Spokesman Press.

Flower, Ken. 1987. *Serving Secretly: An Intelligence Chief on Record, Rhodesia into Zimbabwe 1964 to 1981*. London: John Murray.

Frankel, Phillip. 1984. *Pretoria's Praetorians: Civil-Military Relations in*

*South Africa*. Cambridge: Cambridge University Press.
Gann, L., and T. Henriksen. 1981. *The Struggle for Zimbabwe*. New York: Praeger.
Gelb, Leslie, with R. Betts. 1979. *The Irony of Vietnam: The System Worked*. Washington, D.C.: Brookings.
Geldenhuys, D. 1984. *The Politics of Isolation: South African Foreign Policy Making*. New York: St. Martin's.
George, A., and T. McKeown. 1985. Case studies and theories of organizational decision making. *Advances in Information Processing* 2: 21–58.
George, Alexander, ed. 1983a. *Managing U.S.-Soviet Rivalry: Problems of Crisis Prevention*. Boulder: Westview.
————. 1983b. Missed opportunities for crisis prevention: The war of attrition and Angola. In *Managing U.S.-Soviet Rivalry*, ed. A. George, 187–221. Boulder: Westview.
————. 1982. Case studies and theory development. Paper presented to the Second Annual Symposium on Information Processing in Organizations, Carnegie-Mellon University, Pittsburgh, October 15–16.
Gilbert, Martin. 1966. *The Roots of Appeasement*. New York: Plume.
Gregory, Martyn. 1980. Rhodesia: From Lusaka to Lancaster House. *The World Today* 36 (January): 11–18.
Grew, Raymond. 1978. The crises and their sequences. In *Crises of Political Development in Europe and the United States*, ed. R. Grew, 3–37. Princeton: Princeton University Press.
Grundy, Kenneth. 1986. *The Militarization of South African Politics*. Bloomington: Indiana University Press.
Gutman, Roy. 1988. *Banana Diplomacy: The Making of American Policy in Nicaragua, 1981–1987*. New York: Simon and Schuster.
Hancock, Ian. 1984. *White Liberals, Moderates and Radicals, 1953–1980*. London: Croom Helm.
Handel, Michael. 1978. *War Termination: A Critical Survey*. Jerusalem Papers on Peace Problems. Jerusalem: Leonard Davis Institute for International Relations, The Hebrew University of Jerusalem.
Hill, Christopher. 1975. *The World Turned Upside Down: Radical Ideas During the English Revolution*. New York: Penguin.
Holderness, Harkness. 1985. *Last Chance: Southern Rhodesia, 1945–1958*. Harare: Zimbabwe Publishing House.
Horne, Alistaire. 1987. *A Savage War of Peace: Algeria 1954–1962*. Rev. ed. New York: Penguin.
Horowitz, Donald. 1985. *Ethnic Groups in Conflict*. Berkeley: University of California Press.
Huntington, Samuel. 1968. *Political Order in Changing Societies*. New Haven: Yale University Press.
Ikle, Fred. 1971. *Every War Must End*. New York: Columbia University Press.
————. 1964. *How Nations Negotiate*. New York: Praeger.
International Defence and Aid Fund for Southern Africa. 1977. *Zimbabwe: The Facts About Rhodesia*. London: International Defence and Aid Fund.
Isaacs, Arnold. 1984. *Without Honor: Defeat In Vietnam and Cambodia*. New York: Vintage.
Jaster, Robert. 1983. *A Regional Security Role for Africa's Front Line States: Experiences and Prospects*. Adelphi Paper 180. London: International Institute for Strategic Studies.
Jeeves, Alan. 1975. South Africa and the politics of accommodation.

*International Journal* 30 (Winter): 504–517.

Kahin, George. 1986. *Intervention: How America Became Involved in Vietnam*. Garden City, N.Y.: Anchor Books.

Laitin, David. 1987. South Africa: Violence, myths, and democratic reform. *World Politics* 40: 258–279.

Lake, Anthony. 1976. *The "Tar Baby" Option: American Policy Towards Southern Rhodesia*. New York: Columbia University Press.

Lapping, Brian. 1985. *End of Empire*. New York: St. Martin's.

Lax, D., and J. Sebenius. 1986a. The power of alternatives or the limits to negotiation. *Negotiation Journal* 1 (April): 163–179.

―――――. 1986b. *The Manager as Negotiator: Bargaining for Cooperation and Competitive Gain*. New York: Free Press.

Legum, Colin. 1980. Southern Africa: The road to and from Lancaster House. In *Africa Contemporary Record, Annual Survey and Documents: 1979-1980*, ed. C. Legum, A3–A31. London: Rex Collins.

―――――. 1977. Southern Africa: The year of the whirlwind. In *Africa Contemporary Record, Annual Survey and Documents: 1976-1977*, ed. C. Legum, A3–A57. London: Rex Collins.

―――――. 1975. *Southern Africa: The Secret Diplomacy of Detente*. New York: Africana.

Leonard, Richard. 1983. *South Africa at War: White Power and the Crisis in South Africa*. Westport, Conn.: Lawrence Hill.

Levine, Steven. 1979. A new look at American mediation in the Chinese civil war: The Marshall Mission and Manchuria. *Diplomatic History* 8: 349–375.

Libby, Ronald. 1987. *The Politics of Economic Power in Southern Africa*. Princeton: Princeton University Press.

Licklider, Roy. 1988. Civil violence and conflict resolution: A framework for analysis. Paper presented at the International Studies Association meeting, St. Louis, Missouri, April.

Lijphart, Arend. 1977. *Democracy in Plural Societies: A Comparative Exploration*. New Haven: Yale University Press.

Luard, Evan, ed. 1972. *The International Regulation of Civil Wars*. New York: New York University Press.

Macauley, Neill. 1967. *The Sandino Affair*. Chicago: Quadrangle.

March, J., and H. Simon. 1958. *Organizations*. New York: Wiley.

Marcum, John. 1978. *The Angolan Revolution*, vol. 2. Cambridge: MIT Press.

―――――. 1969. *The Angolan Revolution*, vol. I. Cambridge: MIT Press.

Martin, D., and P. Johnson. 1981. *The Struggle for Zimbabwe: The Chimurenga War*. London: Faber and Faber.

Mastny, V. 1979. *Russia's Road to the Cold War*. New York: Columbia University Press.

Matthews, R. Talking without negotiating: the case of Rhodesia. *International Journal* 35, 1 (Winter 1979–1980): 91–117.

McPherson, James. 1988. *Battle Cry of Freedom: The Civil War Era*. Oxford History of the United States. Oxford: Oxford University Press.

Meredith, Martin. 1979. *The Past Is Another Country: Rhodesia, 1890–1979*. London: Andre Deutsch.

Middlemas, Keith. 1975. *Cabora Bassa: Engineering and Politics in Southern Africa*. London: Weidenfeld and Nicolson.

Minter, W., and E. Schmidt. 1988. When sanctions worked: The case of Rhodesia reexamined. *African Affairs* 87 (April): 207–237.

Mitchell, Christopher. 1981. *The Structure of International Conflict*. New York: St. Martin's.

Mitchell, Christopher, and M. Nicholson. 1983. Rational models and the ending of wars. *Journal of Conflict Resolution* 27 (September): 495–520.

Modelski, George. 1964. International settlements of internal war. In *International Aspects of Civil Strife*, ed. J. Rosenau, 122–153. Princeton: Princeton University Press.

Moorcroft, P., and P. McLaughlin. 1982. Chimurenga! *The War in Rhodesia 1965–1980*. Marshaltown, South Africa: Sygma/Collins.

Moore, Barrington. 1978. *Injustice: The Social Origins of Obedience and Revolt*. London: Macmillan.

Muzorewa, Abel. 1978. *Rise Up and Walk*. London: Evans Brothers.

Naipaul, Shiva. 1980. *North of South*. London: Penguin.

Napper, Larry. 1983. The African terrain and U.S.-Soviet conflict in Angola and Rhodesia: Some implications for crisis prevention. In *Managing U.S.-Soviet Rivalry*, ed. A. George, 155–186. Boulder: Westview Press.

Newhouse, John. 1983. Profiles: Lord Carrington. *New Yorker* (February 14): 47.

Nkomo, Joshua. 1984. *The Story of My Life*. London: Methuen.

North, Robert. 1990. *War, Peace, Survival*. Boulder: Westview Press.

O'Meara, Patrick. 1975. *Rhodesia: Racial Conflict of Coexistence?* Ithaca: Cornell University Press.

Organski, A. K., and J. Kugler. 1980. *The War Ledger*. Chicago: University of Chicago Press.

Pfeffer, Jeffrey. 1981. *Power in Organizations*. Cambridge, Mass.: Ballinger.

Pillar, Paul. 1983. *Negotiating Peace: War Termination as a Bargaining Process*. Princeton: Princeton University Press.

Pruitt, D. 1986. Trends in the scientific study of negotiation and mediation. *Negotiation Journal* 2: 237–244.

Pruitt, D., and J. Rubin. 1986. *Social Conflict: Escalation, Stalemate, and Settlement*. New York: Random House.

Raiffa, Howard. 1982. *The Art and Science of Negotiation*. Cambridge, Mass.: Harvard University Press.

Ranger, T. 1985. *Peasant Consciousness and Guerrilla War in Zimbabwe*. Berkeley: University of California Press.

————. 1980. The changing of the old guard: Robert Mugabe and the revival of ZANU. *Journal of Southern African Studies* 7: 71–90.

Renwick, Robin. 1981a. *The Rhodesia Settlement*. Cambridge, Mass.: Harvard University Center for International Affairs.

————. 1981b. *Economic Sanctions*. Harvard Studies in International Affairs, no. 45. Cambridge, Mass.: Harvard University Center for International Affairs.

Riker, William. 1985. *The Art of Political Manipulation*. New Haven: Yale University Press.

————. 1962. *The Theory of Political Coalitions*. New Haven: Yale University Press.

Rosenau, James, ed. 1964. *International Aspects of Civil Strife*. Princeton: Princeton University Press.

Rotberg, R., et al. 1985. *South Africa and Its Neighbors: Regional Security and Self-Interest*. Lexington, Mass.: D.C. Heath.

Rothchild, Donald. 1986. Hegemonial exchange: An alternative model for managing conflict in middle Africa. In *Ethnicity, Politics, and Development*, ed. D. Thompson and D. Ronen, 65–104. Boulder: Lynne Rienner.

————. 1979. U.S. policy styles in Africa: From minimal engagement to liberal internationalism. In *Eagle Entangled: U.S. Foreign Policy in a Complex World*, ed. K. Oye, D. Rothchild, and R. Lieber, 304–335. New York: Longman.

Rubin, Barry. 1980. *Paved with Good Intentions: The American Experience in Iran*. Oxford: Oxford University Press.

Schelling, Thomas. 1966. *Arms and Influence*. New Haven: Yale University Press.

————. 1960. *The Strategy of Conflict*. Cambridge, Mass.: Harvard University Press.

Schmidt, Dana. 1972. The civil war in Yemen. In *The International Regulation of Civil Wars*, ed. E. Luard, 125–147. New York: New York University Press.

Service, John. 1974. *Lost Chance in China: The World War II Dispatches of John S. Service*, ed. Joseph Esherick. New York: Random House.

Shakespeare, Nicholas. 1988. In pursuit of Guzman. *Granta* 23 (Spring): 149–195.

Sick, Gary. 1985. *All Fall Down: America's Tragic Encounter with Iran*. 2d ed. New York: Penguin.

Sigal, Leon. 1988. *Fighting to a Finish: The Politics of War Termination in the United States and Japan, 1945*. Ithaca: Cornell University Press.

Singer, D., and M. Small. 1982. *Resort to Arms: International and Civil Wars, 1816–1980*. Beverly Hills: Sage.

Sithole, Masipula. 1977. *Zimbabwe: Struggles Within the Struggle*. Harare: Rujeko.

Sithole, Ndabaningi. 1968. *African Nationalism*. 2d ed. London: Oxford University Press.

Sivard, Ruth. 1988. *World Military and Social Expenditures*. Leesburg, Va.: World Priorities.

Skocpol, Theda. 1979. *States and Social Revolutions*. Cambridge: Cambridge University Press.

Smith, D., and C. Simpson. 1981. *Mugabe*. London: Sphere Books.

Smoke, Richard. 1977. *War: Controlling Escalation*. Cambridge, Mass.: Harvard University Press.

Thompson, Carol. 1985. *Challenge to Imperialism: The Frontline States in the Liberation of Zimbabwe*. Harare: Zimbabwe Publishing House.

Tilly, Charles. 1984. *Big Structures, Large Processes, Huge Comparisons*. New York: Russell Sage Foundation.

————. 1975. *The Formation of Nation-States in Western Europe*. Princeton: Princeton University Press.

Touval, Saadia, and I. W. Zartman. 1985. Introduction: Mediation in theory. In *International Mediation in Theory and Practice*, ed. Touval and Zartman, 7–17. Boulder: Westview Press.

Vance, Cyrus. 1983. *Hard Choices: Critical Years in America's Foreign Policy*. New York: Simon and Schuster.

Wheeler-Bennett, J. W., and A. Nicholls. 1974. *The Semblance of Peace: The Political Settlement After the Second World War*. New York: Norton.

Wilkinson, A. R. 1980. The impact of the war. *Journal of Commonwealth and Comparative Politics* 38:110–123.

Windrich, Elaine. 1979. The Anglo-American initiative on Rhodesia: An interim assessment. *The World Today* 35 (July): 294–305.

Wittman, Donald. 1979. How a war ends: A rational model approach. *Journal of Conflict Resolution* 23 (December): 743–763.

Womack, John. 1969. *Zapata and the Mexican Revolution*. New York: Knopf.

Wriggens, W. H. 1976. Up for auction: Malta bargains with Great Britain, 1971. In Zartman, I. W. (ed.), *The 50% Solution*. New Haven: Yale University Press.

Wright, Peter. 1986. *Spycatcher: The Candid Autobiography of a Senior Intelligence Officer*. New York: Dell.

Wright, Quincy. 1965. *A Study of War*. 2d ed. Chicago: University of Chicago Press.

Zartman, I. W. 1985. *Ripe for Resolution: Conflict and Intervention in Africa*. New York: Oxford University Press.

————. 1983. The strategy of preventive diplomacy in third world conflicts. In *Managing U.S.-Soviet Rivalry*, ed. A. George, 341–364. Boulder: Westview.

# Index

# About the Book
# and the Author

Challenging the literatures on war termination, civil war, and revolution—which typically dismiss the possibility of negotiated settlement—Stephen Stedman examines the problem of negotiations during civil wars and demonstrates that third party mediation can help resolve such conflicts.

Stedman analyzes four international attempts to mediate a settlement to the Zimbabwean civil war of the 1970s and compares the three failed negotiations—the 1974–1975 Kenneth Kaunda/ John Vorster "détente" exercise, the Henry Kissinger mediation that led to the Geneva conference of 1976, and the Anglo-American initiatives of David Owen and Cyrus Vance in 1977–1978—with the successful 1979 Lancaster House Conference on Rhodesia, chaired by Lord Carrington. Drawing on primary sources not available previously, his discussion of the factors that distinguish the failures from the successfull attempt is a major contribution to conflict resolution theory, particularly with reference to the work of William Zartman.

Stephen John Stedman is assistant professor in African studies and comparative politics at the Johns Hopkins School of Advanced International Studies.